amy butler's

INSTITCHES

Text and projects by AMY BUTLER
Photographs by COLIN McGUIRE
Illustrations by JACOB REDINGER

amy butler's

INSTITCHES

MORE THAN 25 Simple and Stylish Sewing Projects

CHRONICLE BOOKS
SAN FRANCISCO

Library of Congress Cataloging-in-Publication Data available.
ISBN-10: 0-8118-5159-1
ISBN-13: 978-0-8118-5159-6

Manufactured in China

Technical writing by DIANNE BARCUS and KIM VENTURA
Designed by WARMBO DESIGN
Styling by MONIQUE KEEGAN of Enjoy Co.
Art direction by AMY and DAVID BUTLER

Distributed in Canada by RAINCOAST BOOKS
9050 Shaughnessy Street
Vancouver, British Columbia V6P 6E5

10 9 8 7 6 5 4

CHRONICLE BOOKS LLC
680 Second Street San Francisco, California 94107
www.chroniclebooks.com

ACKNOWLEDGMENTS

This book is dedicated to my grandmother Velma Heymann for stirring my passion for sewing and giving me my first fabric "stash."

Many thanks to everyone who contributed to this book. Without you this project would not have been possible.

A special thanks to the following individuals: My husband, David, for all of his support and help in writing this book. Dianne Barcus and Kim Ventura, two powerhouse ladies who developed the instructions for the projects I designed—their talent and support are incredibly inspiring. Jake Redinger, our "anchor" in the studio, for his amazing illustrations. All of the seamstresses who tested the projects and turned in beautiful work time after time: Nichole Redinger, Dorothy Hughes, Suzanne Aschenbeck, Tracey Swisher, Joyce Burrows, Paula Bevier, Thea Lewis, Donna Thompson, Joy Jung, Kathie Harding, Arlene Donnelly, Tammie Hedglin, and Kim Redding. Colin McGuire for his gorgeous photography. Monique Keegan for her awesome styling abilities and friendship. Diane Capaci for keeping us organized. Kevin Reiner of www.firmlyplanted.net, for providing us with incredible plants. Green Velvet for lending us some lovely accessories for our photo shoot. Jeannie and Will Zink for allowing us to shoot in their home. Randy Levengood and Donna Howard of Colonial Coin Laundry for allowing us to photograph the Oversized Laundry Bag in their facility. Thanks to our models, Maxfield Keegan, Sharon Sinsabaugh, Kevin Reiner, and Sarah Baker. Kokka Ltd. of Japan for providing us with beautiful fabrics. Thine Bloxham of Timtex, Inc. for providing us with loads of her great interfacing. Husqvarna Viking for my sewing machine. Chris Timmons for her much appreciated technical assistance. And Jodi and Mikyla from Chronicle Books for their encouragement, support, and vision.

Contents

89 BATHROOM PROJECTS

91 Kimono-Style Bathrobe
97 Hanging Toiletry Basket
107 Oversized Laundry Bag
113 Decorative Hanging Towels

116 OFFICE PROJECTS

118 CD Holder and Desktop Organizer
125 Document Duvet and Photo File
131 Fashion Checkbook Clutch

144 PERSONAL STYLE PROJECTS

146 Clutch Handbag with Fabric Flower
153 Sash with Beaded Fringe
157 Simple Leather-Handled Shoulder Bag
161 Patchwork Handbag with Zipper Charm

170 SIMPLE TECHNIQUES AND BASIC EQUIPMENT

Sewing basics, as well as some advanced techniques where applicable. Illustrations depicting types of stitches to use. The explanations of terms, stitches, equipment, and techniques.

173 RESOURCE GUIDE

175 INDEX

INTRODUCTION

If you've ever had the pleasure of stitching a seam or finishing a hem, then you know about the deep satisfaction that comes with sewing. As a fabric and sewing-pattern designer, I am fortunate enough to experience that satisfaction every day. I love making beautiful, one-of-a-kind creations by hand, and sharing them with the people closest to me. And I'm thrilled to be able to share my love for sewing with you. Let *In Stitches* be your guide to creating gorgeous, stylish, useful pieces for every room in your home.

This book features patterns for beautiful accessories—from a decorative patchwork throw for the living room, to chic placemats and napkins for the kitchen, a hanging toiletry basket for the bath, and a glamorous sleeping mask for your bedroom. But don't worry—I haven't neglected your wardrobe. You'll find patterns for a perky pleated apron, a luxurious kimono-style bathrobe, and a sleek clutch for nights on the town. And, of course, all of the pieces make great gifts too.

The projects in this book are geared toward the beginning or intermediate sewer, but if you have a more experienced hand you'll also find them fun and useful. If you're new to sewing, you'll want to read "Simple Techniques and Basic Equipment" (page 170) before you start; you may also find the glossary of common sewing terms to be helpful. The book begins with a discussion of how to choose the right fabrics, notions, and trims, and how to care for both vintage and new fabrics, so take a peek at that section before you shop.

While fashion trends are forever changing, the art of sewing is timeless. Once you learn how to sew, you'll never again be restricted to buying off-the-rack, cookie-cutter garments that others have dreamed up. Instead, you'll enjoy the freedom of creating pieces that reflect your own personal style, however modern or retro it may be, while tapping into the history of this ancient art.

Allow the patterns in *In Stitches* to inspire your creativity. Let your personality shine through in the fabrics you choose and the adornments you make. Maybe you'll even find yourself chanting my favorite creativity mantra:

Utility can be beautiful.
Comfy can be stylish.
Organization is healthy.
My personality is unique.
Handmade is best!

Enjoy.

—Amy

FABRICS

Fabrics have attitude. They are graceful, exciting, quiet, or loud. They can set a mood, or even take your mind to a certain place, such as a tropical beach or your favorite garden. They are as colorful and varied as the person who uses them. Culturally, their stories are as old as human history. They can point to simpler times or futuristic ideals. Astonishingly, they can do all of this at once.

My fabric collection, twenty years in the making, would take over my studio if I didn't use the materials in my projects. In my work as a fabric designer, I draw vast inspiration from both vintage pieces and new designs, and I use them both when I create new pieces. Vintage fabrics lend a certain charisma, warmth, and sometimes patina to my projects. New fabrics can offer added durability as well as a fresh attitude to the same work. When you combine fabrics, you allow your personality, warmth, and spirit to shine through. Choose fabrics that you love— that suit your taste and style.

THE FABRIC SEARCH

Finding vintage fabrics requires some digging around. Antique shops, flea markets, garage sales, thrift stores, vintage clothing shops, textile shows, and maybe even your own closet or attic are all possible sources of vintage fabrics. There's also an entire world of traders and sellers on the Internet, but be prepared to dig just as hard online as you would at a flea market on a sunny afternoon! Curtains are another often-overlooked source of fabrics. Just cut away the bad spots and use the curtain fabric

just as you would any other material. The beauty of finding and using vintage textiles is that you are not only allowing their story to be told in a different way but also repurposing and recycling a material resource.

New fabrics can be found at fabric stores and quilting shops. There are so many options! Another great way to get new fabrics is to purchase bed sheets and covers, or tablecloths, which tend to be wider than fabrics sold by the yard and so are especially useful for large projects. Depending on where you search, you can find linens with everything from reproduction vintage prints to super-hip, modern designs. I combine them all. Be sure to check the resource guide for places to start looking for the best vintage and new textiles.

CARE AND USE OF VINTAGE AND NEW FABRICS

As charming as vintage fabrics are, they come with their own set of special needs that must be attended to prior to use. That neatly folded yardage you've found at a garage sale may still have a considerable amount of sizing (starch or another fabric stiffener) in it. Other finds will be aggressively wrinkled from having lived in a bag for

years. For this reason, all fabrics (old and new) should be washed before you start working with them. Most cottons and linens can be machine washed in cold water on the gentle cycle. If your fabric hasn't been exposed to water in a while, soak it in cold water for a day or so to rehydrate the fibers before you clean it. If it seems too fragile for the machine, you might want to think about substituting another fabric for your project. But if you simply must use it, hand wash it in warm water with a mild, phosphate-free soap.

Here are some other great fabric care tips I've learned along the way:

• You can put discolored cotton and linens through a series of long-term baths in Biz detergent. The process could take several days or weeks, depending on how stained the fabric is. Leave it in the initial bath for a week, agitating regularly. If needed, follow with a second bath for another week. This technique is especially good for yellowed whites.

• Don't put bleach directly on stains; it will turn the fabric yellow. Instead soak soiled or yellowed linens in RIT Bright White or in a solution of water and hydrogen peroxide.

• Dark draperies, bark cloth, and fine textiles like velvet and non-colorfast embroidered work should be professionally cleaned.

• Bleach tablecloths and bed linens by spraying them with water and lemon juice. Lay them flat in the sunshine to dry. Avoid hanging heavy items on lines, since this would stretch the fibers.

• Wash small quilting scraps and other small pieces in a bound cotton bag or pillowcase to keep them from getting torn.

• Don't put crochet or lace in the washing machine! If it's stained or needs brightening, wash it by hand using any of the whitening techniques listed above. Air dry it on a flat surface, keeping it taut to retain its shape.

• Dry clean silk and wool. You can also use Woolite and cold water for wool blankets, laying them flat to dry.

• Not everything needs an arduous cleaning. With some fabrics that have become yellow in storage, you may be able to get away with just a gentle machine washing by cutting away any discolored edges. There's likely good material toward the center.

• Sunlight is hard on fabric, just like it is on your skin! Pillows and other textiles left near windows and outdoors will lose their luster quickly, so keep them away from direct sunlight.

• Be sure to press your fabrics before beginning any project to ensure proper measurements and cuts!

TYPES OF FABRICS WE'LL USE

Depending on your mood, your personal tastes, and what's available, you'll likely use a combination of new and vintage textiles in both light and heavy weights. The wearable garments, as well as a few of the kitchen and bedroom projects, should be constructed using mainly finer dress fabrics and quilting-weight cottons or linens. The pieces that will get a lot of wear, like those for the living room and home office, will need fabrics made for use in home decorating. Use your judgment about how much use the item will get.

Pay heed to the combinations of textures in your projects as well. A beefy wool tweed might look a bit odd alongside a delicate cotton. In addition, the two types of fibers tend to sew up differently, which could cause unwanted puckering or folds—not to mention the fact that you'd have a finished project made of fabrics with conflicting washing needs.

NOTIONS AND TRIMS

Embellishment is key to making your project sing. While you're searching for sumptuous, one-of-a-kind fabrics at garage sales, antique shops, and the like, you'll want to also watch for vintage and new buttons, beads, ribbons, and trims. Vintage French ribbon, Indian trims, and English buttons can bring an old-world charm to modern designs. Jewelry can also be a fantastic source of adornments for your sewn pieces. I often steal from my jewelry stash to tweak a cute bag or pillow cover. So make sure to check out beading shops, craft and hobby stores, and ethnic shops for groovy, stylish accents.

CHAPTER 1

LIVING ROOM Projects

With their rich colors and varied textures, fabric accessories are probably the most stylish and versatile way to bring personality to your living spaces. Bold, cutting-edge artwork on your walls is great, but you can't snuggle up under a painting on a rainy night like you can with a patchwork throw or fluffy pillow. Endlessly flexible, fabric artwork can be tossed about in different arrangements and can even move from room to room when the redecorating urge strikes.

DECORATIVE PATCHWORK THROW

FINISHED SIZE: 54" WIDE X 72" LONG

Sturdy, soft, colorful, and comfy, this throw is made with heavier home-decor-weight fabrics for increased warmth and coziness. But you don't have to keep it on your couch—it makes a great wall hanging, or even an extra-special picnic blanket.

FABRICS AND SUPPLIES

- 2 yards (44"-wide) heavyweight cotton fabric ("fabric A")

- 1 yard each of 9 coordinating (44"-wide) heavyweight cotton fabrics ("fabrics B through J"; you will have fabric left over from some of these pieces to use for another project.)

- 3¼ yards (44"-wide) muslin for the foundation

- 1 package (81" x 96") cotton batting

- 4½ yards (44"-wide) heavyweight cotton fabric for the backing and bias binding (This fabric should coordinate with the fabrics A through J used on the front of the throw.)

- Coordinating cotton thread

- Yardstick or ruler

- Chalk pencil or fabric marker

- Masking tape

- Scissors

- Approximately 30 large safety pins

- Straight pins

- Hand sewing needle

NOTES

- All seams are ½" unless otherwise stated. (The ½" seam allowance is included in all cutting measurements.)

- The sample shown was created using a heavy cotton fabric. We do not suggest using lightweight cotton, since some prints may show through after additional blocks are placed over them.

- Preshrink your fabric by washing, drying, and pressing it before starting your project.

Step 1. Cut out all patchwork pieces from fabrics A through J.

a. Measure and mark the dimensions below directly onto the **Wrong** side of the fabric, using a yardstick and a chalk pencil. Using your scissors, cut out all of the pieces following the marked lines on the fabric. (FIGURE 4B)

FROM FABRIC A
- *Cut 1 each. A-1: 10" x 11", A-2: 7" x 9", A-3: 21" x 37"*

FROM FABRIC B
- *Cut 1 each. B-1: 7" x 6", B-2: 20" x 5", B-3: 25" x 11"*

FROM FABRIC C
- *Cut 1 each. C-1: 22" x 22", C-2: 25" x 6"*

FROM FABRIC D
- *Cut 1 each. D-1: 7" x 18", D-2: 11" x 19"*

FROM FABRIC E
- *Cut 1 each. E-1: 9" x 17", E-2: 21" x 28"*

FROM FABRIC F
- *Cut 1 each. F-1: 7" x 8", F-2: 7" x 12", F-3: 25" x 9"*

FROM FABRIC G
- *Cut 1 each. G-1: 11" x 11", G-2: 9" x 16", G-3: 15" x 11"*

FROM FABRIC H
- *Cut 1 each. H-1: 9" x 18", H-2: 20" x 12", H-3: 10" x 16"*

FROM FABRIC I
- *Cut 1 each. I-1: 14" x 18", I-2: 7" x 5"*

FROM FABRIC J
- *Cut 1. J-1: 26" x 28"*

~ CONTINUED

b. In order to keep your pieces organized, mark each piece by writing the name of the piece (A-1, C-2, and so on) on a small piece of masking tape and attaching it to the piece of fabric as it is cut.

Step 2. Cut the muslin foundation, the batting, and the fabric backing.

a. Cut 2 lengths of the muslin, each 58" long. Attach the 2 pieces by stitching a ¼" seam along one long selvage edge*. Now, mark and cut a piece of the joined muslin you created to measure 58" x 76".

* See page 171 for an explanation of a selvage edge.

b. Measure, mark, and cut a piece of cotton batting to measure 58" x 76".

c. Now, as in step 2a, cut and join the 2 lengths of the heavyweight cotton fabric for the backing, and then mark and cut the joined fabric to measure 58" x 76".

Step 3. Prepare the patchwork pieces for the throw.

a. First, using patchwork pieces A-2, C-2, E-1, F-1, G-1, G-2, and H-3, fold under ½" toward the **Wrong** side of the fabric on all 4 raw edges and press. These pieces will be the second layer of pieces that you will stitch onto the throw. Set them aside for now.

b. Then, refer to the pressing guide diagram (FIGURE 3B). Each patchwork piece is shown in its approximate position. The dotted lines in the diagram indicate an unfinished, raw edge. The solid lines indicate a finished, folded, and pressed edge. Be careful to align each patchwork piece in the proper direction, as shown in FIGURE 3B. On each patchwork piece needing a pressed edge, first fold under ½" toward the **Wrong** side of the fabric and then press. Continue pressing all the patchwork pieces needing a ½" folded edge before moving on to step 4.

Step 4. Place and attach the first layer of patchwork pieces.

a. Spread the 58" x 76" piece of muslin on a hard, flat surface, either an uncarpeted floor or a large table. The muslin will be used as a foundation on which to create the Decorative Patchwork Throw. It does not matter whether the muslin faces **Right** side up or down.

b. Then, referring to FIGURE 4B, lay the patchwork pieces, with the **Right** sides facing up, on the muslin in the positions shown in the diagram. Place the pieces 2" from the edges of the muslin. The unfinished raw edges of the patchwork pieces will be placed under the pressed edges of adjoining patchwork pieces. To do this, overlay the pressed edge of each patchwork piece, covering ½" of the unfinished raw edge of the piece next to it. For example, in the top left corner of the throw, the folded and pressed edges of D-1 and H-1 will be placed so that they overlap the raw edge of piece I-1 by ½". (FIGURE 4B)

c. Continue placing the first layer of patchwork pieces until all pieces shown in the diagram are in place. There will be approximately 2" of muslin showing on each edge.

NOTE: *Reserve the 7 pieces you pressed in step 3a. They will be the second layer of the throw.*

d. Once you have the first layer of patchwork pieces in place, you are ready to begin securing them to the muslin foundation. Using large safety pins, secure the patchwork pieces in place.

e. Now, machine stitch each pressed edge, stitching close to the folded edge and backstitching at each end. Stitch through all layers. As you stitch the folded, pressed edges, the ½" seam allowance of the hidden raw edge under it will also be stitched in place.

FIGURE 3B

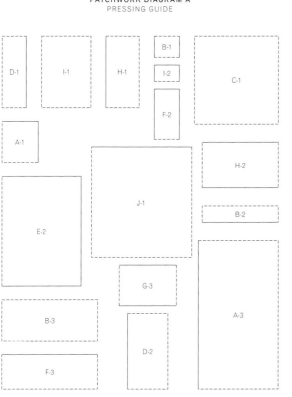

PATCHWORK DIAGRAM A
PRESSING GUIDE

FIGURE 4B

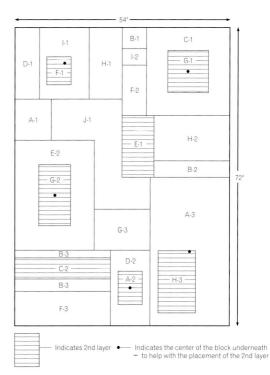

PATCHWORK DIAGRAM B

Indicates 2nd layer   •— Indicates the center of the block underneath
to help with the placement of the 2nd layer

NOTE: The illustration above shows the layout of the design.
The muslin panel behind the patchwork panel is not shown.

FIGURE 9A

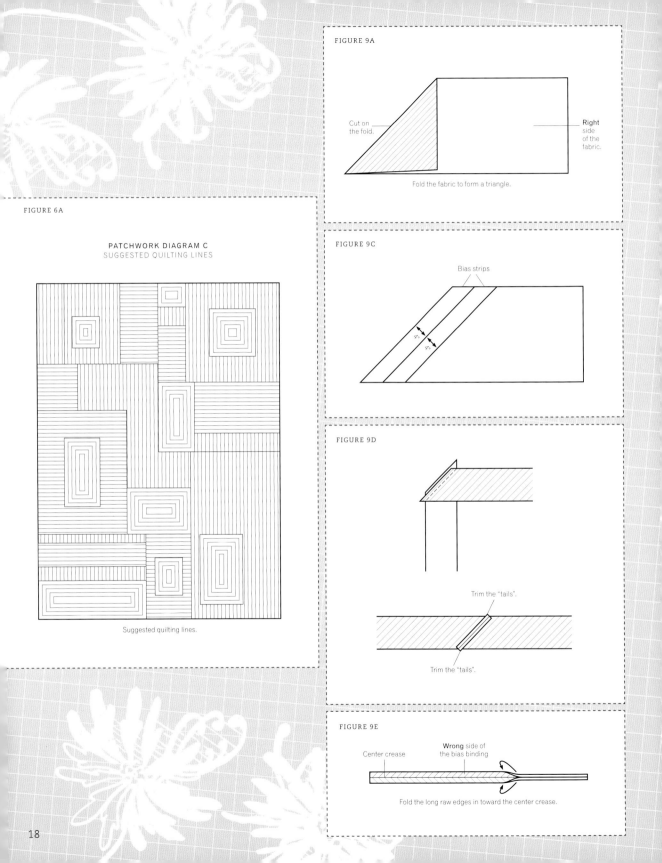

Cut on the fold.

Right side of the fabric.

Fold the fabric to form a triangle.

FIGURE 6A

PATCHWORK DIAGRAM C
SUGGESTED QUILTING LINES

Suggested quilting lines.

FIGURE 9C

Bias strips

4" 4"

FIGURE 9D

Trim the "tails".

Trim the "tails".

FIGURE 9E

Center crease

Wrong side of the bias binding

Fold the long raw edges in toward the center crease.

Step 5. Place and attach the second layer of patchwork pieces.

a. Take the 7 patchwork pieces, all 4 edges turned and pressed, and place them on top of the first layer of the throw in the positions shown in FIGURE 4B, with the **Right** side of the pieces facing up.

b. Using large safety pins as you did in step 4d, secure the pieces in the proper places. Then, stitch the pieces in place by stitching around all 4 pressed edges, stitching close to the folded edge and backstitching at each end. Stitch through all layers.

Step 6. Mark the throw for machine quilting.

a. Using a yardstick and a chalk pencil or fabric marker, draw quilting lines directly on the front of the throw. See FIGURE 6A for suggested quilting lines, or use your imagination to create a quilting pattern that pleases you.

NOTE: *Quilting has two functions: first, to add visual interest to the throw, and, second, to join the layers of the throw together. Quilting lines should be no more than 2" apart in order to hold the layers together securely.*

Step 7. Layer the backing, batting, and the patchwork front of the throw.

a. First, spread the 58" x 76" piece of backing fabric on a flat, hard surface, with the **Wrong** side of the fabric facing up. Smooth the backing fabric flat.

b. Next, place the 58" x 76" piece of batting on the top of the backing fabric. Smooth the batting flat, beginning at the center and working your way out to the edges.

c. Then, place the patchwork front, **Right** side facing up, onto the batting. Smooth the front flat.

d. Using large safety pins in many positions on the throw, secure all 3 layers together.

Step 8. Machine quilt the throw.

a. Beginning in the center of the throw, machine stitch around each patchwork piece to secure the layers together and prevent shifting. Use the presser foot of your machine as a guide by placing the edge of the presser foot along the edge of the patchwork piece as you stitch, backstitching at each end.

b. Now, using the quilting lines you marked in step 6a, quilt the throw by machine stitching along the lines. Begin at the center of the throw and work toward the outer edges, completing one patchwork piece before moving to another. Remember to backstitch at each end, and clip all thread tails as you work.

NOTE: *Due to the size of the throw, you will need to fold or roll it in order to fit it into the sewing machine.*

Step 9. Make the bias binding for the patchwork throw.

a. The bias* binding for the throw is cut on the bias of the fabric. To find the bias, take the extra yardage of the backing fabric and open it flat, **Right** side up. Fold one corner of it with **Right** sides together, matching one selvage edge with one of the cut edges to make a triangle shape. Press a crease on the fold. Then, open the fabric and cut along the pressed crease. (FIGURE 9A)

* See page 171 for an explanation of the bias of your fabric.

b. Now, starting at one end of the cut line, measure over 4" on the fabric's **Right** side and make a mark. Make another mark 4" over on the fabric from the opposite end of the cut line.

c. Then, take your yardstick and match up the 2 marks. With a chalk pencil, mark down the side of the yardstick, drawing a line between the 2 marks. This creates a 4"-wide bias strip marked on the fabric, parallel to the newly cut bias edge. Continue to measure and mark bias strips until you have enough to make 270" of bias tape. (FIGURE 9C)

d. To join the strips into one continuous piece, lay the strips perpendicular to each other with the **Right** sides together. Stitch across the diagonal edges of the strips with a ½" seam. Then, trim the seam allowance to ¼" and press the seam open. Trim any small "tails" of fabric at the seam of the bias binding. Repeat until you have joined all of the strips into one long bias strip. (FIGURE 9D)

e. Then, fold the bias strip in half lengthwise, with the **Wrong** sides together, and press. Open the bias strip and fold each long raw edge in to meet the center crease and press again. Finally, fold the bias strip together on the original center crease and press well. The completed bias strip will be 1" wide and all long raw edges will be hidden. (FIGURE 9E)

~ CONTINUED

Step 10. Attach the bias binding to the throw.

a. First, using a ruler, make certain that the corners of the throw are straight and square. Trim off the excess batting and backing fabric, cutting them even with the edges of the front of the throw.

b. Using the longest stitch on your machine, machine baste* a ½" seam completely around the outer edges of the throw. This will make it easier to attach the bias binding.

See page 171 for an explanation of machine basting.

c. Now, open up the pressed bias binding. Fold the short raw end ½" in toward the **Wrong** side of the binding and press. On the back of the throw at the middle of the bottom raw edge place the folded end of the binding. With **Right** sides together, match one long raw edge of the bias binding to the bottom raw edge on the back of the throw. Pin the binding in place.

d. To attach the binding to the throw, stitch a ½" seam along the binding fold line that's closest to the throw's raw edge.

e. Stop stitching 1" from the first corner, backstitching at the end, and then clip the threads, lift the needle and presser foot. To make a nice, neat mitered corner, first fold the binding strip away from the corner of the throw, forming a 45-degree angle. Then, fold the binding back, even with the adjacent raw edge of the throw, and pin it in place. Begin stitching again at the upper edge of the throw. Miter all 4 corners in this way. (FIGURE 10E)

f. After the fourth corner, place the rest of the binding along the bottom raw edges, overlapping the beginning of the binding by 1", and pin it in place. Cut away any extra binding and then stitch the rest of the binding in place, and backstitch at each end. When the binding is turned to the front of the throw, the fold will conceal the raw edge at the end of the binding. (FIGURE 10F)

Step 11. Complete the throw.

a. Now, wrap the binding over the raw edge of the throw to the front. Fold under the raw edge of the binding at the outer pressed fold line. The center fold of the binding will be the outer edge of the throw. Pin the binding in place, covering the stitch line made when you stitched the binding to the backing. (FIGURE 11A, B, C)

b. On the front of the throw, fold the mitered corners, forming a 45-degree angle, and pin them in place. (FIGURE 11A, B, C)

c. Then, using the hand sewing needle, topstitch* the binding to the front of the throw, stitching close to the folded edge of the binding. (FIGURE 11A, B, C)

See page 172 for an explanation of topstitching.

d. To finish your throw, slip stitch* the folded edges of the mitered corners together by hand on both the front and the back of the throw. (FIGURE 11D)

See page 171 for an explanation of slip stitching.

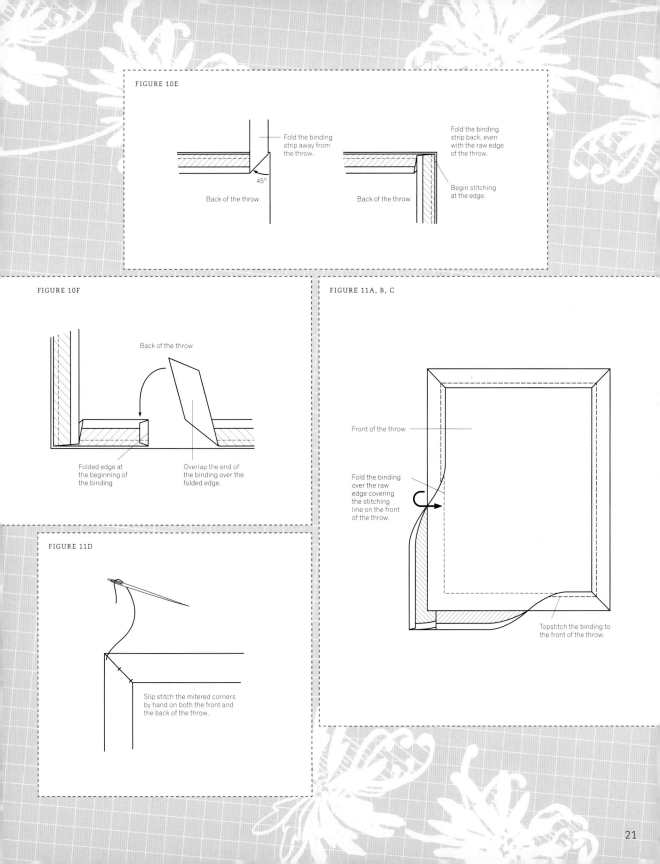

FIGURE 10E

Fold the binding strip away from the throw.

45°

Back of the throw

Fold the binding strip back, even with the raw edge of the throw.

Begin stitching at the edge.

Back of the throw

FIGURE 10F

Back of the throw

Folded edge at the beginning of the binding

Overlap the end of the binding over the folded edge.

FIGURE 11A, B, C

Front of the throw

Fold the binding over the raw edge covering the stitching line on the front of the throw.

Topstitch the binding to the front of the throw.

FIGURE 11D

Slip stitch the mitered corners by hand on both the front and the back of the throw.

FLOOR CUSHIONS

Not just for teenagers' rooms, these soft and comfy portable seats have so many uses. The big ones, sized for lounging friends and napping children, can be stacked or tossed wherever you need some extra seating. The small ones make smart chair cushions or pet beds.

FABRICS

FOR THE SMALL FLOOR CUSHION

- 1¾ yards (44"-wide) heavyweight cotton fabric or ¾ yard (60"-wide) heavyweight cotton fabric for the exterior
- 1½ yards (44"-wide) muslin for the pillow form
- 1½ pounds polyester polyfill

FOR THE LARGE FLOOR CUSHION

- 3 yards (44"-wide) heavyweight cotton fabric or 1½ yards (60"-wide) heavyweight cotton fabric for the exterior

- 3 yards (44"-wide) muslin for the pillow form
- 3½ pounds polyester fiberfill

OTHER SUPPLIES

- Buttons to cover (size 1½); 2 for Small Floor Cushion, 4 for Large Floor Cushion
- ⅝" flat 2-hole buttons; 2 for Small Floor Cushion, 4 for Large Floor Cushion
- Coordinating thread
- 5" doll-maker's hand sewing needle
- Carpet or upholstery thread

- Yardstick
- Chalk pencil or fabric marker
- Scissors
- Straight pins
- Sharp hand sewing needle

NOTES

- All seams are ½" unless otherwise stated. (The ½" seam allowance is included in all cutting measurements.)
- Preshrink your fabric by washing, drying, and pressing it before starting your project.

Step 1. Cut out all pieces from the fabric.

a. FOR THE SMALL FLOOR CUSHION

First, fold the fabric in half lengthwise, **Wrong** sides together, matching the selvage edges, and press. Then, open out the fabric **Right** side down and, using a yardstick and a chalk pencil, measure and mark the following dimensions directly onto the **Wrong** side of your fabric.

FROM THE FABRIC FOR THE EXTERIOR

- *Cut 2 panels: 26˝ wide x 26˝ long*

FROM THE MUSLIN

- *Cut 2 panels: 26˝ wide x 26˝ long*

FOR THE LARGE FLOOR CUSHION

First, fold the fabric in half lengthwise, **Wrong** sides together, matching the selvage edges, and press. Then, open out the fabric **Right** side down and, using a yardstick and a

chalk pencil, measure and mark the following dimensions directly onto the **Wrong** side of your fabric.

FROM THE FABRIC FOR THE EXTERIOR

- *Cut 2 panels: 26˝ wide x 49˝ long*

FROM THE MUSLIN

- *Cut 2 panels: 26˝ wide x 49˝ long*

b. Using your scissors, cut out all of the pieces by cutting on the marked lines on the fabric. Save the scraps of fabric left over from the heavyweight cotton to use in covering the buttons.

Step 2. Make the pillow form.

NOTE: *The instructions in steps 2 and 3 are the same for both the small and the large pillow forms. The illustrations depict the large Floor Cushion.*

~ CONTINUED

a. First, place the muslin panels **Right** sides together, matching the raw edges, and pin them in place.

b. Measure 4" in from one side edge on the short end of the muslin panel and make a mark. (On the small Floor Cushion, all sides are the same size.) Repeat this step for the other side of the panel. Starting at the 4" mark, machine stitch a ½" seam to the corner, then down one long edge, along the short end, and back up the other long edge, turning at the corner and stitching to the second 4" mark, backstitching at each end. Leave the raw edge between the 4" marks open. Using your scissors, trim the corners, making sure not to clip into the stitching line. (FIGURE 2B)

c. Now, turn the pillow form **Right** side out and press.

d. Fold under the ½" seam allowance on each side of the form on the open end, toward the **Wrong** side, and press. (FIGURE 2D)

e. Stuff the pillow form with the polyester fiberfill, using small amounts at a time and filling the corners evenly.

f. Pin the open end closed and slip stitch by hand using the sharp hand sewing needle or machine stitch close to the edge to close the opening. (FIGURE 2F)

Step 3. Make the Floor Cushion.

a. Place the 2 heavyweight cotton panels with **Right** sides together, matching the raw edges, and pin them in place.

b. Repeat step 2b to stitch the Floor Cushion panels together.

c. Now, turn the Floor Cushion **Right** side out and press.

d. Fold under the ½" seam allowance on each side of the form on the open end, toward the **Wrong** side, and press. (REFER TO FIGURE 2D)

Step 4. Mark the button placement on the Floor Cushion.

FOR THE SMALL FLOOR CUSHION

a. First, fold the sewn Floor Cushion panels in half, matching up the top and bottom edges. Gently press a crease along the fold on the panels. Then, unfold the sewn Floor Cushion panels.

b. Starting at the left-side edge, using a yardstick and a chalk pencil, measure 8" in along the center crease and make a mark. Then, from the right-side edge, measure 8" in along the center crease and make another mark. These are the placement marks for attaching the buttons. (FIGURE 4B SMALL CUSHION)

FOR THE LARGE FLOOR CUSHION

a. First, fold the Floor Cushion panels in half across the width matching up long edges on the top and bottom. Gently press a crease along the fold on the panels. Then, unfold the Floor Cushion.

b. Starting at the left-side edge, using your yardstick and chalk pencil, measure along the center crease and mark the following measurements; 6", 18", 30", and 42". These are the placement marks for attaching the buttons. (FIGURE 4B LARGE CUSHION)

Step 5. Fill and close the Floor Cushion.

a. Now, insert the pillow form into the Floor Cushion.

b. Pin the open end of the Floor Cushion closed and slip stitch by hand or machine stitch close to the edge to close the opening. (FIGURE 2F)

Step 6. Attach the buttons and tuft the Floor Cushion.

NOTE: *Adding the buttons and tufting the Floor Cushion will give it dimension and keep the pillow form from shifting.*

a. Follow the manufacturer's instructions to cover the buttons with the leftover heavyweight cotton fabric.

b. Thread a doll-maker's needle with a double strand of carpet or upholstery thread.

c. Tie the ends of the thread to the loop on the back of the covered button. (FIGURE 6C)

d. Push the needle down into the Floor Cushion at the first mark you made, pulling the covered button onto the front of the cushion.

e. Then, on the back of the Floor Cushion, stitch through the back plate of the button. Take the needle back up through the cushion again, stitch through the loop in the covered button, and push the needle through the cushion one more time. Pull the thread to pull the 2 buttons together, creating the tuft. (FIGURE 6E)

f. Knot the thread securely on the back flat button and clip the ends of the thread.

g. To finish, repeat steps 6c through 6f to attach the remaining buttons to the Floor Cushion. (FIGURE 6G)

FIGURE 2B

Trim corner

Wrong side of the muslin panel

Trim corner

4"

Leave open for turning **Right** side out.

4"

Trim corner

Trim corner

FIGURE 2D

Right side of the muslin panel

Fold the seam allowance ½" under at the opening.

FIGURE 2F

Right side of the muslin pillow form

Pin the opening closed and machine stitch close to the edge.

FIGURE 4B SMALL CUSHION

Small Floor Cushion

Center crease

8"   8"

Button placement

FIGURE 4B LARGE CUSHION

Large Floor Cushion

6"   18"   30"   42"

Center crease

Button placement

FIGURE 6C

Tie the thread to the covered button.

FIGURE 6E

Side view of the large Floor Cushion showing how to attach the top covered button to the bottom flat button for all 4 placement marks.

Top covered button

Bottom flat button

FIGURE 6G

Marks for the button placement

Covered button

Side view of the large Floor Cushion

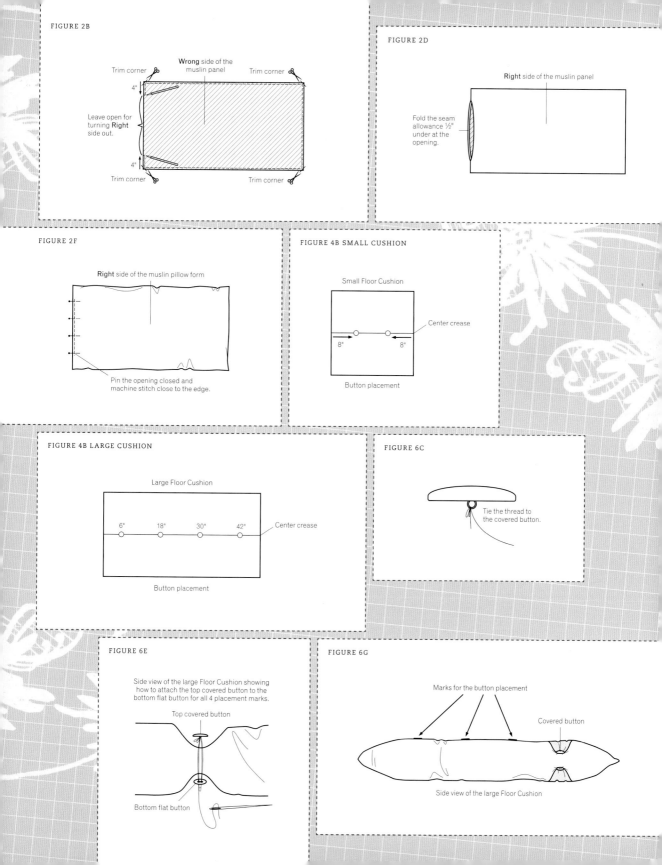

KITTY TUNNEL

My cats have always loved to tunnel under my quilts when they're draped over the couch. I got this idea after I had cleaned cat hair off of it for the umpteenth time! Lined with fake fur, this irresistible tunnel has an adjustable drawstring that can be closed for a cozy nest, or left open for a great pass-through. My feline friends now have a perfect location for their mischief, and I no longer have to vacuum fur off my couch!

FABRICS

- 1⅜ yards (44"-wide) heavyweight cotton fabric for the exterior
- 1⅛ yards (58"-wide) fake fur for the lining

OTHER SUPPLIES

- Coordinating thread
- Yardstick
- Chalk pencil or fabric marker
- Scissors
- Straight pins
- Large safety pin

NOTES

- All seams are ½" unless otherwise stated. (The ½" seam allowance is included in all cutting measurements.)
- Preshrink your exterior fabric by washing, drying, and pressing it before starting your project. (Do not prewash the fake fur.)

Step 1. Cut out all pieces from the fabric.

First, simply measure and mark the dimensions below directly onto the **Wrong** side of the fabric, using a yardstick and a chalk pencil. Then, using your scissors, cut out each panel following the marked lines.

FROM THE FABRIC FOR THE EXTERIOR
- *Cut 1 drawstring: 4" wide x 49" long*
- *Cut 1 main panel: 37" wide x 37" long*

FROM THE FUR FABRIC FOR THE LINING
- *Cut 1 main panel: 37" wide x 37" long*

Step 2. Make the exterior tunnel with an opening on one end for the drawstring.

Fold the exterior main panel in half lengthwise with the **Right** sides together, matching up the side raw edges, and pin them in place. Starting at the top raw edge of the folded panel, using your yardstick and chalk pencil, measure ¾" down the side raw edge and make a mark.

Measure down again 1½" and make another mark. Now, starting at the top raw edge, stitch a ½" seam from the top raw edge to the first mark you made (¾" down), backstitching at each end. Then, leave a 1½" space and begin stitching at the second mark you made (1½" down from the first). Continue to stitch the rest of the side seam down the length of the panel, backstitching at each end. Press the seam allowance open. (FIGURE 2)

Step 3. Finish the opening for the drawstring casing.

On the **Wrong** side of the exterior main panel, topstitch* with a ⅛" seam completely around the 1½" opening on the side seam, and backstitch at each end and across the top and bottom of the opening for added reinforcement. (FIGURE 3)

* See page 172 for an explanation of topstitching.

~ CONTINUED

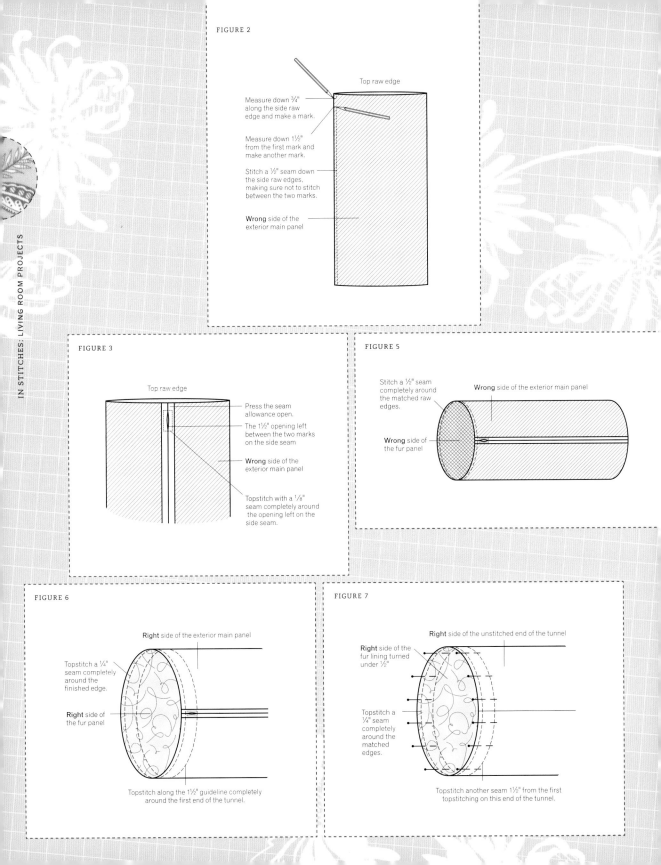

FIGURE 2

Top raw edge

Measure down ¾"
along the side raw
edge and make a mark.

Measure down 1½"
from the first mark and
make another mark.

Stitch a ½" seam down
the side raw edges,
making sure not to stitch
between the two marks.

Wrong side of the
exterior main panel

FIGURE 3

Top raw edge

Press the seam
allowance open.

The 1½" opening left
between the two marks
on the side seam

Wrong side of the
exterior main panel

Topstitch with a ⅛"
seam completely around
the opening left on the
side seam.

FIGURE 5

Stitch a ½" seam
completely around
the matched raw
edges.

Wrong side of the exterior main panel

Wrong side of
the fur panel

FIGURE 6

Right side of the exterior main panel

Topstitch a ¼"
seam completely
around the
finished edge.

Right side of
the fur panel

Topstitch along the 1½" guideline completely
around the first end of the tunnel.

FIGURE 7

Right side of the unstitched end of the tunnel

Right side of the
fur lining turned
under ½"

Topstitch a
¼" seam
completely
around the
matched
edges.

Topstitch another seam 1½" from the first
topstitching on this end of the tunnel.

Step 4. Make the fur lining.

Fold the fur in half lengthwise with **Right** sides together, matching up the side raw edges. Starting at the top raw edge of the folded fur lining, stitch a ½" seam down the length of the panel, backstitching at each end. Turn the fur lining **Right** side out.

Step 5. Attach the exterior main panel to the fur lining.

With the exterior tunnel **Wrong** side facing out and the fur lining **Right** side facing out, slip the exterior tunnel over the fur lining, making sure to match up the side seams. Pin the panels together at the end of the exterior tunnel with the drawstring opening that you made in step 2. Attach this end of the tunnel by stitching a ½" seam completely around the matched raw edges. (FIGURE 5)

Step 6. Make the drawstring casing on the first end of the tunnel.

Turn the tunnel **Right** side out so that the exterior side faces out. Topstitch a ¼" seam around the finished edges on the first end of your tunnel, backstitching at each end. Then, measure 1½" down from the topstitching and mark a guideline all the way around this end of the tunnel. Stitch another seam, following the 1½" guideline, completely around the first end of the tunnel. This will make a casing for your drawstring. (FIGURE 6)

Step 7. Finish the unstitched end of the tunnel.

First, turn the tunnel around so the unstitched end is facing you. Then, fold under the raw edges of the exterior tunnel ½" in toward the **Wrong** side and press. Fold under the raw edges of the fur lining ½" in toward the **Wrong** side and pin these folded edges in place.

Then, match up the folded edges of the exterior tunnel and the fur lining, lining up the seams, and pin the folded edges together. Topstitch completely around the pinned edge with a ¼" seam. Measure 1½" down from the topstitching and make another seam completely around this end of the tunnel. This will make both ends of the tunnel look the same. (FIGURE 7)

Step 8. Make the drawstring.*

First, fold the drawstring in half lengthwise, with the **Wrong** sides together, matching up the long side raw edges, and press a center crease. Open the drawstring, keeping the **Wrong** side facing up. Fold each of the long side raw edges in to meet the center crease and press. Then, fold each short end of the drawstring ½" in and press. Finally, refold the entire drawstring in half along the original center crease to enclose the raw edges and press. Topstitch completely around the drawstring with a ⅛" seam, backstitching at each end.

* See page 170 for more details on how to make a drawstring.

Step 9. Feed the drawstring through the casing.

First, attach a large safety pin to one end of the drawstring and close the pin. With the exterior of the tunnel facing out, insert the closed pin into the opening of the casing. Push the drawstring completely around the casing, using the safety pin to guide it through. Pull the safety pin end of the drawstring out of the same opening and then remove the safety pin. To finish your tunnel, even up the ends of the drawstring, and tie a knot at each end.

BIG DOT PILLOW

Here are three fabulous pillows with multiple looks for your ever-changing moods. The Big Dot Pillow provides a modern backdrop for your favorite scraps and cherished tidbits. The feminine **ROUND RUFFLE PILLOW** (page 34) has an elegant, sculptural feel. And the **POM-POM PILLOW** (page 37) is simple, quirky, and fun.

FABRICS

- 1¾ yards (44"-wide) mid- to heavyweight solid cotton fabric for the pillow panels
- ⅛ yard each of 14 (44"-wide) coordinating fabrics for the circle appliqués
- 1 yard Wonder Under (double-sided fusible webbing)
- 28" square pillow form (or, to make your own pillow form, 1 yard [60"-wide] cotton muslin and 5 large bags of polyester fiberfill)

OTHER SUPPLIES

- Coordinating thread
- Yardstick
- Chalk pencil or fabric marker
- Scissors
- Straight pins
- Turning tool (such as a closed pair of scissors)

NOTES

- All seams are ½" unless otherwise stated. (The ½" seam allowance is included in all cutting measurements.)
- Preshrink your fabric by washing, drying, and pressing it before starting your project.

Step 1. Cut out all pieces from the fabric.

First, simply measure and mark the dimensions below directly onto the **Wrong** side of the fabric, using a yardstick and a chalk pencil. Then, using your scissors, cut out each panel following the marked lines.

FROM THE FABRIC FOR THE PILLOW PANELS

- *Cut 2 panels: 29″ wide x 29″ long*

FROM THE WONDER UNDER

- *Cut 9 circles: Use the pattern piece provided in the pocket at the front of this book.*

FROM THE 14 FABRICS

- *For the patchwork fabric: Cut 2 strips of fabric from each of the 14 coordinating fabrics at different widths. For example, from the first fabric, cut a first strip that is 2¼″ wide by 45″ long and a second that is 1½″ wide by 45″ long. Vary the widths of the strips (you'll use them to make a fun pattern for the patchwork fabric in step 3). Cut out widths anywhere from 1¼″ to 2¾″ wide by 45″ long.*

- *For the circles: First, make the patchwork fabric in step 3; then cut out 9 circles as indicated in step 4, using the circle pattern piece provided in the pocket at the front of this book.*

FROM THE OPTIONAL MUSLIN FOR THE PILLOW FORM

- *Cut 2 pillow panels: 29″ wide x 29″ long*

Step 2. Make the muslin pillow form (optional).

a. First, take the 2 muslin pillow panels and place them **Right** sides together. Stitch a ½" seam around the panels, leaving a 10" opening in the center of one side. Then, trim the 4 corners in the seam allowance, making sure not to clip your stitching.

b. Turn the muslin pillow form **Right** side out and press. Fill the pillow form with polyester fiberfill to your desired firmness. Fold under the ½" seam allowance at the opening and pin the opening closed. Then, slip stitch the opening closed by hand or machine stitch close to the folded edge.

~ CONTINUED

Step 3. Make the patchwork fabric.

First, take the strips that you cut out in step 1 for the patchwork fabric and lay them out in a pleasing horizontal pattern. Then, take the top 2 strips of fabric from your fabric pattern and place them with **Right** sides together. Stitch a ¼" seam across the matched raw edges and press the seam allowance toward one side. Then, take the next strip of fabric in the fabric pattern and place it onto the other raw edge of the second strip of fabric, with **Right** sides together. Again, stitch a ¼" seam across the matched raw edges and press the seam allowance the same way. Repeat this process until you have attached all of the strips of fabric from your fabric pattern.

Step 4. Cut out the circles from the patchwork fabric.

Using the pattern piece provided, cut out 9 circles from the patchwork fabric you made in step 3. Cut the circles from different areas of the patchwork fabric to achieve a varied look.

Step 5. Press the Wonder Under to the back of each circle.

Take the 9 circles of the Wonder Under and press one onto the back of each of the 9 patchwork circles, following the manufacturer's instructions.

Step 6. Mark the placements for the circles on the front pillow panel.

Starting at the top left corner on the first pillow panel, mark the following measurements across the top raw edge: 5½", 14½", and 23½". Then, measure and mark the same increments across the bottom raw edge. Using your yardstick, line up each of the 2 coordinating marks and draw a line between them. Repeat this process and mark the same measurements along both of the side raw edges, lining up the 2 coordinating marks and drawing a line between them.

Step 7. Attach the circles to the marked pillow panel.

Place the circles onto the front of the pillow panel in a pleasing arrangement, centering each over the cross marks. Press the circles in place following the manufacturer's instructions for fusing on the Wonder Under. Then, machine appliqué* completely around the outside edge of each circle with a tight satin stitch (a very close zigzag stitch), backstitching at each end. (FIGURE 7)

* See page 171 for an explanation of machine appliqué.

Step 8. Attach the front and back pillow panels together.

With the **Right** sides together place the front pillow panel onto the back pillow panel, matching up the raw edges, and pin them in place. Stitch a ½" seam around the raw edges on the pillow panels, leaving a 14" opening centered on the bottom of the panels and backstitching at each end. Trim all 4 corners of the pillow panels, being careful not to clip into your stitching. Then, turn the panels **Right** side out, using a turning tool to push out the corners and press the panel flat.

* See page 172 for an explanation of a turning tool.

Step 9. Finish the pillow.

Insert the pillow form through the bottom opening of the pillow cover, matching up the corners on each. Fold the bottom opening in ½" and pin the opening closed. Slip stitch* the opening closed by hand. (FIGURE 9)

* See page 171 for an explanation of slip stitching.

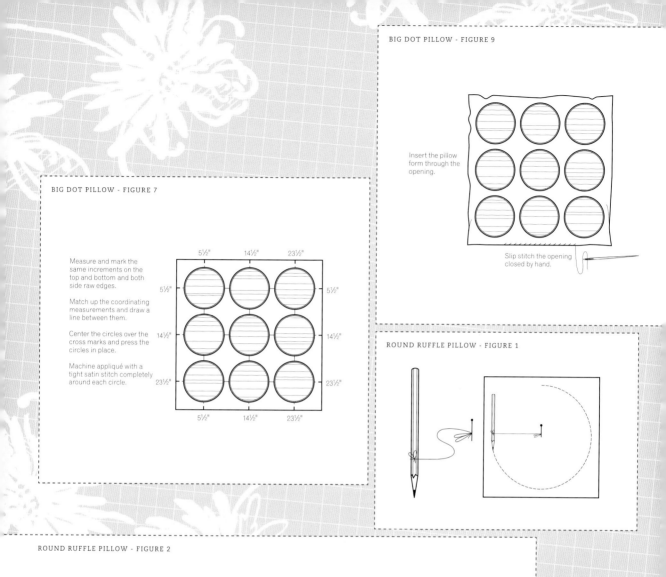

BIG DOT PILLOW - FIGURE 9

Insert the pillow form through the opening.

Slip stitch the opening closed by hand.

BIG DOT PILLOW - FIGURE 7

Measure and mark the same increments on the top and bottom and both side raw edges.

Match up the coordinating measurements and draw a line between them.

Center the circles over the cross marks and press the circles in place.

Machine appliqué with a tight satin stitch completely around each circle.

5½"   14½"   23½"

5½"   5½"

14½"   14½"

23½"   14½"   23½"

5½"   14½"   23½"

ROUND RUFFLE PILLOW - FIGURE 1

ROUND RUFFLE PILLOW - FIGURE 2

LAYOUT FOR THE ROUND RUFFLE PILLOW

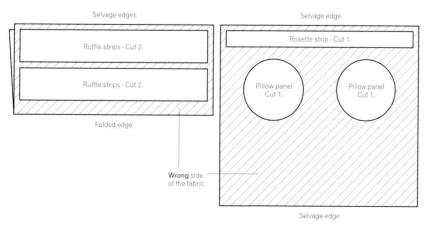

Selvage edges

Ruffle strips - Cut 2.

Ruffle strips - Cut 2.

Folded edge

Selvage edge

Rosette strip - Cut 1.

Pillow panel Cut 1.

Pillow panel Cut 1.

Wrong side of the fabric

Selvage edge

ROUND RUFFLE PILLOW

FINISHED SIZE: 18" DIAMETER

FABRICS

- 3½ yards (44"-wide) mid-weight cotton for the pillow
- 18" round pillow form

OTHER SUPPLIES

- Coordinating thread
- 1 small spool of button/carpet thread for gathering the ruffles
- Freezer paper or any heavier paper, 18" wide

- 12" piece of string
- Pencil
- Yardstick
- Chalk pencil or fabric marker
- Scissors
- Turning tool (such as a closed pair of scissors)
- Straight pins
- Hand sewing needle

NOTES

- All seams are ½" unless otherwise stated. (The ½" seam allowance is included in all cutting measurements.)
- Preshrink your fabric by washing, drying, and pressing it before starting your project.

Step 1. Make the pillow pattern piece.

First, make a 19" circle on the dull side of the freezer paper by taking the string and tying one end to the pencil. Measure from the point on the pencil down the string 9½" and make a knot. Push a long straight pin through the knot and place it in the middle of the freezer paper. Next, using your pencil like a compass, draw a circle while keeping the string taut. Cut out the circle. (FIGURE 1)

Step 2. Cut out all pieces from the fabric.

With **Right** sides together, fold your fabric in half lengthwise, matching up the selvage edges. Using a yardstick and a chalk pencil, and following the measurements below, measure and mark the ruffle strips on the **Wrong** side of the fabric and cut out each panel. Then open up the rest of your fabric and place it **Wrong** side facing up. Measure and mark the rosette strip parallel to the selvage edge but not including it. Then, using the round pillow pattern piece you made in step 1, cut 2 pillow panels out of the rest of the fabric. (FIGURE 2)

- *Cut 4 ruffle strips: 10˝ wide x 60˝ long*
- *Cut 1 rosette strip: 5˝ wide x 60˝ long*
- *Cut 2 round pillow panels: Use the pattern piece you made in step 1.*

Step 3. Attach the ruffle strips together.

First, take 2 ruffle strips and place them **Right** sides together matching up the short side raw edges. Attach by stitching a ½" seam across one of the short ends of the strips. Then, take the next 2 strips and repeat this step to attach them to each other and then to the other strips to make one long ruffle. Press each seam allowance open. (FIGURE 3)

Step 4. Make the ruffle.

a. First, fold the long ruffle strip in half lengthwise with **Right** sides together and pin in place. Stitch a ½" seam down both short ends and along the long side raw edge, leaving a 10" opening. Then, trim all 4 corners in the seam allowance, making sure not to clip the stitching. (FIGURE 4A)

b. Next, turn the ruffle strip **Right** side out, using a turning tool to push out the corners. Then, fold the seam allowances under ½" at the opening and press.

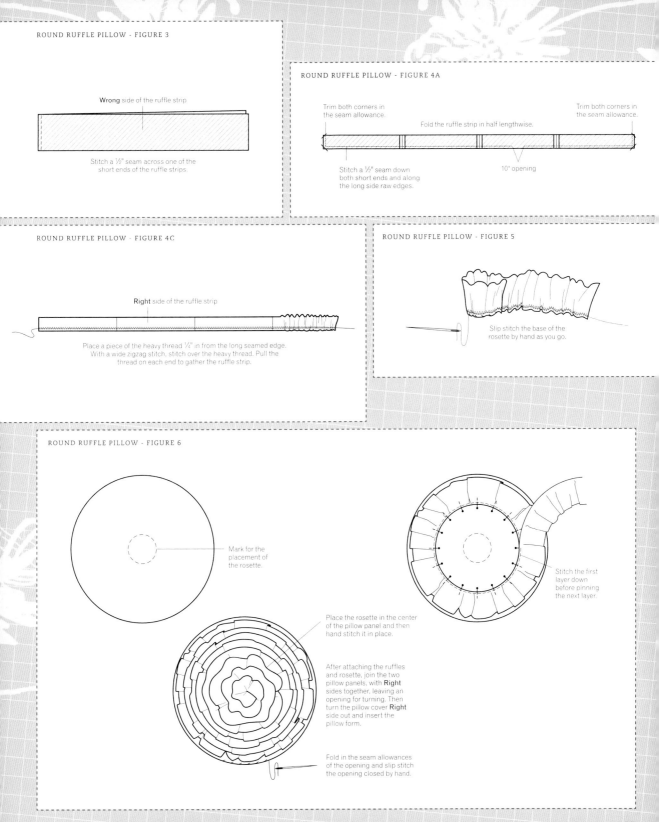

ROUND RUFFLE PILLOW - FIGURE 3

Wrong side of the ruffle strip

Stitch a ½" seam across one of the
short ends of the ruffle strips.

ROUND RUFFLE PILLOW - FIGURE 4A

Trim both corners in
the seam allowance.

Fold the ruffle strip in half lengthwise.

Trim both corners in
the seam allowance.

Stitch a ½" seam down
both short ends and along
the long side raw edges.

10" opening

ROUND RUFFLE PILLOW - FIGURE 4C

Right side of the ruffle strip

Place a piece of the heavy thread ¼" in from the long seamed edge.
With a wide zigzag stitch, stitch over the heavy thread. Pull the
thread on each end to gather the ruffle strip.

ROUND RUFFLE PILLOW - FIGURE 5

Slip stitch the base of the
rosette by hand as you go.

ROUND RUFFLE PILLOW - FIGURE 6

Mark for the
placement of
the rosette.

Stitch the first
layer down
before pinning
the next layer.

Place the rosette in the center
of the pillow panel and then
hand stitch it in place.

After attaching the ruffles
and rosette, join the two
pillow panels, with **Right**
sides together, leaving an
opening for turning. Then
turn the pillow cover **Right**
side out and insert the
pillow form.

Fold in the seam allowances
of the opening and slip stitch
the opening closed by hand.

c. To gather the ruffle, place the button/carpet thread on top of your fabric, ¼" in from the long seamed edge of the ruffle, leaving about 8" to 10" extra on the end of the ruffle strip. Then, with a wide zigzag stitch, stitch back and forth across the heavy thread, along the long seamed edge of the ruffle strip, backstitching at each end. The zigzag stitching makes a casing over the thread. Be careful not to stitch through the heavy thread; otherwise you won't be able to pull the thread to gather the ruffle. (FIGURE 4C)

d. Pull the button/carpet thread on each end of the strip, gathering in the ruffle strip tight, and moving the gathers in toward the center of the strip.

e. Then, to tie off the ends of the gathering thread in order to keep the gathering from loosening up, place a straight pin at the end of the ruffle. Taking the heavy thread used to gather the ruffle, loop it around the ends of the straight pin in a figure 8 pattern (up and around the top of the straight pin and down and across the bottom part of the pin). Do this a number of times to hold the gathering in place. Repeat this step to tie off the other end of the gathering thread on the other end of the ruffle. Keep the straight pins in place until after you stitch the ruffle to the pillow top.

Step 5. Make the rosette for the center of the pillow.

Repeat steps 4a through 4d. To form the rosette, coil the gathered strip for the rosette in a continuous circle, slip stitching* by hand at the bottom of the base as you go to keep the base of the rosette from uncoiling. (FIGURE 5)

See page 171 for an explanation of slip stitching.

Step 6. Attach the ruffle and rosette to the pillow.

a. On the **Right** side of the front pillow panel, place your rosette in the center of the panel and pin it in place. Using your chalk pencil, draw a circle around the base of the rosette to leave room for it when attaching the ruffle. Remove the rosette.

b. Then, starting 5½" in from the outside raw edge, take the gathered ruffle and pin it onto the front pillow panel in a continuous circle, slowly working the ruffle toward the center of the pillow. Once you pin the ruffle around the pillow in one complete turn, stop pinning and machine stitch the first row of ruffle in place. Then, continue pinning the ruffle in a continuous spiral shape, stopping and sewing each time you complete one turn around the panel. You can vary the tightness of the ruffle by taking tucks in the ruffle or overlapping it as you go. Remove any pins that you used to tie off the gathering stitches on the ruffles and trim away the long ends of the gathering threads.

c. Then, place the rosette in the center of the pillow again and slip stitch the rosette to the pillow top by hand completely around the base of the rosette. (FIGURE 6)

Step 7. Attach the front and back pillow panels together.

a. First, fold the ruffle in on the front pillow panel so you don't catch the ruffle in your stitching. Then place the pillow panels with **Right** sides together and pin them in place. Stitch a ½" seam around the pillow panels, leaving a 10" opening to turn the pillow **Right** side out.

b. Now, turn the pillow cover **Right** side out and insert the pillow form. Then, fold under the seam allowances of the opening and pin the opening closed. Slip stitch the opening closed by hand.

POM-POM PILLOW

FINISHED SIZE: 16" WIDE X 28" LONG

FABRICS

- 1 yard (36"-wide) mid- to heavy-weight cotton fabric for the pillow panels
- 1 yard (36"-wide) cotton muslin for the pillow form

OTHER SUPPLIES

- Coordinating thread
- 1 1-lb. bag shredded foam
- 1⅛" x 5" piece stiff cardboard

- 4 (65m/50g) balls coordinating yarn, or 200 grams "chunky" coordinating yarn*
- Yardstick
- Chalk pencil or fabric marker
- Scissors
- Hand sewing yarn needle (size 11)
- Straight pins
- Turning tool (such as a closed pair of scissors)

NOTES

- All seams are ½" unless otherwise stated. (The ½" seam allowance is included in all cutting measurements.)
- Preshrink your fabric by washing, drying, and pressing it before starting your project.

We used a yarn thickness that is suitable for size 11 knitting needles.

Step 1. Cut all pieces from the fabric.

Simply measure and mark the dimensions below directly onto the **Wrong** side of your fabric, using your yardstick and chalk pencil. Then, using your scissors, cut out each panel following the marked lines.

FROM THE FABRIC FOR THE PANELS
- *Cut 2 panels: 17˝ wide x 29˝ long*

FROM THE FABRIC FOR THE PILLOW FORM
- *Cut 2 panels: 17˝ wide x 29˝ long*

Step 2. Make the muslin pillow form.

First, take the 2 muslin pillow panels and place them **Right** sides together. Stitch a ½" seam around the panels, leaving a 6" opening on one of the long sides. Then, trim the 4 corners in the seam allowance, making sure not to clip into your stitching.

Step 3. Finish the pillow form.

Turn the muslin pillow form **Right** side out and press. Fill the pillow form with the shredded foam to your desired firmness. Fold under the ½" seam allowance on the opening and pin the opening closed. Then, slip stitch the opening closed by hand or machine stitch close to the folded edge.

Step 4. Make the pom-poms for the pillow top.

a. Wind your yarn around the 1⅛" width of the cardboard approximately 100 times. (FIGURE 4A)

b. Then, take an 18" piece of yarn and thread it onto a yarn needle, pulling through about 4" of the yarn. Slide the needle underneath the wrapped yarn on the cardboard along the bottom long side and pull the needle through, leaving 4" of the yarn hanging out on each side. Tie the ends of the yarn tight in a single knot at the center of the yarn along the bottom edge of the cardboard to hold it securely in place. (FIGURE 4B)

c. Using your scissors, cut the yarn along the top edge of the cardboard, releasing the yarn from the cardboard. Now, tighten up the knot you made in the center of the cut yarn and tie a double knot to secure the strands of yarn. Fluff up the pom-pom to make a half sphere and trim the long ends and long strands of yarn to make a rounded shape. Repeat this step to make a total of 18 pom-poms and then set them aside. The pom-poms will be attached to the front of the pillow by stitching the flat side of the sphere onto the pillow front. (FIGURE 4C)

Step 5. Mark the placement for the pom-poms on the front pillow panel.

On the **Right** side of the first pillow panel, starting at the top left corner, measure and mark the following increments across the top raw edge: 4½", 8½", 12½", 16½", 20½", 24½". Then, starting at the bottom left corner, measure and mark the same increments across the bottom raw edge. Using your yardstick and a chalk pencil, line up the coordinating marks and draw a line between them. Then, measure and mark the first three increments (4½", 8½", and 12½") down both sides of the front pillow panel. Line up the coordinating marks and draw a line between them. **(FIGURE 5)**

Step 6. Attach the pom-poms to the front pillow panel.

Center the pom-poms where the marks intersect and pin them in place. Doubling up the thread in your needle for strength, slip stitch* each pom-pom firmly in place by hand.

See page 171 for an explanation of slip stitching.

Step 7. Attach the front and back pillow panels together.

Place the 2 pillow panels **Right** sides together, matching up the side raw edges, and pin them in place. Stitch a ½" seam around the panels, leaving a 15" opening in the center of one of the long side raw edges. Trim each of the corners in the seam allowance, making sure not to clip the stitching.

Step 8. Finish the Pom-pom Pillow.

Turn the pillow **Right** side out and press. Insert the muslin pillow form you made in steps 2 and 3 inside the pillow cover. Fold under the ½" seam allowance in the opening and pin the opening closed. Slip stitch the opening closed by hand.

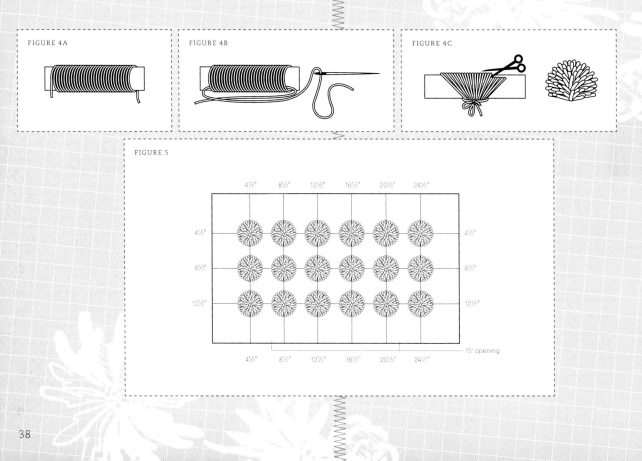

FIGURE 4A

FIGURE 4B

FIGURE 4C

FIGURE 5

CHAPTER 2

KITCHEN

Projects

The projects that follow will bring some vintage charm to your culinary efforts Remember your grandma's white tile and chrome kitchen? These placemats, napkins, aprons, and pot holders have all of that retro homeyness, with a little modern flair to boot. Plus, they make great gifts for new home-owners, moms, and amateur chefs alike. So awaken your inner June Cleaver and start heating up that kitchen—with style!

PLACEMATS

FINISHED SIZE: 4 PLACEMATS: EACH 20" WIDE X 15" LONG

A lovely, personal housewarming or wedding gift, these reversible placemats and large, dinner-sized reversible **NAPKINS** (page 43) are truly a modern heirloom to be cherished.

FABRICS

• 2 yards (44"-wide) home-decor-weight cotton for the centers and backs of the Placemats

• ½ yard (44"-wide) coordinating mid-weight cotton for the sides of the Placemats

• 2 yards (22"-wide) Timtex* or similar extra-heavyweight interfacing

See page 172 for an explanation of Timtex.

OTHER SUPPLIES

• Coordinating thread

• Yardstick

• Chalk pencil or fabric marker

• Scissors

• Masking tape

• Straight pins

• Turning tool (such as a closed pair of scissors)

• Hand sewing needle

NOTES

• All seams are ½" unless otherwise stated. (The ½" seam allowance is included in all cutting measurements.)

• Preshrink your fabric by washing, drying, and pressing it before starting your project. To wash Timtex after completing your project, machine wash warm, then reshape your project and air dry. Your project will press back into shape with a steam iron. Once you steam the project, lay it flat while air drying.

Step 1. Cut out all pieces from the fabric.

a. Simply measure and mark the dimensions below directly onto the **Wrong** side of your fabric, using a yardstick and a chalk pencil. Then, using your scissors, cut out each panel following the marked lines.

FROM THE FABRIC FOR THE CENTERS AND BACKS
• Cut 4 center panels: 15" wide x 16" long
• Cut 4 back panels: 21" wide x 16" long

FROM THE FABRIC FOR THE SIDES
• Cut 8 side panels: 4" wide x 16" long

FROM THE TIMTEX
• Cut 4 panels: 15" wide x 20" long

b. In order to keep your pieces organized, mark each piece by writing the name on a piece of masking tape and attaching it to the **Wrong** side of each panel as it is cut.

Step 2. Make the front of the Placemat.

First, with **Right** sides together, place one side panel onto one center panel, matching up the left side raw edge of the center panel with the right side raw edge of the first side panel, and pin it in place. Attach by stitching a ½" seam down the matched side raw edges, backstitching at each end. Then, press the seam allowance toward the side panel. Repeat this step to attach another side panel onto the right side raw edge of the first center panel. (FIGURE 2)

~ CONTINUED

Step 3. Attach the front and back panels together.

With **Right** sides together, pin the front of the Placemat and the first back panel together. Attach by stitching a ½" seam around the Placemat, leaving an 8" opening centered on one of the short ends. Next, trim all 4 corners in the seam allowance, making sure not to clip your stitching. **(FIGURE 3)**

Step 4. Inserting the Timtex.

First, turn your Placemat **Right** side out, using a turning tool to push out the corners, and press. Then, starting with the long edge of the Timtex, roll it up just enough so it will slide in through the 8" opening. Then, with the front of the Placemat facing up, insert the Timtex through the opening and smooth it flat, lining up all 4 corners. Place the Timtex on top of the seam allowances to make the front of the Placemat appear smooth.

Step 5. Finishing the Placemat.

Next, fold under the raw edges ½" at the 8" opening and pin them in place. Then, slip stitch* the opening closed by hand. Press the Placemat flat, using steam to smooth out and flatten the Timtex. Finally, topstitch completely around the Placemat with a ¼" seam to secure the Timtex and give the Placemat a finished look.

See page 171 for an explanation of slip stitching.

Step 6. Follow the instructions in steps 2 through 5 to make the other 3 Placemats.

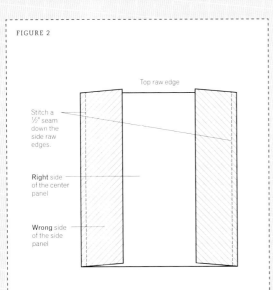

FIGURE 2

Top raw edge

Stitch a ½" seam down the side raw edges.

Right side of the center panel

Wrong side of the side panel

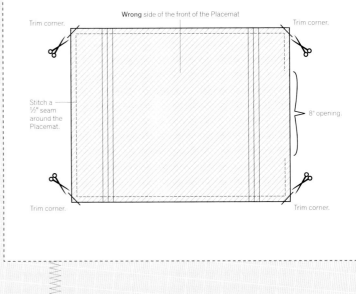

FIGURE 3

Trim corner.

Wrong side of the front of the Placemat

Trim corner.

Stitch a ½" seam around the Placemat.

8" opening.

Trim corner.

Trim corner.

NAPKINS

FINISHED SIZE: 4 NAPKINS: EACH 21" WIDE X 23" LONG

FABRICS

- 1½ yards (44"-wide) mid-weight cotton for the fronts
- 1½ yards (44"-wide) coordinating mid-weight cotton for the reversible backs

OTHER SUPPLIES

- Coordinating thread
- Yardstick
- Chalk pencil or fabric marker
- Scissors
- Straight pins
- Turning tool (such as a closed pair of scissors)

NOTES

- All seams are ½" unless otherwise stated. (The ½" seam allowance is included in all cutting measurements.)
- Preshrink your fabric by washing, drying, and pressing it before starting your project.

Step 1. Cut out all pieces from the fabric.

Simply measure and mark the dimensions directly onto the **Wrong** side of your fabric, using your yardstick and chalk pencil. Then, using your scissors, cut out each panel following the marked lines.

FROM THE FABRIC FOR THE FRONTS

- *Cut 4 panels: 22˝ wide x 24˝ long*

FROM THE COORDINATING FABRIC FOR THE REVERSIBLE BACKS

- *Cut 4 panels: 22˝ wide x 24˝ long*

Step 2. Make the Napkins.

Place the first front panel and the first reversible side panel with **Right** sides together, matching up the raw edges, and pin them in place. Stitch a ½" seam around the Napkin, leaving a 3" opening centered on one side, backstitching at each end. Next, trim all 4 corners in the seam allowance, making sure not to clip your stitching. Then, turn your Napkin **Right** side out, using a turning tool* to push out the corners.

* See page 172 for an explanation of a turning tool.

Step 3. Finish the Napkins.

Fold under the raw edges ½" at the 3" opening and press. Pin the opening closed. Then, topstitch* with a ⅛" seam completely around the Napkin to close the opening, and then press the Napkin flat.

* See page 172 for an explanation of topstitching.

Step 4.

Follow the instructions in steps 2 and 3 to make the other 3 Napkins.

GIFTABLE RECIPE CARD BAGS

FINISHED SIZES: SMALL GIFTABLE RECIPE CARD BAG: 3¾" WIDE X 6¾" TALL (FITS 3" X 5" CARDS)
LARGE RECIPE CARD BAG: 4¾" WIDE X 7¾" TALL (FITS 4" X 6" CARDS)

Every chef needs a place to keep her favorite recipes. When you're organizing, storing, or gifting your prized pie recipes, you can whip up these lovely recipe card bags, which make any recipe even more special.

FABRICS

- ¼ yard (44"-wide) light- to mid-weight cotton for the top panel
- ¼ yard (44"-wide) coordinating light- to mid-weight cotton for the bottom panel
- ¼"-wide ribbon for the drawstring (16" for the small bag; 24" for the large bag)
- ⅝"-wide ribbon for the trim (8" for the small bag; 10" for the large bag)

OTHER SUPPLIES

- Coordinating cotton thread
- Straight pins
- Scissors
- Ruler
- Chalk pencil or fabric marker
- Turning tool (such as a closed pair of scissors)
- Small safety pin

NOTES

- All seams are ½" unless otherwise stated. (The ½" seam allowance is included in all pattern pieces and cutting measurements provided.)
- Preshrink your fabric by washing, drying, and pressing it before starting your project.

Step 1. Cut out all pieces from the fabric.

NOTE: *The following instructions are the same for making both sizes of the Giftable Recipe Card Bags.*

a. First, determine which size bag you are making and cut out the correct Recipe Card Bag pattern pieces provided in the pocket at the front of this book.
- *Large or Small Giftable Recipe Card Bag Top Panel*
- *Large or Small Giftable Recipe Card Bag Bottom Panel*

b. Then pin the pattern pieces to the fabrics and, using your scissors, cut out each panel according to the outlines on the pattern pieces.

FROM THE FABRIC FOR THE TOP PANEL
- *Cut 1 top panel on the fold:* Use top panel pattern piece provided in the pocket at the front of this book.

FROM THE FABRIC FOR THE BOTTOM PANEL
- *Cut 1 bottom panel on the fold:* Use bottom panel pattern piece provided in the pocket at the front of this book.

  * To cut the pattern piece on the fold of your fabric, lay your pattern piece so that the edge to be placed on the fold is even with the folded edge of your fabric. Once this pattern piece is cut out of your fabric, open it up to make one full panel.

Step 2. Attach the top and bottom panels together.

a. With **Right** sides together, pin the bottom raw edge of the top panel to the top raw edge of the bottom panel. Attach the panels by stitching a ¼" seam across the matched raw edges, backstitching at each end. Serge or zigzag across the panels in the seam allowance to finish the raw edge, and then press the seam allowance down.

~ CONTINUED

b. Now, open up the attached panels, and with the **Right** side facing up, center the ⅝"-wide ribbon over the seam and pin the ribbon in place, making sure to keep it straight and centered over the seam. Then, edge stitch* along both long edges of the ribbon, stitching close to the edge of the ribbon, and press. (FIGURE 2B)

See page 170 for an explanation of edge stitching.

Step 3. Measure, mark, and prepare the drawstring casing.

a. With the **Wrong** side of the panels facing up, start on the left-side raw edge of the top panel, measure down from the top raw edge 1¼", and make a mark with your chalk pencil. Repeat this step to mark the right-side raw edge of the top panel.

b. On the **Wrong** side of the attached top panel, at the left 1¼" mark, sew a 1"-long stitch line ½" in from the raw edges to reinforce the cut you will make in the seam allowance. Repeat this step for the right side of the top panel.

c. Then, clip into the seam allowance at the 1¼" mark, just to the reinforced stitching* line on both sides of the panel. (FIGURE 3C)

See page 171 for an explanation of a reinforcement stitch.

d. Now, take the left-side raw edge above the 1¼" clip, fold it in ¼" toward the **Wrong** side, and press it in place. Then, fold the edge in again ¼" and press. Topstitch* along the inner folded edge, backstitching at each end. Repeat this step to finish the right-side raw edge of the casing. (FIGURE 3D)

See page 172 for an explanation of topstitching.

e. With the **Wrong** side of the panel still facing up, fold the top raw edge ¼" in toward the **Wrong** side of the panel and press. Fold the top edge in again ½" and press. Pin in place and topstitch across the inner folded edge to make the casing, backstitching at each end. (FIGURE 3E)

Step 4. Finish the Recipe Card Bag.

a. First, fold the panel in half lengthwise with the **Right** sides together. Pin along the side and bottom raw edges, matching up the ribbon stitched over the seam, and matching the top finished edge.

b. Stitch the panel together by sewing a ½" seam down the side and across the bottom raw edges, backstitching at each end. (FIGURE 4B)

c. Now, using your scissors, trim the 2 bottom corners* in the seam allowance, making sure not to clip the stitching. Then, serge or zigzag the seam allowance and press.

See page 172 for an explanation of trimming corners.

d. Turn the bag **Right** side out, using a turning tool* to push out the bottom corners, and then press it flat.

See page 172 for an explanation of a turning tool.

e. Using the small safety pin, attach the pin to one end of the ¼" drawstring ribbon and thread it through the casing at the top of the bag. Then, remove the safety pin, and tie a knot on each end of the ribbon.

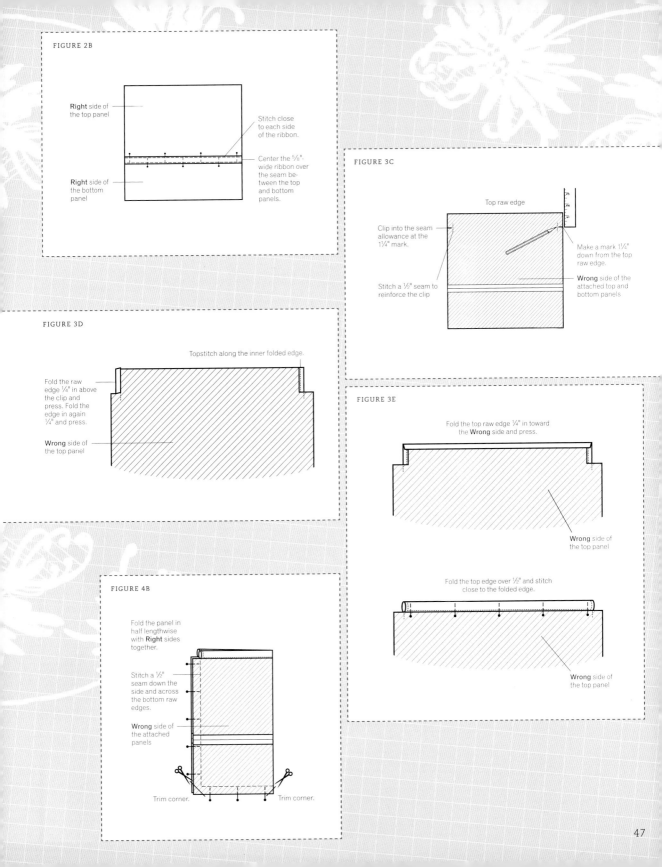

FIGURE 2B

Right side of the top panel

Stitch close to each side of the ribbon.

Center the ⅝"-wide ribbon over the seam between the top and bottom panels.

Right side of the bottom panel

FIGURE 3C

Top raw edge

Clip into the seam allowance at the 1¼" mark.

Make a mark 1¼" down from the top raw edge.

Wrong side of the attached top and bottom panels

Stitch a ½" seam to reinforce the clip

FIGURE 3D

Topstitch along the inner folded edge.

Fold the raw edge ¼" in above the clip and press. Fold the edge in again ¼" and press.

Wrong side of the top panel

FIGURE 3E

Fold the top raw edge ¼" in toward the **Wrong** side and press.

Wrong side of the top panel

Fold the top edge over ½" and stitch close to the folded edge.

Wrong side of the top panel

FIGURE 4B

Fold the panel in half lengthwise with **Right** sides together.

Stitch a ½" seam down the side and across the bottom raw edges.

Wrong side of the attached panels

Trim corner.   Trim corner.

SHORT PLEATED APRON

FINISHED SIZE: 31½" ACROSS THE BOTTOM X 24¾" LONG, WITH 31"-LONG TIES; FITS MOST ADULTS.

You'll make your grandma proud when you don this traditional pleated apron, and you can give it your signature look by choosing bright and beautiful fabrics. We've put a towel loop right where you need it, and a pocket for you to stash recipes. Now twirl about the kitchen in style!

FABRICS

- ¾ yard (44"-wide) light- to mid-weight cotton print for the apron panel, pocket, and towel loop
- ¾ yard (44"-wide) coordinating light- to mid-weight solid cotton for the trim, waistband, and ties

OTHER SUPPLIES

- Coordinating thread
- Yardstick
- Chalk pencil or fabric marker
- Scissors
- Masking tape
- Straight pins
- Hand sewing needle

NOTES

- All seams are ½" unless otherwise stated. (The ½" seam allowance is included in all cutting measurements.)
- Preshrink your fabric by washing, drying, and pressing it before starting your project.

Step 1. Cut out all pieces from the fabric.

a. Simply measure and mark the dimensions below directly onto the **Wrong** side of the fabric, using a yardstick and a chalk pencil. Then, using your scissors, cut out each panel following the marked lines.

FROM THE FABRIC FOR THE APRON PANEL, POCKET, AND TOWEL LOOP (FIGURE 1A-01)

- *Cut 1 apron panel: 33½" wide x 22½" long*
- *Cut 1 pocket: 5¼" wide x 6" long*
- *Cut 1 towel loop: 2½" wide x 7" long*

FROM THE FABRIC FOR THE TRIM, WAISTBAND, AND TIES (FIGURE 1A-02)

- *Cut 1 apron trim: 3" wide x 33½" long*
- *Cut 1 waistband: 5½" wide x 21½" long*
- *Cut 2 ties: 6½" wide x 32½" long*
- *Cut 1 pocket trim: 1¾" wide x 5¼" long*

b. In order to keep your pieces organized, mark each piece by writing the name on a piece of masking tape and attaching to the **Wrong** side of each panel as it is cut.

Step 2. Make and attach the pocket.

a. First, place the **Right** side of the pocket trim facing down onto the **Wrong** side of the pocket at the top raw edge. Pin the trim in place. Stitch a ½" seam across the matched raw edges, backstitching at each end.

b. Then, fold the pocket trim over onto the **Right** side of the pocket and press the top seam flat.

c. Fold ½" under at the bottom raw edge of the pocket trim, toward the **Wrong** side of the trim, and press. Topstitch* along the inner folded edge on the trim to enclose the raw edges and attach the trim. (FIGURE 2C)

* See page 172 for an explanation of topstitching.

d. Now, turn the pocket over so the **Wrong** side is facing up. Fold in ½" toward the **Wrong** side of the fabric down both sides and across the bottom raw edge of the pocket and press.

~ CONTINUED

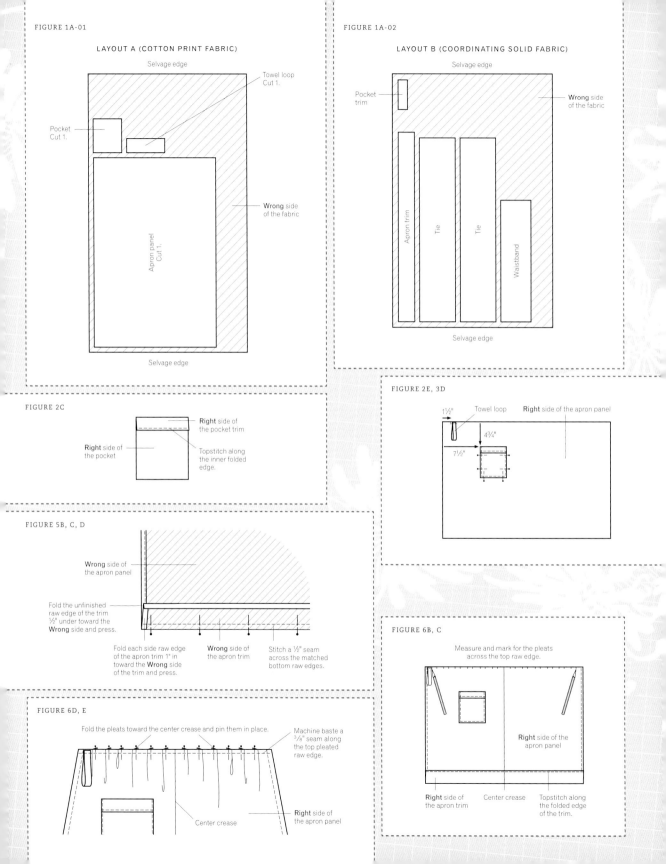

FIGURE 1A-01

LAYOUT A (COTTON PRINT FABRIC)

Selvage edge

Towel loop
Cut 1.

Pocket
Cut 1.

Wrong side
of the fabric

Apron panel
Cut 1.

Selvage edge

FIGURE 1A-02

LAYOUT B (COORDINATING SOLID FABRIC)

Selvage edge

Pocket
trim

Wrong side
of the fabric

Apron trim

Tie

Tie

Waistband

Selvage edge

FIGURE 2C

Right side of
the pocket trim

Right side of
the pocket

Topstitch along
the inner folded
edge.

FIGURE 2E, 3D

1½"

Towel loop

Right side of the apron panel

4¾"

7½"

FIGURE 5B, C, D

Wrong side of
the apron panel

Fold the unfinished
raw edge of the trim
½" under toward the
Wrong side and press.

Fold each side raw edge
of the apron trim 1" in
toward the Wrong side
of the trim and press.

Wrong side
of the apron trim

Stitch a ½" seam
across the matched
bottom raw edges.

FIGURE 6B, C

Measure and mark for the pleats
across the top raw edge.

Right side of the
apron panel

Right side of
the apron trim

Center crease

Topstitch along
the folded edge
of the trim.

FIGURE 6D, E

Fold the pleats toward the center crease and pin them in place.

Machine baste a
³⁄₈" seam along
the top pleated
raw edge.

Right side of the apron panel

Center crease

e. With the **Right** side of the apron panel facing up, place the pocket **Wrong** side facing down, with the top edge of the pocket 4¾" from the top edge of the apron panel and the left edge of the pocket 7½" in from the left raw edge of the apron panel. Pin the pocket in place and then attach the pocket to the apron panel by stitching close to the folded edges, down both sides and across the bottom edge of the pocket, backstitching at each end. (FIGURE 2E, 3D)

Step 3. Make and attach the towel loop to the apron panel.

a. First, find the center of the towel loop by folding it in half lengthwise with the **Wrong** sides facing each other, and gently press a center crease.

b. Unfold the towel loop and fold the long side raw edges in toward the center crease and press.

c. Now, refold the entire towel loop together along the original center crease to enclose the raw edges, and press. Edge stitch* down both sides of the towel loop close to the folded edges.

See page 170 for an explanation of edge stitching.

d. Place the towel loop on the **Right** side of the apron panel with the matched raw ends of the loop even with the top raw edge of the apron panel, and the left edge of the loop 1½" in from the left raw edge of the apron panel. (FIGURE 2E/3D)

e. Pin the towel loop in place and machine baste it to the apron panel with a ¼" seam across the raw ends.

Step 4. Finish the side raw edges of the apron panel.

a. With the **Wrong** side of the apron panel facing up, fold the left side raw edge in ½" and press. Fold in again ½" and pin along the inner folded edge.

b. Topstitch close to the inner folded edge of the apron panel to finish the side edge.

c. Repeat steps 4a and 4b to finish the right side raw edge of the apron panel.

Step 5. Attach the apron trim to the apron panel.

a. First, fold the short raw ends of the apron trim 1" in toward the **Wrong** side and press.

b. With the **Right** side of the trim facing the **Wrong** side of the apron panel, line up the folded edge of the apron trim so that it's even with the finished side edge of the apron panel, matching up the bottom raw edges. Pin the trim in place. (FIGURE 5B, C, D)

c. Stitch a ½" seam across the matched raw edges, backstitching at each end. (FIGURE 5B, C, D)

d. Then, fold ½" under on the unfinished raw edge of the apron trim, toward the **Wrong** side of the trim, and press. (FIGURE 5B, C, D)

e. Now, turn the apron panel over so that the **Right** side is facing up.

f. Fold the apron trim over onto the **Right** side of the bottom of the apron panel and press the trim flat. Pin the top folded edge of the apron trim in place.

g. On the **Right** side of the apron panel, edge stitch across the inner folded edge of the trim to enclose the raw edges, backstitching at each end.

Step 6. Make the pleats on the apron panel.

a. First, find the center of the apron panel by folding it in half lengthwise, and gently press a center crease.

b. Then, starting at the top left corner of the top raw edge, measure over toward the center of the apron panel and make marks at the following increments: 1⅜", 2⅜", 3¾", 4¾", 6", 7", 8½", 9½", 11", 12", 13½", 14½" (FIGURE 6B, C)

c. Repeat step 6b, measuring from the top right corner of the top raw edge of the apron panel. There will be 24 marks across the top raw edge of the apron panel. (FIGURE 6B, C)

d. Now, you will make 6 pleats on each side of the center crease at the top of the apron panel. Match up the first 2 marks with the **Right** sides together. Fold the pleat that forms on the **Wrong** side of the fabric toward the center of the apron, and pin the pleat in place. Repeat this step to pleat each set of 2 marks until you have made 6 pleats on each side of the center crease of the apron panel. (FIGURE 6D, E)

e. Press all the pleats toward the center crease and machine baste a ⅜" seam across the top pleated raw edge to secure the pleats. (FIGURE 6D, E)

~ CONTINUED

Step 7. Attach the waistband to the apron panel.

a. First, find the center of the waistband by folding it in half crosswise, matching the short raw ends. Gently press a crease to mark the center.

b. Now, place one long raw edge of the waistband on the top raw edge of the pleated apron panel **Right** sides together, matching the center crease of the waistband with the center crease of the apron panel. (There will be ½" of the waistband left on each side of the apron panel. This is the seam allowance for attaching the ties.)

c. Then, attach the waistband by stitching a ½" seam along the matched raw edges, backstitching at each end.

d. Fold under ½" on the long raw edge of the waistband toward the **Wrong** side and press.

e. Now, fold the waistband in half, matching the long folded edge to the stitching attaching the apron panel, and gently press a crease to mark the center. (FIGURE 7E)

Step 8. Make and pleat the ties.

a. Fold the first tie in half lengthwise with **Right** sides together, matching up the raw edges, and pin the sides in place. Stitch a ½" seam down the long side raw edges and along one end.

b. Then, trim the 2 bottom corners* in the seam allowance, making sure not to clip the stitching.

See page 172 for an explanation of trimming corners.

c. Turn the tie **Right** side out and press.

d. At the open end of the tie, machine baste* a ¼" seam across the matched raw edges. Then, find the center of the raw end of the tie by folding the tie in half lengthwise and pressing a crease. Measure ½" to the right of the center crease and make a mark. Measure ½" to the left of the center crease and make another mark.

See page 171 for an explanation of machine basting.

e. Make a pleat in the center of the raw edge of the tie, matching the 2 marks you just made, and pin the pleat toward the folded edge. Machine baste the pleat in place.

f. Repeat steps 8a through 8d to make and pleat the second tie. (FIGURE 8F)

Step 9. Attach the ties and finish the waistband.

a. With the **Right** side of the apron and attached waistband facing up, start on the left side of the waistband and line up the folded edge of the first tie, so that the folded edge is even with the center crease mark on the waistband. Match the raw edges and pin the tie in place.

b. Then, machine baste the tie to the waistband with a ½" seam along the matched raw edges.

c. Repeat steps 9a and 9b to attach the second tie to the other side of the waistband. (FIGURE 9C)

d. Now, fold the waistband in half over the ties, with the **Right** sides together and matching up the raw edges. Stitch a ½" seam across the matched raw edges on each end of the waistband. (FIGURE 9D)

e. Then, turn the waistband **Right** side out by pulling both of the ties out. Press the waistband flat.

f. Turn the apron over, so that the **Wrong** side is facing up. Pin the folded edge of the waistband even with the seam that attached the waistband to the apron panel.

g. Turn the apron so the **Right** side is facing up and top-stitch ¼" from the lower edge of the waistband, back-stitching at each end to finish the waistband. (FIGURE 9G)

Step 10. Make a point at the end of each tie.

a. With the back of the ties facing up, take the top, finished end of the tie and fold it in a triangle, matching up the end with the seamed edge of the tie.

b. Slip stitch* the matched seamed edges of the tie together by hand, leaving the folded edge unattached. (FIGURE 10B)

See page 171 for an explanation of slip stitching.

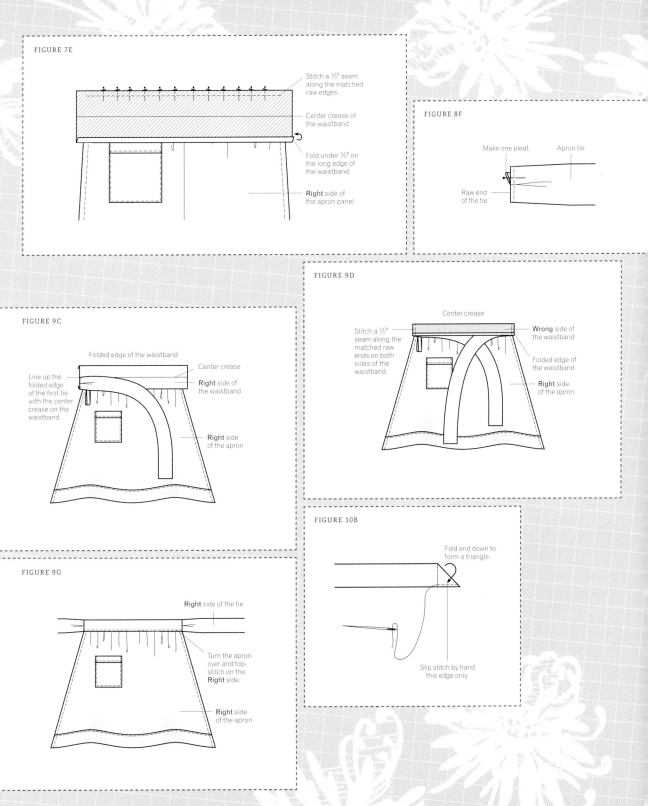

FIGURE 7E

Stitch a ½" seam along the matched raw edges.

Center crease of the waistband

Fold under ⅛" on the long edge of the waistband.

Right side of the apron panel

FIGURE 8F

Make one pleat.

Apron tie

Raw end of the tie

FIGURE 9C

Folded edge of the waistband

Line up the folded edge of the first tie with the center crease on the waistband.

Center crease

Right side of the waistband

Right side of the apron

FIGURE 9D

Center crease

Stitch a ½" seam along the matched raw ends on both sides of the waistband.

Wrong side of the waistband

Folded edge of the waistband

Right side of the apron

FIGURE 10B

Fold end down to form a triangle.

Slip stitch by hand this edge only.

FIGURE 9G

Right side of the tie

Turn the apron over and top-stitch on the **Right** side.

Right side of the apron

SQUARE POT HOLDER

FINISHED SIZE: 9" SQUARE

I'll bet you've never thought pot holders could be cool. Well, think again. In this design, modern patchwork style dresses up the kitchen workhorse. The pot holder has protective hand-cover backs and a grommet for hanging—so convenient. And it's just the thing to bring a whole lot of cool to your next sizzling dinner party.

FABRICS

- ¼ yard (44"-wide) light- to mid-weight cotton print for 2 of the patchwork panels and the hand covers

- ⅛ yard (44"-wide) light- to mid-weight coordinating solid-color cotton for 2 of the patchwork panels

- ¼ yard (44"-wide) light- to mid-weight coordinating solid-color cotton fabric for the back panel

- ½ yard (44"-wide) light- to mid-weight coordinating cotton print for the bias binding

- ¼ yard (45"-wide) cotton batting

OTHER SUPPLIES

- Coordinating thread
- 1 (½") grommet
- Scissors
- Straight pins
- Ruler
- Chalk pencil or fabric marker

- 1"-wide masking tape
- Hand sewing needle

NOTES

- All seams are ½" unless otherwise stated. (The ½" seam allowance is included in all cutting measurements and the pattern pieces.)

- Preshrink your fabric by washing, drying, and pressing it before starting your project.

Step 1. Cut out all pieces from the fabric.

a. First, cut out the Square Pot Holder pattern pieces provided in the pocket at the front of this book.

- *Square Pot Holder patchwork panels A, B, C, and D*

b. Then pin the pattern pieces to the fabric and, using your scissors, cut out each panel according to the outlines on the pattern pieces.

FROM THE PRINTED FABRIC FOR 2 PATCHWORK PANELS AND HAND COVERS

- *Cut 1 panel: Use pattern piece A.*
- *Cut 1 panel: Use pattern piece D.*
- *Cut 2 hand covers: 8" wide x 9" long (Mark these dimensions directly onto the Wrong side of your fabric, using your yardstick and chalk pencil. Then, using your scissors, cut out the hand covers following the marked lines.)*

FROM THE SOLID-COLOR FABRIC FOR THE OTHER 2 PATCHWORK PANELS

- *Cut 1 panel: Use pattern piece B.*
- *Cut 1 panel: Use pattern piece C.*

c. To cut out the back panel, bias binding, and batting panels, simply measure and mark the dimensions below directly onto the **Wrong** side of your fabric, using your ruler and chalk pencil. Then, using your scissors, cut out each panel following the marked lines.

FROM THE SOLID-COLOR FABRIC FOR THE BACK PANEL

- *Cut 1 back panel: 9" wide x 9" long*

FROM THE PRINTED FABRIC FOR THE BIAS BINDING

- *Follow the instructions in step 6 to cut and make the bias binding.*

FROM THE COTTON BATTING

- *Cut 2 panels: 9" wide x 9" long*
- *Cut 2 panels: 4" wide x 9" long*

~ CONTINUED

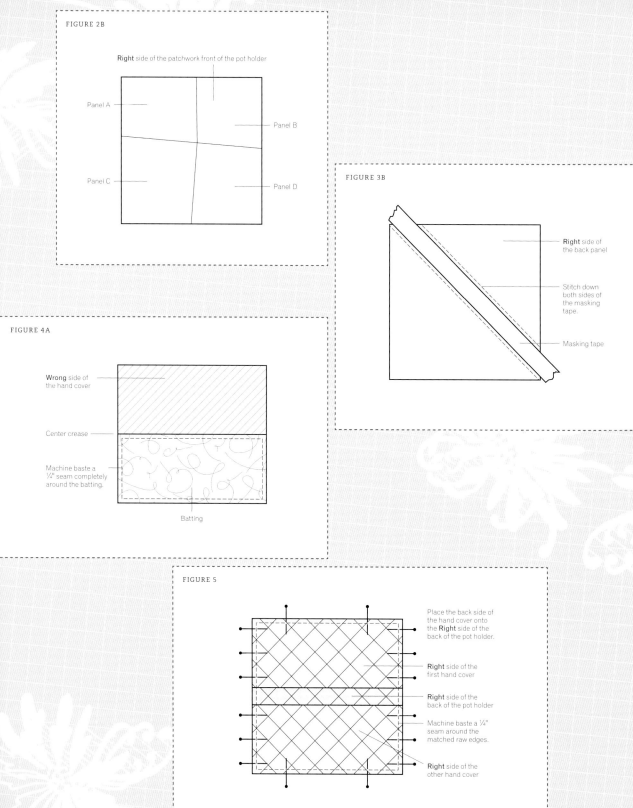

FIGURE 2B

Right side of the patchwork front of the pot holder

Panel A

Panel B

Panel C

Panel D

FIGURE 3B

Right side of the back panel

Stitch down both sides of the masking tape.

Masking tape

FIGURE 4A

Wrong side of the hand cover

Center crease

Machine baste a ¼" seam completely around the batting.

Batting

FIGURE 5

Place the back side of the hand cover onto the Right side of the back of the pot holder.

Right side of the first hand cover

Right side of the back of the pot holder

Machine baste a ¼" seam around the matched raw edges.

Right side of the other hand cover

Step 2. Make the patchwork front of the pot holder.

a. Place panel A and panel B with **Right** sides together, matching up the side raw edges, and pin them in place. Stitch a ¼" seam along the matched raw edges, back-stitching at each end. Press the seam allowance to one side. Then, repeat this step, attaching panels C and D together.

b. With **Right** sides together, place panel A/B on panel C/D, matching up the long, side raw edges, and pin them in place. Attach by stitching a ¼" seam across the matched raw edges, backstitching at each end. Press the seam allowance to one side. (FIGURE 2B)

Step 3. Quilt the front of the pot holder.

a. Place both layers of batting onto the **Wrong** side of the front panel, matching up the raw edges. Then, place the back panel with **Right** side facing up on top of the batting layers and pin through all of the layers to hold the panels in place.

b. On the **Right** side of the back panel, place a piece of masking tape diagonally across the back panel. Using the masking tape as a guideline, stitch down both sides of the tape, backstitching at each end. Now move the tape, lining up one side of the tape with one of the stitching lines, and stitch down the opposite side of the tape. Repeat this process all the way across the width of the back panel, with the diagonal stitching lines all going the same way. Then, place the tape on the opposite diagonal and repeat, stitching the quilting lines across the width of the back panel, back-stitching at each end. This will make a diamond-shaped quilting pattern on your pot holder. (FIGURE 3B)

c. Using your scissors, trim around the cut edge of the patchwork panel to cut away any excess batting and threads.

Step 4. Make the quilted hand covers.

a. With **Wrong** sides together, fold the first cover in half across the 8" side and press a crease. Then, open up the cover. Place your first 4" x 9" piece of batting onto the **Wrong** side of the hand cover along the center crease, matching up the side and bottom raw edges, and pin it in place. Machine baste* with a ¼" seam completely around the batting to hold it in place. (FIGURE 4A)

See page 171 for an explanation of machine basting.

b. Then, fold the hand cover again at the center crease over the batting and pin the raw edges in place.

c. On the **Right** side of the hand cover with the batting attached, place a piece of masking tape diagonally across the hand cover, and follow the instructions in step 3b to create a diamond-shaped quilting pattern on your hand cover.

d. Follow the instructions in steps 4a through 4c to make the other hand cover.

Step 5. Attach the hand covers to the back of the pot holder.

Place the back side of the first hand cover onto the **Right** side of the back of the pot holder, matching up the top and side raw edges, and pin them in place. Then, machine baste a ¼" seam around the matched raw edges. Repeat this step to attach the other hand cover to the other side of the pot holder. (The finished edges on the hand covers will be across the width of the pot holder facing each other, with a 1" gap between them.) (FIGURE 5)

~ CONTINUED

Step 6. Make the bias binding.

a. First, open up your fabric for the bias binding. Fold it on the bias by taking one of the selvage edges* and matching it up with one of the cut edges to make a triangle shape, and press along the folded edge. You will measure and mark your bias binding directly on the **Right** side of your fabric. **(FIGURE 6A)**

* See page 171 for an explanation of the selvage edge.

b. Open up your fabric. Using the crease for the bias fold* as your starting point, measure 2" over, parallel to the bias fold at each end of the fabric panel, and make a mark with your chalk pencil. Using your ruler and chalk pencil, match up the 2 marks and draw a line connecting them. Repeat this step, measuring 2" over, parallel to the chalk line, to make another strip for the bias binding. **(FIGURE 6B)**

* See page 171 for an explanation of the bias fold.

c. Then, cut along the folded edge and down the chalk lines you just made. You will have 2 bias strips.

d. Attach the bias strips together by placing them **Right** sides together, matching up the angled raw edges. (This will form a V shape.) Stitch the bias strips together across the matched raw edges with a ¼" seam, backstitching at each end. Press the seam allowance to one side, pressing the strip flat. Trim any small "tails" of fabric at the seam of the bias binding. **(FIGURE 6D)**

e. Fold the bias strip in half lengthwise with the **Wrong** sides together and press a center crease. Open up the strip. Using the center crease as a guideline, fold the long, side edges of the bias strip toward the center crease and press. Then, fold the bias strip at the center crease again and press. This will enclose the raw edges. You will need approximately 38" of binding to go around the Square Pot Holder.

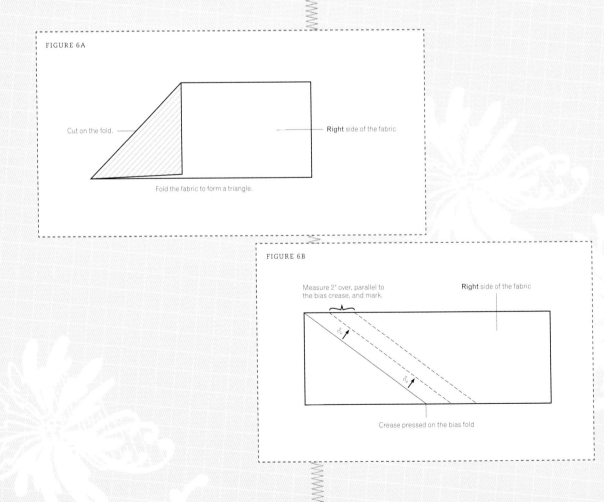

FIGURE 6A

Cut on the fold.

Right side of the fabric

Fold the fabric to form a triangle.

FIGURE 6B

Measure 2" over, parallel to the bias crease, and mark.

Right side of the fabric

2"

2"

Crease pressed on the bias fold

Step 7. Attach the bias binding to the pot holder.

a. First, take the 38" piece of bias binding, and open it up at the center crease. Then, completely open one of the long, side folded edges, leaving the other folded edge in place. To finish the first cut end of the binding, fold the first cut end ½" toward the **Wrong** side of the binding and press.

b. Starting in the center, at the bottom raw edge on the back of the pot holder, place the folded end of the **Right** side of the bias binding onto the **Right** side of the back of the pot holder. Line up the edge of the bias binding that you just opened, so it is even with the raw edges of the pot holder, and pin it in place. (**FIGURE 7B**)

c. Then, stitch a ½" seam across the bias binding (on the crease on the binding you made in step 6e), stopping ½" in from the first side raw edge, backstitching at each end.

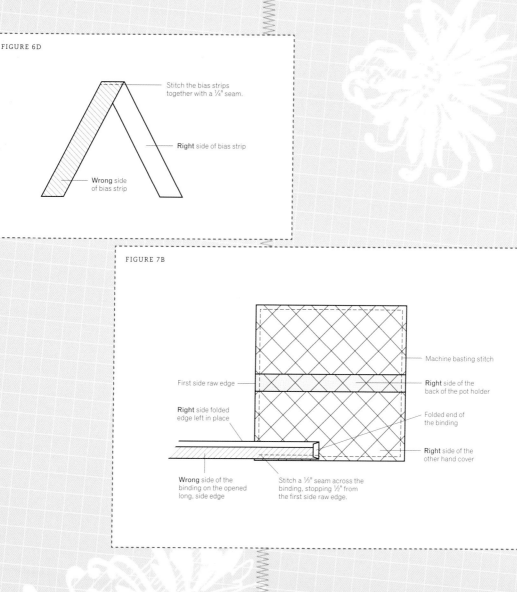

FIGURE 6D

Stitch the bias strips together with a ¼" seam.

Right side of bias strip

Wrong side of bias strip

FIGURE 7B

Machine basting stitch

First side raw edge

Right side of the back of the pot holder

Right side folded edge left in place

Folded end of the binding

Right side of the other hand cover

Wrong side of the binding on the opened long, side edge

Stitch a ½" seam across the binding, stopping ½" from the first side raw edge.

d. To make the first mitered corner, fold the binding away from the corner of the pot holder, forming a 45-degree angle. (FIGURE 7D)

e. Then, fold the binding back, even with the raw edge on the first side of the pot holder, and pin it in place. Stitch a ½" seam starting at the bottom edge and continue up the raw side edge, repeating this process at each of the corners of the pot holder. (FIGURE 7E)

f. After the fourth corner, place the rest of the binding along the bottom raw edges, overlapping the beginning of the binding by ½", and pin it in place. Cut away any extra binding and then stitch the rest of the binding in place. (FIGURE 7F)

g. Turn the pot holder over so the front of the pot holder is facing up. Then, fold the binding over the raw edges, matching up the other long, folded edge of the binding with the stitching line showing on the front of the pot holder, and pin it in place along the stitching. Fold the extra binding under at each corner, mitering each angle.

h. Next, attach the binding to the front of the pot holder by stitching completely around the pot holder close to the inner folded edge, backstitching at each end. Then, slip stitch* the mitered corners by hand on both the front and back of the pot holder. (FIGURE 7H)

See page 171 for an explanation of slip stitching.

i. Turn your pot holder over so the back is facing up. Measure 2" in along the finished edge of each of the hand covers on both the right and left sides and place a pin at the 2" measurements. Slip stitch 4 or 5 times in place by hand to tack the hand cover to the back of the pot holder. (Do not stitch completely through your pot holder; only catch the back fabric. This is slip stitched by hand to keep your stitches from showing through on the front of the pot holder.) Tie off your thread a couple of times in the same place and then cut your thread to free your needle. (FIGURE 7I)

j. On the top right corner of the pot holder, place a ½" grommet with the finished side of the grommet onto the patchwork side of the pot holder. Use the marking on the pattern piece for patchwork panel B as a guide in placing your grommet. Follow the manufacturer's instructions to attach the grommet to the corner of your pot holder.

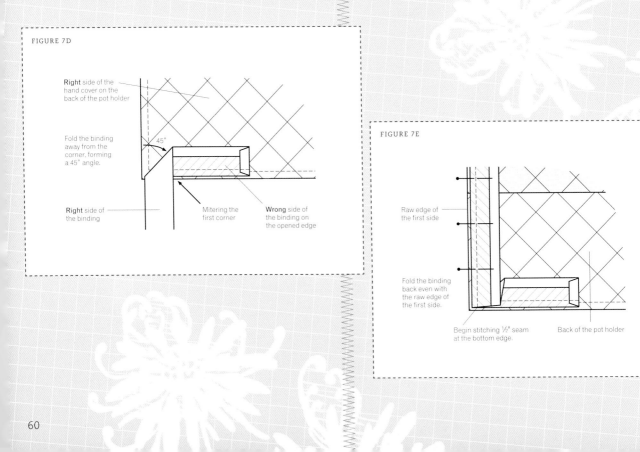

FIGURE 7D

Right side of the hand cover on the back of the pot holder

Fold the binding away from the corner, forming a 45° angle.

45°

Right side of the binding

Mitering the first corner

Wrong side of the binding on the opened edge

FIGURE 7E

Raw edge of the first side

Fold the binding back even with the raw edge of the first side.

Begin stitching ½" seam at the bottom edge.

Back of the pot holder

FIGURE 7F

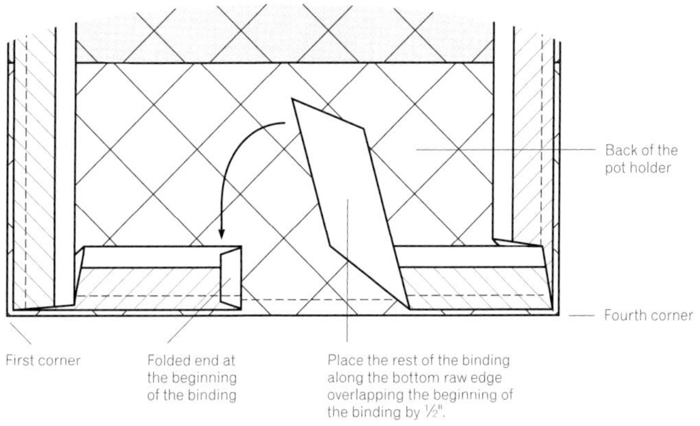

Back of the
pot holder

Fourth corner

First corner

Folded end at
the beginning
of the binding

Place the rest of the binding
along the bottom raw edge
overlapping the beginning of
the binding by ½".

FIGURE 7H

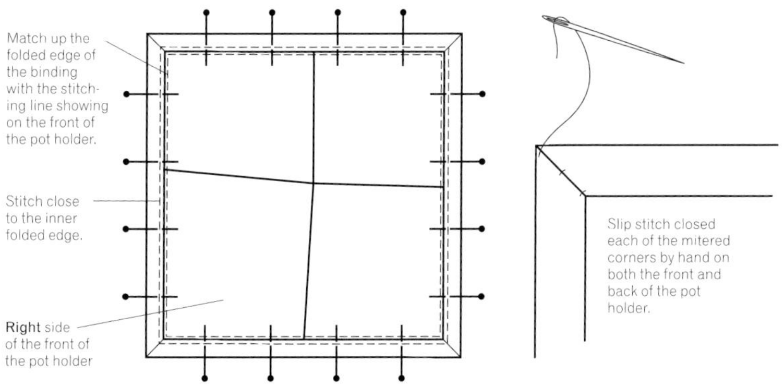

Match up the
folded edge of
the binding
with the stitch-
ing line showing
on the front of
the pot holder.

Stitch close
to the inner
folded edge.

Right side
of the front of
the pot holder

Slip stitch closed
each of the mitered
corners by hand on
both the front and
back of the pot
holder.

FIGURE 7I

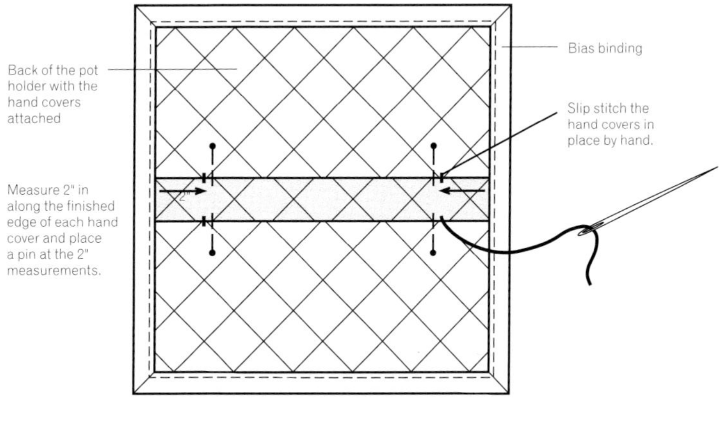

Back of the pot
holder with the
hand covers
attached

Bias binding

Slip stitch the
hand covers in
place by hand.

Measure 2" in
along the finished
edge of each hand
cover and place
a pin at the 2"
measurements.

CHAPTER 3

BEDROOM

Projects

Your bedroom should be a relaxing retreat, a soothing environment where you can forget all about the pressures of day-to-day life. To help you turn your bedroom into an oasis of comfort, here are all the things you need—a beautiful duvet cover to adorn your bed, a bedside organizer to keep your sleeping area clutter free, cool lounge pants and a sophisticated sleeping mask so you can sleep in on Saturday morning. Now, if we could just stitch up someone to bring us breakfast in bed . . .

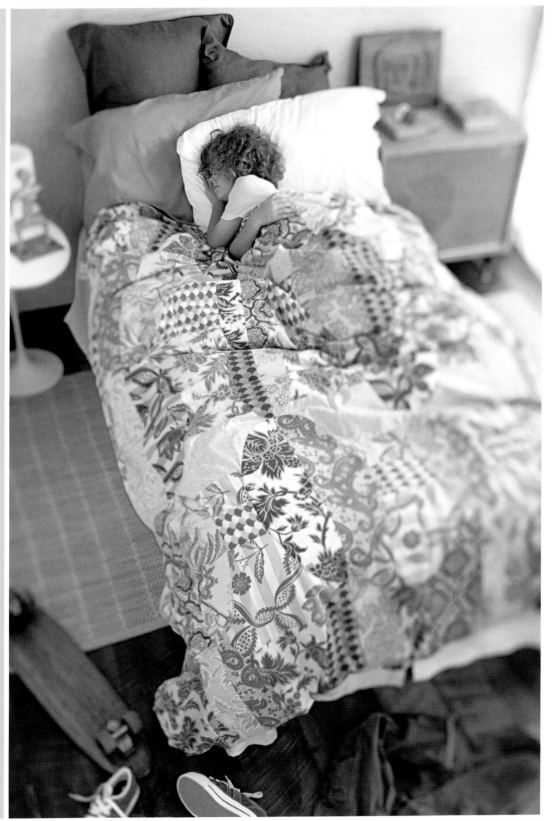

PATCHWORK DUVET COVER

FINISHED SIZES: TWIN: 67½" WIDE X 86" LONG | FULL/QUEEN: 87½" WIDE X 92" LONG | KING: 103½" WIDE X 92" LONG

The mod design of this super-cool duvet cover (see photo, page 63) can be customized to highlight your favorite fabric and color combinations, and to fit any size comforter. Easy piecing of ovals on stripes makes for unlimited possibilities and tons of style.

FABRICS

• 44"-wide quilting-weight to mid-weight cotton fabric for the duvet foundation (the front of the duvet cover) back, and bobbles (the decorative shapes to be attached to the foundation) (Please use the charts below to determine the amount of yardage you will need for the size of duvet cover you are making.)

OTHER SUPPLIES

• Comforter in the size of your choice

• Coordinating thread

• ¾" flat buttons (5 for twin, 7 for full/queen, 8 for king)

• Tape measure

• Yardstick

• Chalk pencil or fabric marker

• Scissors

• Rotary cutter and self-healing mat (optional)

• Masking tape

• Straight pins

• Template plastic or freezer paper

• Turning tool (such as a closed pair of scissors)

• Hand sewing needle

• Large safety pins (optional)

FOR THE FOUNDATION	TWIN	FULL/QUEEN	KING
Fabric 1	2 yards	2½ yards	2½ yards
Fabric 2	1⅛ yards	1¾ yards	1¾ yards
Fabric 3	1 yard	1⅛ yards	1⅜ yards
Fabric 4	1⅛ yards	1⅛ yards	1⅜ yards
Fabric 5	1 yard	1⅝ yards	1⅝ yards

FOR THE BACK	TWIN	FULL/QUEEN	KING
Coordinating cotton	5¼ yards	8¼ yards	8¼ yards

FOR THE BOBBLES	TWIN	FULL/QUEEN	KING
4 different coordinating light printed cotton fabrics			
4 different coordinating dark printed cotton fabrics			
Light prints	⅝ yard each	¾ yard each	1¼ yards each
Dark prints	⅝ yard each	¾ yard each	1¼ yards each

8½ yards (22"-wide) medium-weight sew-in interfacing

2 yards (¼"-wide) ribbon

NOTES

• All seams are ¼" in the construction of the front foundation, the back cover, and the bobbles. The seams are ½" for attaching the front foundation and the back cover together. Both the ¼" and ½" seam allowances are included in all cutting measurements. The ¼" seam allowance is included in the bobble pattern piece.

• This project takes some time to do, but it is not at all difficult. Relax and follow the step-by-step instructions, and you will soon have a beautiful Patchwork Duvet Cover that you will be proud to display!

• Comforter sizes vary among manufacturers. Please measure your comforter carefully before starting your project. Instructions in step 1 will guide you in customizing the Patchwork Duvet Cover to fit your comforter. Unless your comforter size varies greatly from the measurements listed above, the yardage requirements should not change.

• Preshrink your fabric by washing, drying, and pressing it before starting your project.

Step 1. Customize the fabric measurements for your comforter, if necessary.

To make a duvet cover for a comforter that is wider or longer than the dimensions listed, first, using a tape measure, measure your comforter and divide the additional width and/or length by 2. Add the additional width and/or length to each side for extra width, or the top and bottom for extra length. For example, if your comforter is 4" wider than the dimensions above, divide by 2 and add the extra 2" to each side of the foundation. You will add this width to the pieces on the outside edges of the foundation. (For example, on the left side of the foundation, add 2" to pieces labeled #1A, #2C, #3L, #4O, #5U, #3L, #2D, #4P, #2G, and #1B, and also #5W if making a full/queen or king size.)

Repeat this step for the right side of the foundation. Use the same procedure to add to the top and bottom if extra length is needed. Dividing the extra width or length by 2 and adding it to each side will keep the duvet cover design balanced.

Step 2. Cut out all pieces from the fabric.

a. Simply measure and mark the dimensions below (or these and the measurements you adjusted in step 1) directly onto the **Wrong** side of your fabric using a yardstick and a chalk pencil. Then, using your scissors or a rotary cutter and self-healing mat, cut out each panel following the marked lines.

	TWIN	FULL/QUEEN	KING
FROM FABRIC 1			
(A) Cut 4: 16½" long	x 30" wide	x 39½" wide	x 42½" wide
(B) Cut 2: 16½" long	x 9½" wide	x 10½" wide	x 20½" wide
FROM FABRIC 2			
(C) Cut 4: 4¼" long	x 28" wide	x 38" wide	x 41" wide
(D) Cut 4: 4¼" long	x 13½" wide	x 13½" wide	x 23½" wide
(E) Cut 2: 9½" long	x 28½" wide	x 38½" wide	x 40½" wide
(F) Cut 2: 9½" long	x 3" wide	x 3" wide	x 5" wide
(G) Cut 2: 9½" long	x 2½" wide	x 2½" wide	x 4½" wide
(H) Cut 1: 9½" long	x 3½" wide	x 3½" wide	x 5½" wide
FROM FABRIC 3			
(I) Cut 4: 7¼" long	x 29¼" wide	x 39¼" wide	x 42¼" wide
(J) Cut 4: 7¼" long	x 2½" wide	x 2½" wide	x 4½" wide
(K) Cut 4: 7¼" long	x 2¼" wide	x 2¼" wide	x 4¼" wide
(L) Cut 4: 7¼" long	x 2" wide	x 2" wide	x 3" wide
FROM FABRIC 4			
(M) Cut 1: 9" long	x 24" wide	x 42½" wide	x 42" wide
(N) Cut 1: 9" long	x 4½" wide	x 4½" wide	x 5" wide
(O) Cut 2: 9" long	x 20¾" wide	x 21½" wide	x 29¼" wide
(P) Cut 2: 4½" long	x 10¼" wide	x 20¼" wide	x 28½" wide
(Q) Cut 2: 4½" long	x 13¾" wide	x 13¾" wide	x 13¾" wide
(R) Cut 2: 4½" long	x 6½" wide	x 6½" wide	x 6½" wide
(S) Cut 2: 4½" long	x 5½" wide	x 5½" wide	x 5½" wide
FROM FABRIC 5			
(T) Cut 2: 16½" long	x 29½" wide	x 39¼" wide	x 42" wide
(U) Cut 2: 16½" long	x 5¼" wide	x 5½" wide	x 10¾" wide
(V) Cut 2: 6½" long	none needed	x 39" wide	x 42¼" wide
(W) Cut 2: 6½" long	none needed	x 5½" wide	x 10½" wide

~ CONTINUED

FROM THE FABRIC FOR THE BACK

FOR TWIN

- *Cut 2: 19˝ wide x 90½˝ long*
- *Cut 1: 33˝ wide x 90½˝ long*

FOR FULL/QUEEN

- *Cut 2: 24˝ wide x 96½˝ long*
- *Cut 1: 43˝ wide x 96½˝ long*

FOR KING

- *Cut 2: 33˝ wide x 96½˝ long*
- *Cut 1: 42˝ wide x 96½˝ long*

FROM THE LIGHT AND DARK COLORED PRINTS FOR THE BOBBLES*

FOR TWIN

- *Cut 5 light and 5 dark: 7˝ strips for the large bobble halves*
- *Cut 4 light and 4 dark: 6˝ strips for the medium bobble halves*
- *Cut 4 light and 4 dark: 4˝ strips for the small bobble halves*

FOR FULL/QUEEN

- *Cut 6 light and 6 dark: 7˝ strips for the large bobble halves*
- *Cut 8 light and 8 dark: 6˝ strips for the medium bobble halves*
- *Cut 6 light and 6 dark: 4˝ strips for the small bobble halves*

FOR KING

- *Cut 7 light and 7 dark: 7˝ strips for the large and small bobble halves*
- *Cut 15 light and 15 dark: 6˝ strips for the medium and small bobble halves*

   * Each bobble is made up of 2 halves, 1 of light and 1 of dark fabric, stitched together. You will be cutting strips of the light and dark fabrics in this step and stitching them together in step 7. Cut or rip strips along the crosswise grain of the fabric. To rip strips of fabric, first measure the length you need along the selvage edge (see page 171 for an explanation of the selvage edge) of your fabric and make a clip into the selvage edge with your scissors. Then pull your fabric apart from either side of the clip. If you pull fast enough you can rip through the other selvage edge, or you may choose to stop at the selvage and clip the end of the fabric apart.

FROM THE INTERFACING

- *Cut out the bobble pattern piece in the pocket at the front of this book. Make a pattern piece for each size bobble, using the pattern piece as a guide. Fold a piece of the freezer paper in half and place the bobble pattern piece on the folded edge as indicated on the pattern piece. Cut along the outlines for the large size. Repeat to make pattern pieces for the other 2 sizes. Unfold the freezer-paper pattern pieces. Then fold the interfacing in half lengthwise and place the pattern pieces (with the edge to be placed on the fold) on the fold of the interfacing, pinning them in place. Using your scissors, cut out each piece according to the outline on the pattern piece and the quantities given below.*

	TWIN	FULL/QUEEN	KING
Large bobbles	9	11	13
Medium bobbles	7	15	17
Small bobbles	8	12	14

b. In order to keep your pieces organized, mark each piece by writing the name on a piece of masking tape and attaching to the **Wrong** side of each panel as it is cut.

Step 3. Lay out the foundation pieces you cut out in step 2.

Lay out your pieces in place according to FIGURE 3, placing them with the **Right** sides facing up. (FIGURE 3)

Step 4. Attach the patchwork pieces together across each row.

   NOTE: *The seams in the patchwork of the foundation are all ¼˝. It is important to remember this to ensure the correct size of the foundation after the piecing is complete.*

Starting at the top left corner of your layout, take the first 2 pieces in the top row and place them **Right** sides together. Stitch a ¼" seam down the side edges and press the seam allowances to one side. Continue across the first row until all of the pieces are attached, pressing the seam allowances toward the same side. Then, place the entire row of attached pieces back in order in your layout. Repeat this step to attach all of the pieces in each of the rest of the rows and lay them back in place.

FIGURE 3

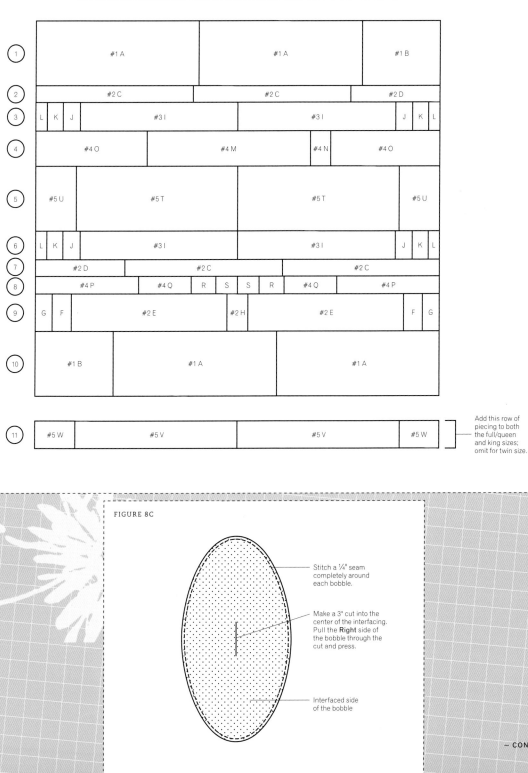

LAYOUT FOR THE FRONT FOUNDATION
(EXAMPLE SHOWN FOR KING-SIZE COVER, FINISHED SIZE 103½" WIDE X 92" LONG)

1 — #1 A #1 A #1 B

2 — #2 C #2 C #2 D

3 — L K J #3 I #3 I J K L

4 — #4 O #4 M #4 N #4 O

5 — #5 U #5 T #5 T #5 U

6 — L K J #3 I #3 I J K L

7 — #2 D #2 C #2 C

8 — #4 P #4 Q R S S R #4 Q #4 P

9 — G F #2 E #2 H #2 E F G

10 — #1 B #1 A #1 A

11 — #5 W #5 V #5 V #5 W

Add this row of piecing to both the full/queen and king sizes; omit for twin size.

PATCHWORK DUVET COVER

FIGURE 8C

Stitch a ¼" seam completely around each bobble.

Make a 3" cut into the center of the interfacing. Pull the **Right** side of the bobble through the cut and press.

Interfaced side of the bobble

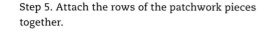

Step 5. Attach the rows of the patchwork pieces together.

Starting at the top of the foundation, place the first and second rows **Right** sides together. Attach by stitching a ¼" seam across the matched raw edges, and press the seam allowances to one side. Repeat this step to attach all of the rows in the order in which you laid them out. Due to the size and weight of the foundation, it is easiest to stitch the top 5 rows together (rows 1 through 5), set them aside, and then stitch together the next 5 rows (or 6 rows, if making the full/queen or king size). Then stitch row 5 to row 6, completing the patchwork foundation.

Step 6. Finish the top raw edge of the foundation.

With the **Wrong** side of the patchwork foundation facing up, fold over 2" of the top raw edge toward the **Wrong** side and press. Then, fold the top edge over again another 2" and press. Topstitch* along the top folded edge with a ½" seam. This will create a flap at the top edge of the foundation. You will attach the buttons to this flap in step 15, which will allow you to close the top of the duvet cover.

See page 172 for an explanation of topstitching.

Set the foundation aside.

Step 7. Make the bobbles.

NOTE: *The seams used to stitch together the bobbles are ¼". It is important to remember this to ensure the correct size bobble.*

a. Take the light and dark strips of fabric that you cut in step 2. Place the first 7"-wide light-colored strip **Right** sides together with the first 7"-wide dark colored strip. Attach by stitching a ¼" seam down the length of the strips, backstitching at each end. Repeat this step to attach the remaining light and dark strips together.

NOTE: *The freezer-paper bobble pattern pieces can be pressed (wax side down) directly onto the fabric strips to make cutting the bobbles easier. You will need to cut several freezer-paper bobble pattern pieces for each size bobble to use this technique.*

b. Using the freezer-paper bobble pattern pieces, refer to the chart below to cut the correct quantities of bobbles from the strips you just made, centering the pattern piece on the seam line, not on the raw edge. The attached strips have not yet been opened up. You will cut through both layers of each strip to create one bobble.

	TWIN	FULL/QUEEN	KING
Large bobbles	9	11	13
Medium bobbles	7	15	17
Small bobbles	8	12	14

c. Then, open up each bobble and press the seam allowance to one side.

Step 8. Finish the bobbles' raw edges.

a. Take the bobble interfacing pieces and place them on the **Right** side of the bobbles you cut in step 7b.

b. With a ¼" seam, stitch completely around each bobble, attaching the interfacing to the bobble.

c. Carefully make a 3" cut into the center of the interfacing only. Then, pull the **Right** side of the bobble through the cut in the interfacing, using a turning tool* to push out the seams. Press each bobble flat. (FIGURE 8C)

See page 172 for an explanation of a turning tool.

Step 9. Check the measurements of the foundation.

First, press the foundation flat, making certain to fold the flap down on the **Wrong** side of the foundation. Do not include the flap in your measurements. Then, measure across the foundation and down the length in many different places to double check your measurements. Your duvet cover should match your finished measurement for the size you are making plus 1" in the width and ½" in the length. The top edge (or flap) of the foundation was finished in step 6.

NOTE: *Now is the time to make adjustments to your measurements, if necessary. On a patchwork panel you can always add more pieces to fill in any length or width you might need, or trim down the length and width to meet the measurements required.*

Step 10. Mark the placement for the bobbles on the foundation.

a. First, measure and mark the placement for the bobbles across the width of the foundation. Be careful at this point to fold the flap up away from the foundation to avoid catching it in the bobble placement. Mark the vertical lines for the bobble placement down the foundation's length, equal distances apart:

4 vertical lines for the twin, at 13½", 27", 40½", and 54"

6 vertical lines for the full/queen, at 12½", 25", 37½", 50, 62½", and 75"

7 vertical lines for the king, at 9¾", 23¾", 37¾", 51¾", 65¾", 79¾", and 93¾"

b. Refer to FIGURE 10B for placing the bobbles down each vertical line. The bobble placement marks begin at the seam line already in place securing the flap. Alternate the light and dark sides, placing the bobbles end to end, and hand baste or pin* them in place. It is easiest to do this with the foundation lying flat on a hard surface such as a large table or on the floor. This process is time consuming but well worth the effort. First, thread your needle, doubling the thread back, matching up the cut ends of the thread, and making a knot at the matched ends of the thread. Stitch close to the edge of the bobble and push the needle through the bobble and the foundation, pulling all of the thread through the back of the foundation, and pushing the needle through the back and out the front of the bobble. Take large stitches with 3" to 4" between each stitch, stitching completely around each bobble. This will hold the bobbles in place while you machine stitch the bobbles to the foundation.

(FIGURE 10B)

To pin the bobbles in place, use large safety pins every 5" to 7", pinning through the bobble and the foundation, keeping the pins about 1" away from the edge of the bobbles. This will allow you to stitch completely around the bobbles without having to stop to take the pins out.

Step 11. Attach the bobbles to the foundation.

a. With the bobbles basted or pinned in place, and starting on the right edge of the foundation, stitch from the seam line at the top of the foundation to the bottom, in order to attach the bobbles by using a satin stitch or stitch with a ⅛" seam. Fold the flap up out of the way when stitching the bobbles to avoid catching it in the stitching. Stitch around the right-hand side of each bobble down the first vertical line in a scalloped pattern.

b. Then, turn the foundation around so you will be stitching from the bottom of the foundation to the top. Stitch around the left sides of the bobbles, using the same stitch as on the other side and stitching in a scalloped pattern. Continue until all of the bobbles have been stitched in place down both sides of all the vertical lines.

NOTE: *To comfortably fit the foundation through the opening in your machine, fold or roll the raw edges in toward the vertical line of bobbles you will be stitching in place. As you turn the foundation to stitch from the bottom to the top, fold or roll in the other side raw edges. Adjust the rolled or folded edges for each line of bobbles to be sewn.*

Step 12. Make the back.

a. Lay the 3 strips of fabric lengths that you cut out in step 2 together, with the wider strip in the center.

b. Then, place the first and second lengths with **Right** sides together. Attach by stitching a ¼" seam down the matched raw edges and press the seam allowances to one side. Repeat this step to attach the third length in the order in which you laid them out.

c. Then, repeat step 6 to finish the top raw edge of the back of the duvet cover to make the flap for placing the buttonholes.

d. Place the back on a large flat surface and smooth it out. Then, place the foundation on top of the back, centering it on top to check the measurements and make sure the size is correct. Trim if necessary.

~ CONTINUED

FIGURE 10B

LAYOUT FOR THE BOBBLES
(EXAMPLE SHOWN FOR KING SIZE COVER, FINISHED SIZE 103½" WIDE X 92" LONG)

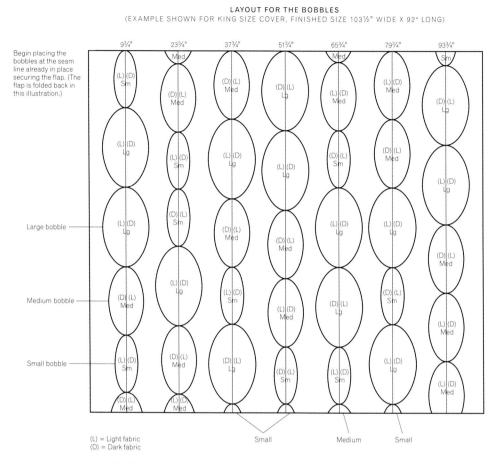

Begin placing the bobbles at the seam line already in place securing the flap. (The flap is folded back in this illustration.)

Large bobble

Medium bobble

Small bobble

(L) = Light fabric
(D) = Dark fabric

NOTE: The illustration above shows the placement of the bobbles on the foundation. The seam lines of the patchwork foundation have been omitted in the illustration for the sake of simplicity. Your bobbles will be placed onto the Right side of the foundation.

FIGURE 17D

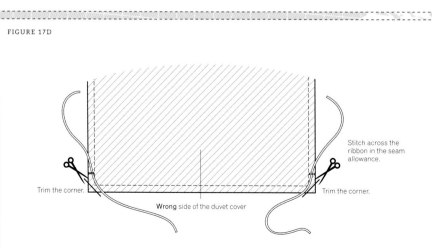

Stitch across the ribbon in the seam allowance.

Trim the corner.

Trim the corner.

Wrong side of the duvet cover

Step 13. Measure and mark for the opening at the top of the duvet cover.

On the **Right** side of the back of the duvet cover, measure 12½" over from the raw edge on the left side across the top finished edge and make a mark. Repeat this step to mark the other end of the opening, measuring 12½" in from the raw edge on the right side.

Step 14. Mark and make the buttonholes.

On the flap, at the top of the back of the duvet, measure and mark the placement for the buttonholes using the measurements below. Begin measuring from the 12½" mark you made in step 13.

King: Mark 8 buttonholes, 9" apart.

Full/queen: Mark 7 buttonholes, 9¼" apart.

Twin: Mark 5 buttonholes, 8" apart.

Center a buttonhole for a ¾" button at each mark, vertically across the flap.

Step 15. Mark the placement of and attach the buttons to the flap at the top finished edge of the foundation.

Repeat step 14 to measure and mark the placement for the buttons on the inside flap of fabric on the foundation. Center a button over each of the marks and slip stitch* each button in place by hand.

See page 171 for an explanation of slip stitching.

Step 16. Attach the foundation and the back together.

a. With the **Right** sides together, match up the top finished edges and the side and bottom raw edges of the foundation and the back and pin them in place. Stitch a ½" seam down one side, across the bottom, and up the other side of the duvet cover, backstitching at each end. Then, turn the duvet cover **Right** side out using a turning tool to push out the corners and press the seams flat.

b. Now, pin the top of the duvet cover **Wrong** sides together, and stitch a ½" seam from the right edge over to the 12½" mark, backstitching at each end. You will be stitching through both the foundation and the back, directly over the seam lines made in steps 5 and 11. If you wish, use a decorative stitch if your machine has one. Repeat this step to stitch from the left edge to the 12½" mark. The center top of the duvet cover will be left open to allow you to insert your comforter.

c. Using your scissors, trim the 2 corners* in the seam allowance, making sure not to clip the stitching.

See page 172 for an explanation of trimming corners.

Step 17. Attach the ribbon to the bottom corners of your duvet cover and comforter to keep the comforter in place inside the cover.

a. Take your ribbon and cut it into 4 pieces, each 18" long.

b. With the **Wrong** side of your duvet cover facing out, fold the first piece of ribbon in half crosswise, place the center of the ribbon in the seam allowance at one of the bottom corners of the duvet cover, and pin it in place.

c. Stitch across the ribbon a few times to secure the ribbon.

d. Repeat steps 17b and 17c to attach a second piece of ribbon to the other bottom corner of the duvet cover. (FIGURE 17D)

e. Repeat steps 17b and 17c to attach a ribbon to each bottom corner of the comforter you will be using inside the duvet cover.

Step 18. Put the final touches on the Patchwork Duvet Cover.

a. Turn the duvet cover **Right** side out and press it flat. Topstitch with a ¼" seam around finished edges of the duvet cover, excluding the finished opening at the top, backstitching at each end. (Be careful not to catch the ribbons on the inside of the bottom corners of the duvet cover when topstitching.)

b. Tie the ribbons at the bottom corners of your Patchwork Duvet Cover to the ribbons at the bottom corners of your comforter insert, in order to keep it from moving. Slip the duvet cover over your comforter and button the top closed.

BEDSIDE ORGANIZER

FINISHED SIZES:
MAGAZINE POCKET (2): 14" WIDE X 14" LONG (ON EACH END OF THE DECK)
EYEGLASS POCKET (2): 3" WIDE X 6" LONG | CD PLAYER POCKET (2): 7" WIDE X 6" LONG
IPOD/PEN POCKET (2): 6" WIDE X 6" LONG | SMALL MISCELLANEOUS POCKET (2): 10" WIDE X 4" LONG
LARGE MISCELLANEOUS POCKET (2): 10" WIDE X 6" LONG

A tidy, serene bedroom environment is key to getting a good night's sleep. And there's nothing serene about a cluttered night table. The solution? Keep your bedtime essentials right at your bedside! This fabric organizer has a place for everything you need—magazines, digital music players, tissues, eyeglasses, lip balm, pens, journals—so you can rest easy. Don't worry, I haven't forgotten your partner—there's an identical set of pockets for the other side of the bed, too!

FABRICS

- 2½ yards (54"-wide) home-decor-weight cotton fabric for the organizer, lining, and deck topper
- ¼ yard (44"-wide) coordinating cotton flannel to line the eyeglass pockets
- 1⅛ yards (60"-wide) cotton canvas for the deck (for any size mattress; cotton duck or twill could also be used)

OTHER SUPPLIES

- Coordinating thread
- Yardstick or ruler
- Chalk pencil or fabric marker
- Scissors
- Masking tape
- Straight pins
- Turning tool (such as a closed pair of scissors)

NOTES

- All seams are ½" unless otherwise stated. (The ½" seam allowance is included in all cutting measurements.)
- The length of the deck is determined by the width of your mattress. Mattress sizes differ slightly from one manufacturer to another. Please measure the width of your mattress before beginning your project.
- Preshrink your fabric by washing, drying, and pressing it before starting your project.

Step 1. Cut out all pieces from the fabric.

a. Simply measure and mark the dimensions below directly onto the **Wrong** side of the fabric, using a yardstick and a chalk pencil. Then, using your scissors, cut out each panel following the marked lines.
(FIGURE BEDSIDE ORGANIZER OVERVIEW)

FROM THE FABRIC FOR THE ORGANIZER, LINING, AND DECK TOPPER (FIGURE 1)

- *Cut 2 magazine pocket panels: 17½" wide x 31½" long*
- *Cut 2 magazine pocket linings: 17½" wide x 31½" long*
- *Cut 2 eyeglass pockets: 4" wide x 7" long*
- *Cut 2 CD pockets: 8" wide x 7" long*
- *Cut 2 iPod/pen pockets: 7" wide x 7" long*
- *Cut 2 small miscellaneous pockets: 11" wide x 5" long*
- *Cut 2 large miscellaneous pockets: 11" wide x 7" long*
- *Cut 2 deck toppers: 16" wide x 7" long*

FROM THE FABRIC FOR THE POCKET LININGS

- *Cut 2 eyeglass pocket linings: 4" wide x 7" long*

FROM THE FABRIC FOR THE DECK

- *Cut 2 decks:* 16" wide x (width of mattress + 29") divided by 2 (For example, if you have a standard queen-size mattress, each piece would be 16" wide x (60" + 29") divided by 2, or 16" wide x 44½" long.)*
- ** Cut these panels with the length going across the width of the canvas.*

~ CONTINUED

b. In order to keep your pieces organized, mark each piece by writing the name on a piece of masking tape and attaching to the wrong side of each panel as it is cut.

Step 2. Mark the folding guidelines on the magazine pocket panel. (FIGURE 2)

a. Lay the first magazine pocket panel on a flat surface with the **Wrong** side of the fabric facing up. Fold the 17½" top raw edge in ½" toward the **Wrong** side and firmly press a crease on the fold. Now open up the fold. Repeat this step for the 17½" bottom raw edge.

b. Next, fold both of the side raw edges in 1¾" toward **Wrong** side and firmly press a crease on both folds. Open up the folds.

c. Then, measure down 14½" from the top raw edge on the right side and make a mark. Move your yardstick over to the left side, measure down 14½" again, and make another mark. Use your yardstick to draw a line connecting the 2 marks. Fold the magazine pocket panel on the line, folding the **Wrong** sides together. Press a firm crease on the fold.

d. Follow the instructions in step 2c to measure, mark, and press 14½" up from the bottom raw edge.

e. Now, fold the magazine pocket panel in half with **Wrong** sides together, matching the top and bottom raw edges, and press a firm crease at the folded edge to mark the center bottom of the magazine pocket panel. Set the magazine pocket panel aside.

Step 3. Make the eyeglass pocket.

a. First, take one eyeglass pocket and eyeglass pocket lining, place them **Right** sides together, matching the raw edges, and pin them together. Then, stitch a ½" seam around the raw edges, leaving a 2" opening centered along the bottom raw edge. Trim all 4 corners* in the seam allowance, being careful not to clip into the stitching.

See page 172 for an explanation of trimming corners.

b. Now, turn the eyeglass pocket **Right** side out, using your turning tool* to push out the corners, and press.

See page 172 for an explanation of a turning tool.

c. Fold the 2" opening ½" under along the bottom edge, toward the **Wrong** side of the fabric, and press.

d. Then, topstitch* with a ¼" seam across the top of the eyeglass pocket. Set the eyeglass pocket aside.

See page 172 for an explanation of topstitching.

Step 4. Make the CD player pocket.

a. First, take one CD player pocket piece, fold under ¼" toward the **Wrong** side at the top (8") raw edge, and press. Fold under ¼" again and stitch close to the inner folded edge.

b. Now, fold under ½" toward the **Wrong** side on both side edges and the bottom raw edge and press. Set the CD player pocket aside.

Step 5. Make the iPod/pen pocket.

a. First, take one iPod/pen pocket piece, fold under the top raw edge ¼" toward the **Wrong** side, and press. Fold under ¼" again and stitch close to the inner folded edge.

b. Now, fold under ½" toward the **Wrong** side on both side raw edges and along the bottom raw edge and press.

c. With the **Right** side of the iPod/pen pocket facing up, use a chalk pencil or fabric marker to draw a line from the top edge to the bottom edge 1" from, and parallel to, the folded left edge. Measure and draw a second parallel line 1" from the first. Measure and draw a third parallel line 1" from the second line. (FIGURE 5C, D)

d. Measure 4" down from the top of the third line and make a mark. Then, measure 4" down from the top right edge of the iPod/pen pocket and make a second mark. Use your yardstick to draw a line connecting the 2 marks. Set the iPod/pen pocket aside. (FIGURE 5C, D)

NOTE: *These drawn lines will be used as stitching guidelines to create smaller compartments for pens and your iPod in step 7d.*

Step 6. Make the small and large miscellaneous pockets.

a. Take one small miscellaneous pocket piece, fold under ¼" toward the **Wrong** side on the long top raw edge, and press. Then fold under ¼" again and press. Stitch close to the inner folded edge.

b. Follow the instructions in step 6a to finish the top long raw edge of the large miscellaneous pocket.

BEDSIDE ORGANIZER OVERVIEW

This illustration shows the Bedside Organizer from above, as it would look lying across the box springs.

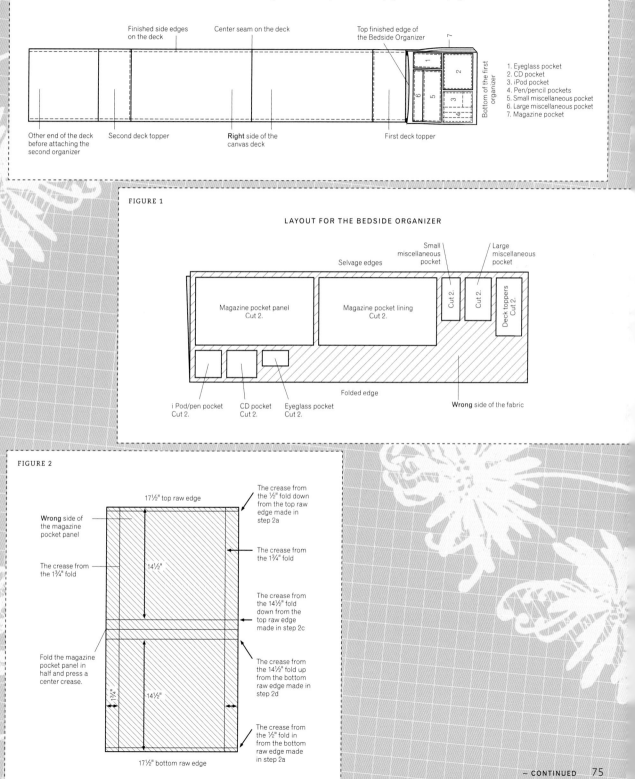

Finished side edges on the deck

Center seam on the deck

Top finished edge of the Bedside Organizer

Bottom of the first organizer

1. Eyeglass pocket
2. CD pocket
3. iPod pocket
4. Pen/pencil pockets
5. Small miscellaneous pocket
6. Large miscellaneous pocket
7. Magazine pocket

Other end of the deck before attaching the second organizer

Second deck topper

Right side of the canvas deck

First deck topper

FIGURE 1

LAYOUT FOR THE BEDSIDE ORGANIZER

Selvage edges

Small miscellaneous pocket

Large miscellaneous pocket

Magazine pocket panel
Cut 2.

Magazine pocket lining
Cut 2.

Cut 2.

Cut 2.

Deck toppers
Cut 2.

i Pod/pen pocket
Cut 2.

CD pocket
Cut 2.

Eyeglass pocket
Cut 2.

Folded edge

Wrong side of the fabric

FIGURE 2

17½" top raw edge

Wrong side of the magazine pocket panel

The crease from the ½" fold down from the top raw edge made in step 2a

The crease from the 1¾" fold

The crease from the 1¾" fold

14½"

The crease from the 14½" fold down from the top raw edge made in step 2c

The crease from the 14½" fold up from the bottom raw edge made in step 2d

Fold the magazine pocket panel in half and press a center crease.

1¾"

14½"

The crease from the ½" fold in from the bottom raw edge made in step 2a

17½" bottom raw edge

~ CONTINUED

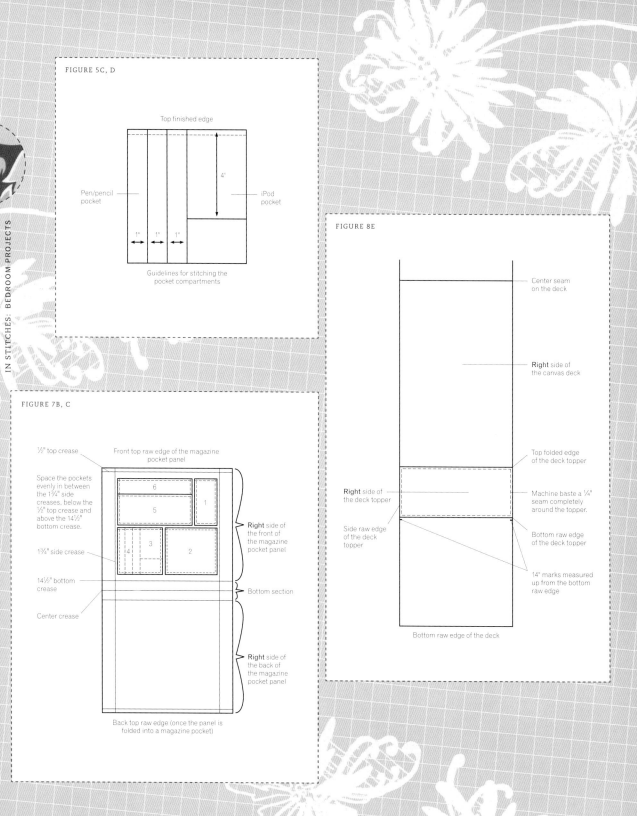

FIGURE 5C, D

Top finished edge

4"

Pen/pencil pocket

iPod pocket

1" 1" 1"

Guidelines for stitching the pocket compartments

FIGURE 8E

Center seam on the deck

Right side of the canvas deck

Top folded edge of the deck topper

Right side of the deck topper

Machine baste a ¼" seam completely around the topper.

Side raw edge of the deck topper

Bottom raw edge of the deck topper

14" marks measured up from the bottom raw edge

Bottom raw edge of the deck

FIGURE 7B, C

½" top crease

Front top raw edge of the magazine pocket panel

Space the pockets evenly in between the 1¾" side creases, below the ½" top crease and above the 14½" bottom crease.

6

5

1

1¾" side crease

4 3

2

14½" bottom crease

Center crease

Right side of the front of the magazine pocket panel

Bottom section

Right side of the back of the magazine pocket panel

Back top raw edge (once the panel is folded into a magazine pocket)

c. Now, with the **Right** sides of both pocket pieces facing up, place the small miscellaneous pocket on top of the large miscellaneous pocket, matching the side and bottom raw edges, and pin in place. Then, machine baste* with a ¼" seam along the matched side and bottom raw edges.

See page 171 for an explanation of machine basting.

d. Then, fold the side and bottom raw edges under ½" toward the **Wrong** side and press.

Step 7. Attach the outside pockets onto the magazine pocket panel.

a. First, place the magazine pocket panel on a flat surface with the **Right** side of the panel facing up.

b. Next, following FIGURE 7B, C, place the **Wrong** sides of the 4 pockets onto the **Right** side of the magazine pocket panel. Place the pockets inside the pressed creases on the magazine pocket panel, spacing the pockets evenly in between the 1¾" side creases, below the ½" top crease and above the 14½" bottom crease. Place the side edges of the pockets ¾" in from, and parallel to, the side pressed creases and pin the pockets in place.

c. Then, attach the pockets by stitching down both sides and across the bottom folded edges of each pocket, backstitching at each end.

d. On the iPod/pen pocket, stitch along the lines drawn in steps 5c and 5d through all the layers, backstitching at each end. Set the magazine pocket panel aside.

Step 8. Make the deck and the deck topper.

a. Place the 2 canvas deck panels **Right** sides together, matching the 2 short raw edges, and pin them in place. Stitch a ½" seam across the matched raw edges and then serge or zigzag the seam allowances together. Press the seam allowance to one side. The joined deck panels will create one long piece that will be referred to as the "deck."

b. With the deck **Right** side up and positioned lengthwise so that one short edge is closest to you, use your yardstick to measure 14" up from the bottom right corner along the long side raw edge and make a mark. Repeat this step to measure and mark 14" up from the bottom left corner.

c. Now, with the first deck topper **Wrong** side up, fold the top long raw edge ½" in toward the **Wrong** side and press.

d. Then, place the deck topper, with the **Right** side facing up, on the deck, lining up the bottom raw edge of the deck topper with the 14" marks you made in step 8b and matching up the side raw edges. The folded edge of the deck topper will be the top edge.

e. Attach the deck topper to the deck by stitching a ¼" seam across the top folded edge. Then, machine baste down both sides and across the bottom raw edges to hold them in place. (FIGURE 8E)

f. Next, turn the deck over to the **Wrong** side, fold both long raw edges of the deck under ½" to the **Wrong** side, and press. Then fold these edges under another ½" and press. Finally, topstitch along the inner folded edges, to finish both the side raw edges of the deck and the side raw edges of the attached deck topper.

Step 9. Attach the magazine pocket panel to the deck.

a. First, find the center of the end of the deck by folding it in half lengthwise, matching the hemmed side edges, and pressing a crease.

b. Then, find the center of the magazine pocket panel by folding it in half lengthwise, matching the side raw edges, and press a center crease.

c. Next, fold the magazine pocket panel along the ½" crease (at the back top raw edge) that you made in step 2a toward the **Wrong** side, and press.

d. Place the **Wrong** side of the deck onto the **Wrong** side of the magazine pocket panel. Match up the bottom raw edge on the deck with the back 14½" fold line on the magazine pocket panel. Then, line up the center creases on each panel. (The side raw edges of the magazine pocket panel will extend past the finished side edges of the canvas deck.) Pin the deck in place. (FIGURE 9D, E)

e. Stitch down one finished side close to the folded edge of the deck, along the bottom raw edge, and back up the other finished side, securing the deck to the magazine pocket panel. Then, turn the panel over so the **Right** side of the magazine pocket panel is facing up, and topstitch across the back top folded edge of the magazine pocket panel. (FIGURE 9D, E)

f. Fold the magazine pocket panel along the ½" crease at the front top raw edge, toward the **Wrong** side, and press it in place again. Topstitch a ⅛" seam close to the folded edge.

Step 10. Make the magazine pocket.

a. First, turn the magazine pocket panel (with the deck already attached) over so the **Right** side of the back of the magazine pocket is facing up. Then, fold the magazine pocket panel in half with **Right** sides together, matching the front top folded edge to the back top folded edge. Stitch a ½" seam down both sides of the panel, backstitching at each end. Trim each of the corners in the seam allowance, making sure not to clip your stitching, and then press the seam allowances open.

b. Now, to give the side of the magazine pocket depth, starting on the left side of the panel, place the side seam on top of the center crease you made in step 2e, forming a triangle shape at the corner panel. Make sure that the side seam and the bottom crease are aligned, then press along the folded side edges and pin securely to avoid shifting.

c. Using a yardstick and a chalk pencil, measure 1¼" in, starting at the corner point along one of the folded edges you made in the previous step, and make a mark. Then measure 1¼" in along the other folded edge from the same corner point and make another mark. Using a yardstick, match up these 2 marks and draw a line between them. This will be your stitching line to make a corner on the left side of the magazine pocket. Then, stitch along the drawn line, backstitching at each end. (FIGURE 10C)

d. Follow the instructions in steps 10b and 10c to stitch the right side bottom corner for the magazine pocket.

e. Now, turn the pocket **Right** side out and fold the formed triangles toward the bottom of the magazine pocket.

Step 11. Make and attach the lining to the Bedside Organizer.

a. First, fold both the top and bottom raw edges of the lining ½" in toward the **Wrong** side and press.

b. Fold the lining in half with the **Right** sides together, aligning the 2 folded edges and matching the side raw edges. Stitch a ½" seam down both sides, backstitching at each end.

c. Follow the instructions in steps 10b through 10d to form and stitch the bottom corners of the lining.

d. Then, place the lining inside the magazine pocket with the **Wrong** sides together. Match the side seams and the top folded edges and pin it in place.

e. Edge stitch* completely around the top edge of the opening of the pocket and lining, stitching on top of the stitching already near the folded edge.

* *See page 170 for an explanation of edge stitching.*

f. Now, stitch a second, decorative row of stitching ¼" in from the first stitching.

Step 12. Make the side pleats on the magazine pocket.

a. First, turn the Bedside Organizer **Wrong** side out.

b. Next, match up the exterior and lining side seams on each side of the magazine pocket and pin along the seams to hold them in place.

c. Then, fold the magazine pocket at the pinned side seams with the exterior sides together, flattening out the top of the organizer. Pin the matched sides of the magazine pocket, which extend past the deck, in place.

d. The pleats line up with the side finished edge of the deck. Starting on the left side of the magazine pocket, place your ruler vertically over the top part of the pocket and line it up with the left side finished edge of the deck. Mark a guideline for the left side pleat by drawing a vertical line that extends 3" down from the top finished edge of the pocket. Then, make the pleat by stitching along the guideline, backstitching at each end. Repeat this step to make the pleat on the right side. (FIGURE 12D)

e. Turn the Bedside Organizer **Right** side out and press.

Step 13. Make the Bedside Organizer for the other end of the deck.

Follow the instructions in steps 2a through 12e (excluding step 8a) to make and attach the second Bedside Organizer to the other end of the deck.

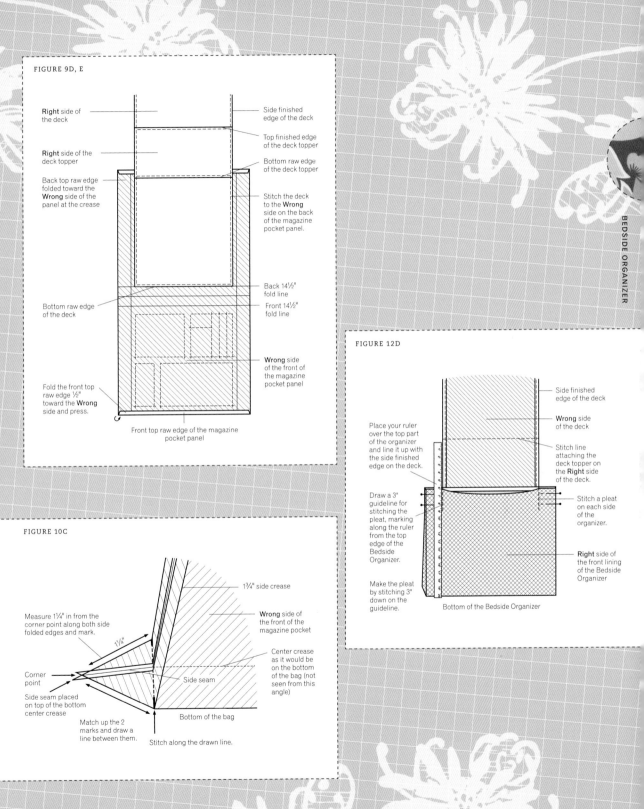

FIGURE 9D, E

Right side of the deck

Right side of the deck topper

Back top raw edge folded toward the **Wrong** side of the panel at the crease

Bottom raw edge of the deck

Fold the front top raw edge ½" toward the **Wrong** side and press.

Side finished edge of the deck

Top finished edge of the deck topper

Bottom raw edge of the deck topper

Stitch the deck to the **Wrong** side on the back of the magazine pocket panel.

Back 14½" fold line

Front 14½" fold line

Wrong side of the front of the magazine pocket panel

Front top raw edge of the magazine pocket panel

FIGURE 12D

Place your ruler over the top part of the organizer and line it up with the side finished edge on the deck.

Draw a 3" guideline for stitching the pleat, marking along the ruler from the top edge of the Bedside Organizer.

Make the pleat by stitching 3" down on the guideline.

Side finished edge of the deck

Wrong side of the deck

Stitch line attaching the deck topper on the **Right** side of the deck.

Stitch a pleat on each side of the organizer.

Right side of the front lining of the Bedside Organizer

Bottom of the Bedside Organizer

FIGURE 10C

Measure 1¼" in from the corner point along both side folded edges and mark.

1¼"

Corner point

Side seam placed on top of the bottom center crease

Match up the 2 marks and draw a line between them.

Stitch along the drawn line.

1¾" side crease

Wrong side of the front of the magazine pocket

Center crease as it would be on the bottom of the bag (not seen from this angle)

Side seam

Bottom of the bag

79

WIDE-LEG LOUNGE PANTS

FINISHED SIZES: SMALL: FITS SIZES 6 AND 8 (33½"–35" HIP) | MEDIUM: FITS SIZES 10 AND 12 (36"–38" HIP)
LARGE: FITS SIZES 14 AND 16 (40"–42" HIP) | LOUNGE PANTS INSEAM: 32"

Need a little silver-screen glamour in your life? These comfortable, easy pants will match your casual style, with a splash of 1940s elegance for good measure. These pants are just the thing for lounging in on Sunday mornings.

FABRICS

- 2¾ yards (44"- or 60"-wide) light- to mid-weight cotton fabric
- 2½ yards trim, in any width, for the hem
- ⅛ yard fusible interfacing

OTHER SUPPLIES

- Coordinating thread
- Scissors
- Cellophane tape
- Freezer paper (or other paper) (2 pieces, each 20" wide x 50" long, for all sizes Lounge Pants)
- Yardstick/ruler
- Pencil
- Straight pins
- Chalk pencil or fabric marker
- Safety pin
- Seam ripper

NOTES

- All seams are ½" unless otherwise stated. (The ½" seam allowance is included in the pattern pieces and cutting measurements provided.)

- If you choose to make a longer or shorter inseam, make the adjustment when cutting your fabric pieces. Cut the fabric to your desired length and add ¾" for the hem. We suggest trying the garment on before hemming to determine the length needed.

- Preshrink your fabric by washing, drying, and pressing it before starting your project.

Step 1. Make the pattern pieces for the Lounge Pants.

a. Use the pattern pieces provided in the pocket at the front of this book. Tape a long piece of the freezer paper to the back of the front pattern piece, making sure that the dull side of the freezer paper is facing up. Place the shorter, inside leg edge against one edge of the freezer paper to allow room for adding extra width on the outside edge if making a size medium or large.

b. Next, place the edge of the yardstick along one side edge of the pattern piece and, using a pencil, extend the side edge by adding 29" to the length. Extend the other side edge in the same way.

c. Now, draw the bottom cutting line by connecting the 2 side cutting lines, using a yardstick and pencil. (FIGURE 1C FRONT)

d. Follow the instructions in steps 1a through 1c to make an extended pattern piece for the back, being sure to match the back pattern piece and the back extension pattern piece at the dotted lines and tape them together to make one complete back pattern piece. (FIGURE 1D BACK)

e. To make a size medium or large, first extend the original pattern piece by following steps 1a through 1c. Then, using a yardstick and a pencil, add the additional width as noted on the pattern pieces by placing your yardstick along the outer side edge of the drawn pattern piece and measuring out the distance needed for the larger size. Use a pencil and yardstick to draw a new side cutting line parallel to the original pattern piece. Be sure to add the additional width to both the front and the back pattern pieces. (The additional width is added only to the outer side edge of the pattern. Do not add extra width to the shorter inside leg edge.) (FIGURE 1E BACK AND 1E FRONT)

~ CONTINUED

f. Using your scissors, cut out the front and back pattern pieces, making sure to follow the newly marked lines if you have made any changes in size.

Step 2. Cut out all pieces from the fabric.

a. First, fold the fabric in half lengthwise with **Wrong** sides together and the selvage edges* aligned. Lay the fabric on a flat surface with the folded edge toward you.

* See page 171 for an explanation of a selvage edge.

b. Pin the pattern pieces to the fabric following the cutting layout provided on the pattern pieces. The long arrows (marked "Lengthwise grain line") on the pattern pieces are to be placed on the lengthwise grain* of the fabric, which means that the long lines of the arrow on the pattern piece will be parallel to the fold and the selvage edges of the fabric. (FIGURE 2B)

* See page 171 for an explanation of lengthwise grain.

c. Then, using your scissors, cut the fabric according to the outlines on the pattern pieces.

d. Now, open up the remaining fabric and cut one strip measuring 1½" wide x 60" long parallel to (but not including) the selvage edge. This strip will be used to make the drawstring for the Lounge Pants.

Step 3. Make the Lounge Pants.

NOTE: *All the seams can be finished by serging them or by trimming the seam allowance to ¼" and zigzag stitching along the trimmed edge. Press all the seams to the side indicated in the directions.*

a. Place one front piece and one back piece with **Right** sides together matching the inner leg raw edge and pin them in place. Attach the front and back by stitching a ½" seam down the inner leg. Press the allowance toward the back. (FIGURE 3A)

b. Follow the instructions in step 3a to attach the second set of front and back pieces.

c. Next, open up both sets of front/back pieces, place them **Right** sides together, and match the inner leg seams and the curved raw edges. Pin the crotch seam and stitch it together with a ½" seam. To reinforce this seam, stitch over the crotch seam again. To help identify the back, make a small mark at the center back seam using a chalk pencil or fabric marker. (FIGURE 3C)

d. Now, open up the front/back pieces so that the **Right** sides are together and the side raw edges are matched, and pin in place. Stitch a ½" seam along both side edges. Press the side seam allowances toward the back. (FIGURE 3D)

Step 4. Make the buttonholes* on the casing for the drawstring.

a. First, turn the Lounge Pants so that the **Right** side is facing out. Now, place your yardstick ½" to the left of the center front seam. Measure down from the top raw edge 3" and make a mark, using a chalk pencil. Move the ruler ½" to the right of the center seam, measure down from the top raw edge 3", and make a second mark. These 2 marks will be the top edge of the buttonholes.

* See page 170 for an explanation of how to make a buttonhole if your sewing machine does not have that feature.

b. Cut a 2" x 2" piece of fusible interfacing and place the fusible side (the shiny or bumpy side) of the interfacing onto the **Wrong** side of the fabric, centering it over the buttonhole marks. Follow the manufacturer's instructions to apply the fusible interfacing to the fabric. This interfacing will add stability for the buttonholes.

c. Make one vertical ½" buttonhole on each side of the center front seam, starting the top of the buttonholes at the marks you made in step 4a. (FIGURE 4C)

d. To cut open the buttonholes start at the bottom bar tack in the middle of the narrow zigzag stitching lines, insert the pointed end of your seam ripper through the fabric, and cut up to the top bar tack. Repeat this step to cut open the other buttonhole.

Step 5: Finish the top edge of the Lounge Pants.

a. Turn the Lounge Pants so that the **Wrong** side is facing out. Now, on the top raw edge, turn under ¼" toward the **Wrong** side of the fabric and press. (FIGURE 5A)

b. Then, turn this edge under again 1¾" and press. Pin the folded edge in place and edge stitch* close to this folded edge, all the way around the top of the Lounge Pants. (FIGURE 5B, C)

* See page 170 for an explanation of edge stitching.

c. Stitch again ¾" from your first row of stitching to create the casing for the drawstring. (FIGURE 5B, C)

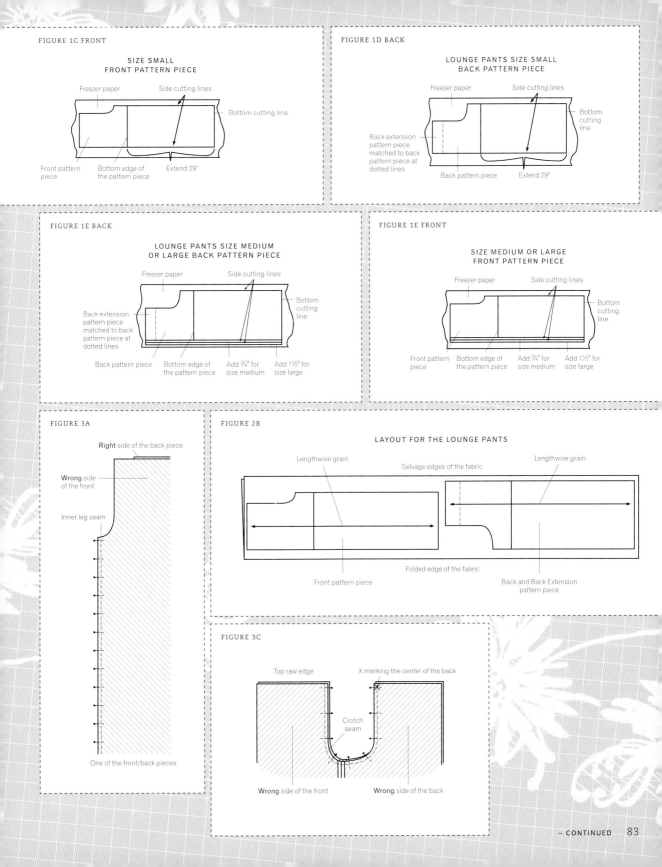

FIGURE 1C FRONT

SIZE SMALL
FRONT PATTERN PIECE

Freezer paper
Side cutting lines
Bottom cutting line
Front pattern piece
Bottom edge of the pattern piece
Extend 29"

FIGURE 1D BACK

LOUNGE PANTS SIZE SMALL
BACK PATTERN PIECE

Freezer paper
Side cutting lines
Bottom cutting line
Back extension pattern piece matched to back pattern piece at dotted lines
Back pattern piece
Extend 29"

FIGURE 1E BACK

LOUNGE PANTS SIZE MEDIUM
OR LARGE BACK PATTERN PIECE

Freezer paper
Side cutting lines
Bottom cutting line
Back extension pattern piece matched to back pattern piece at dotted lines
Back pattern piece
Bottom edge of the pattern piece
Add ¾" for size medium
Add 1½" for size large

FIGURE 1E FRONT

SIZE MEDIUM OR LARGE
FRONT PATTERN PIECE

Freezer paper
Side cutting lines
Bottom cutting line
Front pattern piece
Bottom edge of the pattern piece
Add ¾" for size medium
Add 1½" for size large

FIGURE 3A

Right side of the back piece
Wrong side of the front
Inner leg seam
One of the front/back pieces

FIGURE 2B

LAYOUT FOR THE LOUNGE PANTS

Lengthwise grain
Selvage edges of the fabric
Lengthwise grain
Front pattern piece
Folded edge of the fabric
Back and Back Extension pattern piece

FIGURE 3C

Top raw edge
X marking the center of the back
Crotch seam
Wrong side of the front
Wrong side of the back

– CONTINUED

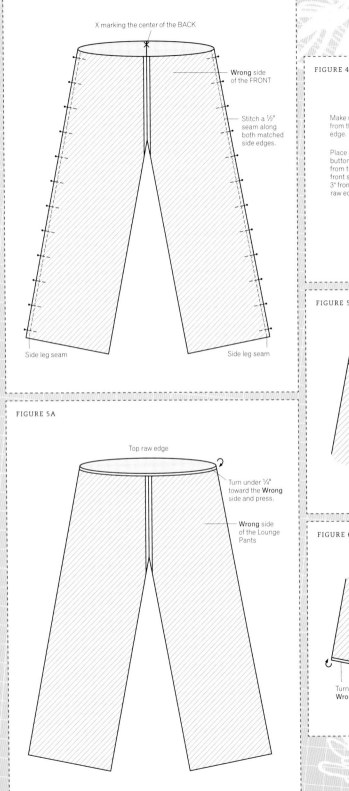

X marking the center of the BACK

Wrong side of the FRONT

Stitch a ½" seam along both matched side edges.

Side leg seam

Side leg seam

FIGURE 5A

Top raw edge

Turn under ¼" toward the **Wrong** side and press.

Wrong side of the Lounge Pants

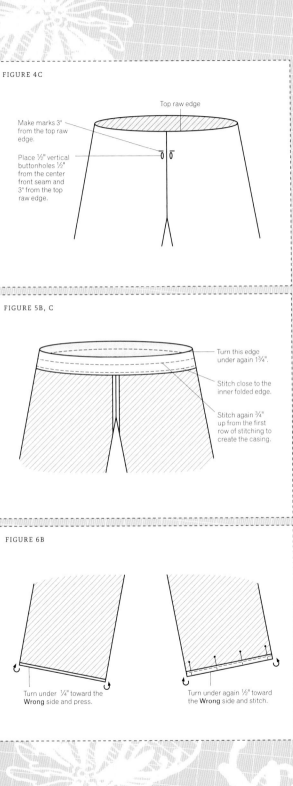

FIGURE 4C

Top raw edge

Make marks 3" from the top raw edge.

Place ½" vertical buttonholes ½" from the center front seam and 3" from the top raw edge.

FIGURE 5B, C

Turn this edge under again 1¾".

Stitch close to the inner folded edge.

Stitch again ¾" up from the first row of stitching to create the casing.

FIGURE 6B

Turn under ¼" toward the **Wrong** side and press.

Turn under again ½" toward the **Wrong** side and stitch.

Step 6. Hem the Lounge Pants and add the trim.

a. With the **Wrong** side of the Lounge Pants still facing out, turn under ¼" on the bottom raw edge of each leg, toward the **Wrong** side of the fabric, and press.

b. Now, turn this edge under ½" again toward the **Wrong** side of the fabric and press. Pin the folded edge in place and stitch close to this folded edge. (FIGURE 6B)

c. Turn the Lounge Pants **Right** side out to apply the trim. Beginning at the inner leg seam, pin the trim with **Right** side facing out around the leg opening at a distance from the hemmed edge that pleases you. When you reach the beginning point, fold the trim under ½" overlapping the raw edge where you began and pin the edge in place. (FIGURE 6C)

d. Stitch the trim in place by topstitching* all the way around the leg opening, close to the edge of the trim at both the top and the bottom edges and then slip stitch the end of the trim in place by hand. (FIGURE 6D)

See page 172 for an explanation of topstitching.

e. Follow the instructions in steps 6a through 6d to hem and attach the trim to the other leg of the Lounge Pants.

Step 7: Make and insert the drawstring.*

a. To make the drawstring, take the 1½"x 60" strip that you cut in step 3d and fold it in half lengthwise. Press a crease on the fold. Now, unfold the strip and fold both long raw edges in to meet the center crease and press. Fold in ¼" at each short end and press. Then, fold the drawstring in half one more time at the center crease, enclosing the long raw edges, and press. Your drawstring will measure approximately ⅜" wide and 59½" long. Topstitch across one short end, down the long double-folded edge and across the other short end. (FIGURE 7A)

b. To finish the pants, insert the drawstring by attaching a safety pin to one end and threading it into one buttonhole, through the casing, and out the buttonhole on the other side. Remove the safety pin. Then, tie a knot at each end of the drawstring.

See page 170 for more details on how to make a drawstring.

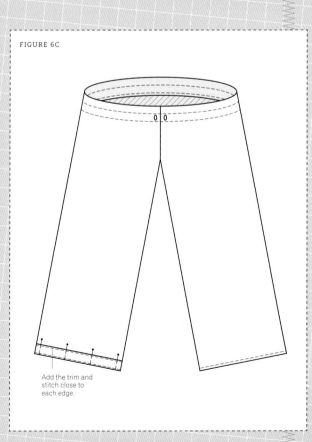

FIGURE 6C

0 0

Add the trim and stitch close to each edge.

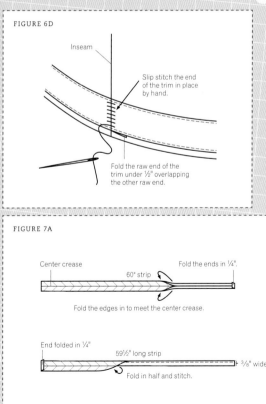

FIGURE 6D

Inseam

Slip stitch the end of the trim in place by hand.

Fold the raw end of the trim under ½" overlapping the other raw end.

FIGURE 7A

Center crease

60" strip

Fold the ends in ¼".

Fold the edges in to meet the center crease.

End folded in ¼"

59½" long strip

⅜" wide

Fold in half and stitch.

SLEEPING MASK

FINISHED SIZE: 3½" WIDE X 9" LONG

Here is everything you need to get your beauty sleep—a chic quilted sleeping mask to shield you from those early-morning rays that come streaming in your window. Toss it in your flight bag next time you're packing for a plane trip, and you'll emerge at your destination rested and energized!

FABRICS

- ¼ yard (36"-wide) soft cotton or washable satin or silk for the Sleeping Mask
- ⅓ yard lightweight polyester batting
- ¼ yard (36"-wide) muslin for the backing
- 1 yard (¾"-wide) satin ribbon

OTHER SUPPLIES

- Coordinating thread
- Scissors
- Quilting ruler
- Chalk pencil or fabric marker
- Straight pins
- Turning tool (such as a closed pair of scissors)

NOTES

- All seams are ½" unless otherwise stated. (The ½" seam allowance is included in all cutting measurements and the pattern piece.)
- Preshrink your fabric by washing, drying, and pressing it before starting your project.

Step 1. Cut out all pieces from the fabric.

a. First, cut out the Sleeping Mask pattern piece provided in the pocket at the front of this book.

b. Simply measure and mark the dimensions below directly onto the **Wrong** side of the fabric, using a yardstick and a chalk pencil. Then, using your scissors, cut out each panel following the marked lines.

FROM THE FABRIC FOR THE SLEEPING MASK EXTERIOR

- *Cut 1 front panel: 6" wide x 12" long*
- *Cut 1 Sleeping Mask back panel: Use the Sleeping Mask pattern piece in the pocket at the front of this book.*

FROM THE LIGHTWEIGHT BATTING

- *Cut 4 panels: 6" wide x 12" long*

FROM THE MUSLIN

- *Cut 1 panel: 6" wide x 12" long*

FROM THE RIBBON

- *Cut 2 lengths: 16" long each*

Step 2. Quilt the front panel for the Sleeping Mask.

a. Place the muslin panel on a hard, flat surface. Using your ruler and chalk pencil, mark diagonal lines across the panel, ½" apart. Then, mark lines on the opposite diagonal ½" apart, making a diamond-shaped quilting pattern.

b. Turn the front panel over so the **Wrong** side is facing up and stack all 4 panels of batting on the front panel, matching up the raw edges. Then, place the muslin panel with the marked quilting lines facing up, on top of the batting layers, and pin the panels in place.

c. Starting with one of the center diagonal lines, machine stitch through all the layers, along the lines you marked in step 2a. Working from the center lines out to the side edges, stitch along all of the quilting lines on both diagonals.

~ CONTINUED

Step 3. Make the Sleeping Mask.

a. Pin the Sleeping Mask pattern piece to the quilted panel you made in step 2. Then, using your scissors, cut the fabric according to the outline on the pattern piece.

b. With the pattern piece in place on the **Right** side of the quilted panel, using your chalk pencil, mark the placement lines for the ribbon on both the right and left sides according to the lines on the pattern piece, onto the **Right** side of the quilted panel. Remove the pattern piece from the quilted Sleeping Mask panel.

c. Place the **Right** sides of the quilted Sleeping Mask panel and the ribbons together at the placement marks on the right and left side of the quilted panel, lining up the raw edges, and pin them in place. Then, machine baste* the ribbons in place by stitching a ¼" seam across the ends of the ribbons. (**FIGURE 3C**)

See page 171 for an explanation of machine basting.

d. Fold up the ends of the ribbons and pin them to the **Right** side of the quilted Sleeping Mask to keep from catching the ribbon when stitching the front and back panels together. Then, place the **Right** sides of the quilted Sleeping Mask and the back Sleeping Mask panels together and pin them in place. Attach by stitching a ½" seam around the Sleeping Mask, leaving a 4" opening centered at the top of the panels, backstitching at each end.

e. Using your scissors, trim the seam allowances* to ¼" around the outside curves of the mask. Then, clip into the seam allowance* around the inside curve of the nose area, making sure not to clip your stitching. This will allow the mask to turn **Right** side out. (**FIGURE 3E**)

See page 172 for an explanation of trimming and clipping the seam allowances.

f. Turn the mask **Right** side out, using a turning tool* to push out the seams of the mask, and press it flat.

See page 172 for an explanation of a turning tool.

g. To finish the Sleeping Mask, fold in the ½" seam allowances of the opening and pin the opening closed. Then topstitch* completely around the Sleeping Mask with a ⅛" seam to close the opening.

See page 172 for an explanation of topstitching.

FIGURE 3C

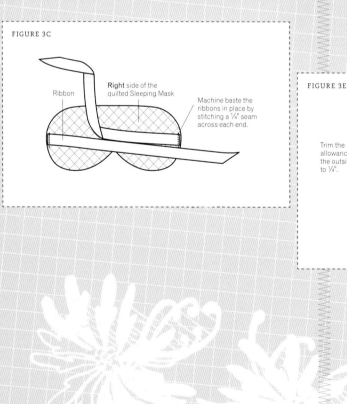

Ribbon

Right side of the quilted Sleeping Mask

Machine baste the ribbons in place by stitching a ¼" seam across each end.

FIGURE 3E

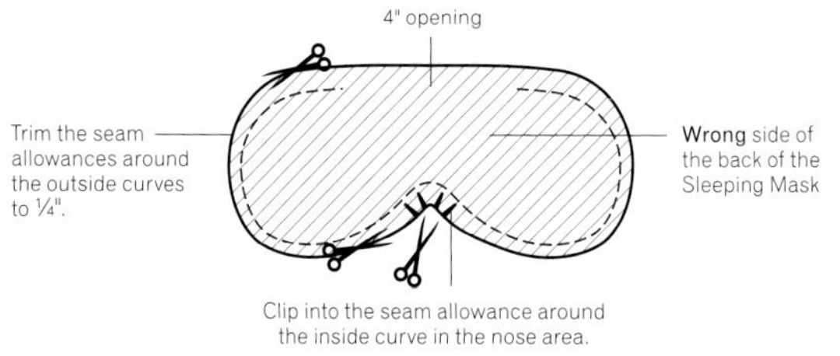

4" opening

Trim the seam allowances around the outside curves to ¼".

Wrong side of the back of the Sleeping Mask

Clip into the seam allowance around the inside curve in the nose area.

This illustration shows the seam allowances around the outside curves on the Sleeping Mask after they have been trimmed to ¼".

CHAPTER 4

BATHROOM

Projects

Whether your bathroom is a tiny water closet or a spacious day spa off of a master suite, the bath is your own private refuge from the bustle of the outside world. Dressing up your little sanctuary is gloriously self-indulgent, but a well-appointed bath also impresses visitors. So you win both ways! Here are some fun projects that'll give your bathroom some extra appeal: a hanging toiletry basket, a really large laundry bag, and an elegant way to dress up plain-Jane towels. And you can even dress yourself up in your own kimono-style bathrobe. It's very comfy and stylish.

KIMONO-STYLE BATHROBE

FINISHED SIZES:
SMALL: BUST: 32"–33½", WAIST: 24"–25", SLEEVE LENGTH: 22" (WITH CUFF UNFOLDED), ROBE LENGTH: 33½"
MEDIUM: BUST: 34"–36", WAIST: 26"–28", SLEEVE LENGTH: 22" (WITH CUFF UNFOLDED), ROBE LENGTH: 35½"
LARGE: BUST: 38"–40", WAIST: 30"–32", SLEEVE LENGTH: 22" (WITH CUFF UNFOLDED), ROBE LENGTH: 37"

The sleek, sophisticated look of this luxurious bathrobe means it works as well at the pool as it does in your home bathroom. A bit saucier than the standard bathrobe, it's wonderful to wear just out of the shower, while lounging in bed on weekend mornings, and relaxing at the spa! Instructions for three sizes are included.

FABRIC (FOR ALL SIZES)

- 3¾ yards 44"-wide light- to mid-weight cotton

OTHER SUPPLIES

- Coordinating thread
- Scissors
- Yardstick
- Chalk pencil or fabric marker

- Straight pins
- Masking tape

NOTES

- All seams are ½" unless otherwise stated. (The ½" seam allowance is included in all cutting measurements and the pattern pieces.)

- Preshrink your fabric by washing, drying, and pressing it before starting your project.

- If your fabric is printed, purchase extra yardage (the length of the repeat in the fabric's design) so you can match up the print at seams.

Step 1. Cut out all pieces from the fabric.

a. First, cut out the Kimono-Style Bathrobe pattern pieces provided in the pocket at the front of this book:

- *Front trim*
- *Neck trim*

b. Referring to FIGURE 1B, first measure and mark the belt along (but not including) one of the selvage edges*, working directly on the **Wrong** side of the fabric and using a yardstick and a chalk pencil. Then, fold the remaining section of fabric in half lengthwise, lining up the other selvage edge with the outside of the belt measurement. Simply measure and mark the dimensions for the front panels, sleeves, and belt loops directly onto the **Wrong** side of your folded fabric. Place and pin the neck trim pattern piece on the fold of the fabric and then, using your scissors, cut out each panel following the marked lines. Open the remaining piece of fabric and measure and mark the back panel. To make the front trim, place the pattern piece onto the **Wrong** side of the fabric, lining up the lengthwise grain on the pattern piece with the lengthwise grain on the fabric, leaving enough fabric below the bottom of the pattern piece to measure and mark the added length for the particular size that you are making. Using your yardstick and chalk pencil, measure and mark the added length. Then, cut out around the pattern piece following the solid line and down the added length to make the front trim. Using the front trim you just made, flip the piece over, matching up the **Wrong** sides of the fabric, and cut out around the front trim. This will give you 2 front trim pieces. Cut out these pieces. **(FIGURE 1B)**

* See page 171 for an explanation of a selvage edge.

~ CONTINUED

FOR SIZE SMALL

- *Cut 1 belt: 8˝ wide x 81˝ long*
  (Measure and mark this piece first.)
- *Cut 2 front panels: 12½˝ wide x 36˝ long*
- *Cut 1 back panel: 27˝ wide x 36˝ long*
- *Cut 2 sleeves: 16˝ wide x 26˝ long*
- *Cut 2 belt loops: 4˝ wide x 4˝ long*
- *Cut 2 front trims: Use front trim pattern piece provided in the pocket at the front of this book; add 20˝ to the bottom of the pattern piece.*
- *Cut 1 neck trim on the fold:* Use neck trim pattern piece provided in the pocket at the front of this book.*

FOR SIZE MEDIUM

- *Cut 1 belt: 8˝ wide x 81˝ long*
  (Measure and mark this piece first.)
- *Cut 2 front panels: 13˝ wide x 38˝ long*
- *Cut 1 back panel: 28˝ wide x 38˝ long*
- *Cut 2 sleeves: 17˝ wide x 26˝ long*
- *Cut 2 belt loops: 4˝ wide x 4˝ long*
- *Cut 2 front trims: Use front trim pattern piece provided in the pocket at the front of this book; add 22˝ to the bottom of the pattern piece.*
- *Cut 1 neck trim on the fold:* Use neck trim pattern piece provided in the pocket at the front of this book.*

FOR SIZE LARGE

- *Cut 1 belt: 8˝ wide x 85˝ long*
  (Measure and mark this piece first.)
- *Cut 2 front panels: 14˝ wide x 40˝ long*
- *Cut 1 back panel: 30˝ wide x 40˝ long*
- *Cut 2 sleeves: 22˝ wide x 26˝ long*
- *Cut 2 belt loops: 4˝ wide x 4˝ long*
- *Cut 2 front trims: Use front trim pattern piece provided in the pocket at the front of this book; add 24˝ to the bottom of the pattern piece.*
- *Cut 1 neck trim on the fold:* Use neck trim pattern piece provided in the pocket at the front of this book.*

* To cut the pattern piece on the fold of your fabric, lay your pattern piece so that the edge to be placed on the fold is even with the folded edge of your fabric. Once this pattern piece is cut out of your fabric, open it up to make one full panel.

c. In order to keep your pieces organized, mark each piece by writing the name on a piece of masking tape and attaching to the **Wrong** side of each panel as it is cut.

d. Using your chalk pencil, transfer the dot* on the neck trim pattern piece onto the **Wrong** side of your fabric piece on each side of the neck trim. The dots will be used as a stopping point for your stitching when attaching the front trim and the point to clip into the seam allowance.

* See page 170 for an explanation of the dot.

FIGURE 1B

LAYOUT FOR THE KIMONO-STYLE BATHROBE

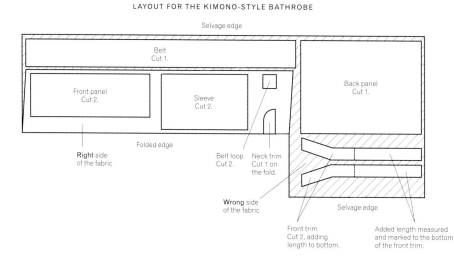

Selvage edge

Belt
Cut 1.

Front panel
Cut 2.

Sleeve
Cut 2.

Back panel
Cut 1.

Belt loop
Cut 2.

Neck trim
Cut 1 on
the fold.

Right side
of the fabric

Folded edge

Wrong side
of the fabric

Selvage edge

Front trim
Cut 2, adding
length to bottom.

Added length measured
and marked to the bottom
of the front trim.

Step 2. Make the neck opening on the front panels.

a. With the **Right** sides of the front panels together, place the front trim pattern piece onto the **Wrong** side of the front panels, lining up the top of the front trim pattern piece with the top raw edge on the front panels. Place the pattern piece so it curves (at the bust line) to the right side raw edge. The lower part of the front trim pattern piece will line up with the raw edges on the right side. Pin the pattern piece in place through both layers of your fabric.

b. Using your scissors, cut the top right corner area of the front panels along the edge of the pattern piece. (FIGURE 2B)

Step 3. Attach the front panels to the back panel.

a. Place the **Right** sides of the 2 front panels onto the **Right** side of the back panel, laying the neck opening on each front panel toward the center, lining up the outside edge on both sides. Match up the top raw edges and pin the panels in place. Attach the panels together by stitching a ½" seam across the top raw edges, backstitching at each end. (FIGURE 3A)

b. Turn the joined pieces over so the **Wrong** side of the back panel is facing up. Clip into the seam allowance* on the back panel at the end of the stitching toward the middle that attached the front panels. Make sure not to clip the stitching. Then, serge or zigzag across the raw edges of the 2 seam allowances, held together, and press the seam allowances toward the back panel. (FIGURE 3B)

See page 170 for an explanation of clipping into the seam allowance.

Step 4. Attach the front trim and neck trim pieces together.

a. Place the front trim pieces with the **Right** sides facing up, laying them so that the curves point inward toward the center. Then, place the **Right** side of the neck trim onto the **Right** sides of the front trim, matching up the raw edges for the shoulder, and pin them in place.

b. Starting on the top left outside raw edge, stitch a ½" seam across the matched raw edges, stopping at the dot (which you transferred from the pattern piece in step 1d) at the neck opening, backstitching at each end. Repeat this step to stitch the top right matched raw edges. (FIGURE 4B, C)

c. Clip the neck trim in the seam allowance to the dots on each side of the neck trim. Then, press the shoulder seam allowances open. (FIGURE 4B, C)

Step 5. Finish the outside raw edge of the trim.

First, stitch a ½" seam around the outside raw edge of the attached front and neck trim pieces. Then, with the **Wrong** side of the trim pieces facing up, using the seam as a guideline, fold the outside raw edges ½" in toward the **Wrong** side of the trim pieces at the seam and press them in place. (FIGURE 5)

Step 6. Attach the trim to the front and back panels.

Place the **Right** side of the trim onto the **Wrong** side of the attached front and back panels, matching up the shoulder seams, and pin in place. Stitch a ½" seam around the inside raw edge of the front and neck trim, backstitching at each end. (FIGURE 6, 7)

Step 7. Trim and clip the seam allowance.

a. Using your scissors, clip into the seam allowance at the corners of the neck opening to the dot (marked on the **Wrong** side of the piece), where the shoulder seams meet. Be careful not to clip your stitching.

b. Then, trim the seam allowance* to ¼" at the curve at the bust line. (FIGURE 6, 7)

See page 172 for an explanation of trimming the seam allowance.

Step 8. Finish attaching the trim to the front and back panels.

a. Fold the trim over onto the **Right** side of the front and back panels and press it flat. Pin the outside folded edge of the trim onto the **Right** side of the front and back panels.

b. Then, with a ⅛" seam, topstitch* around the outside folded edge of the trim to attach it to the panels, and then topstitch another ⅛" seam in from the inside finished edge. (FIGURE 8B)

See page 172 for an explanation of topstitching.

Step 9. Attach the sleeves to the front and back panels.

a. First, find the center of the sleeve by folding the sleeve in half lengthwise and gently pressing a crease.

b. Then, with the front and back panels **Right** sides facing out, center the crease on the sleeve over the shoulder seam on the left side of the panels and pin it in place. Make sure to match the raw edges on the sleeve along the left side raw edges on both the front and back panels. (FIGURE 9B)

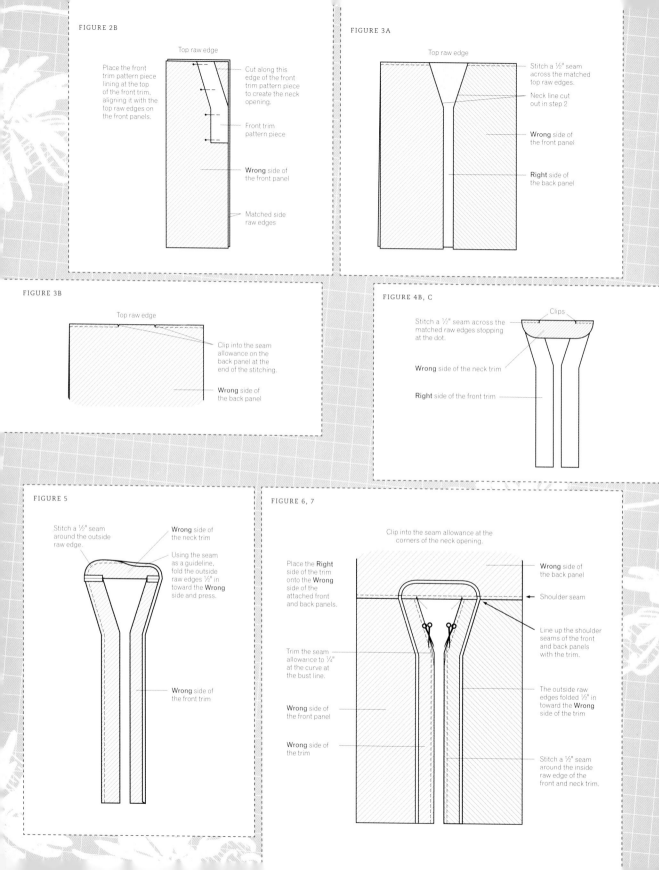

FIGURE 2B

Place the front trim pattern piece lining at the top of the front trim, aligning it with the top raw edges on the front panels.

Top raw edge

Cut along this edge of the front trim pattern piece to create the neck opening.

Front trim pattern piece

Wrong side of the front panel

Matched side raw edges

FIGURE 3A

Top raw edge

Stitch a ½" seam across the matched top raw edges.

Neck line cut out in step 2

Wrong side of the front panel

Right side of the back panel

FIGURE 3B

Top raw edge

Clip into the seam allowance on the back panel at the end of the stitching.

Wrong side of the back panel

FIGURE 4B, C

Clips

Stitch a ½" seam across the matched raw edges stopping at the dot.

Wrong side of the neck trim

Right side of the front trim

FIGURE 5

Stitch a ½" seam around the outside raw edge.

Wrong side of the neck trim

Using the seam as a guideline, fold the outside raw edges ½" in toward the **Wrong** side and press.

Wrong side of the front trim

FIGURE 6, 7

Clip into the seam allowance at the corners of the neck opening.

Place the **Right** side of the trim onto the **Wrong** side of the attached front and back panels.

Trim the seam allowance to ¼" at the curve at the bust line.

Wrong side of the front panel

Wrong side of the trim

Wrong side of the back panel

Shoulder seam

Line up the shoulder seams of the front and back panels with the trim.

The outside raw edges folded ½" in toward the **Wrong** side of the trim

Stitch a ½" seam around the inside raw edge of the front and neck trim.

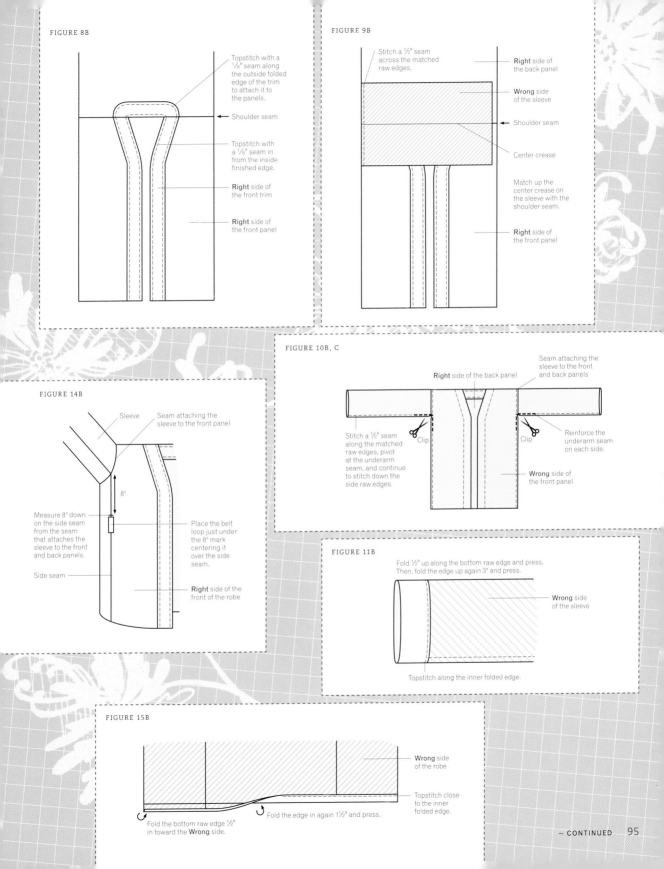

FIGURE 8B

Topstitch with a ⅛" seam along the outside folded edge of the trim to attach it to the panels.

← Shoulder seam

Topstitch with a ⅛" seam in from the inside finished edge.

Right side of the front trim

Right side of the front panel

FIGURE 9B

Stitch a ½" seam across the matched raw edges.

Right side of the back panel

Wrong side of the sleeve

← Shoulder seam

Center crease

Match up the center crease on the sleeve with the shoulder seam.

Right side of the front panel

FIGURE 10B, C

Right side of the back panel

Seam attaching the sleeve to the front and back panels

Stitch a ½" seam along the matched raw edges, pivot at the underarm seam, and continue to stitch down the side raw edges.

Clip

Clip

Reinforce the underarm seam on each side.

Wrong side of the front panel

FIGURE 14B

Sleeve

Seam attaching the sleeve to the front panel

8"

Measure 8" down on the side seam from the seam that attaches the sleeve to the front and back panels.

Side seam

Place the belt loop just under the 8" mark centering it over the side seam.

Right side of the front of the robe

FIGURE 11B

Fold ½" up along the bottom raw edge and press. Then, fold the edge up again 3" and press.

Wrong side of the sleeve

Topstitch along the inner folded edge.

FIGURE 15B

Wrong side of the robe

Topstitch close to the inner folded edge.

Fold the bottom raw edge ½" in toward the **Wrong** side.

Fold the edge in again 1½" and press.

~ CONTINUED

c. Attach by stitching a ½" seam across the matched raw edges, backstitching at each end. Serge or zigzag across the seam allowance and press the seam allowance toward the sleeve.

d. Follow the instructions in steps 9a through 9c to attach the other sleeve onto the right-hand side of the attached front and back panels.

Step 10. Attach the sides of the robe.

a. First, place the front and back panels with **Right** sides together. Match up the side raw edges of the front panel and sleeve with the side raw edges of the back panel and sleeve on both sides of the robe and pin them in place.

b. Starting on the left side of the robe, stitch a ½" seam across the matched raw edges on the sleeve, pivot* at the underarm seam, and continue to stitch down the side raw edges of the matched front and back panels, backstitching at each end. (FIGURE 10B, C)

See page 171 for an explanation of pivoting.

c. To reinforce the seam* under the arm, stitch again over your stitching for about 2" on each side of the seam that attaches the sleeve to the front and back panels, backstitching at each end. (FIGURE 10B, C)

See page 171 for an explanation of a reinforcement stitch.

d. Next, clip into the seam allowance where the seams attaching the sleeve to the main panels connect, making sure not to clip your stitching.

e. Then, serge or zigzag across raw edges of the underarm and side seam allowances held together and press the seam allowances toward the back of the robe.

f. Follow the instructions in steps 10b through 10e to attach and finish the raw edges on the right side of the robe.

Step 11. Hem the sleeves.

a. First, try on your robe. Place a pin at the point on the sleeve to mark where your arm ends. Take off the robe and measure 3½" past the length you marked on the sleeve and cut away any excess sleeve length.

b. Then, starting with the left sleeve, fold ½" up toward the **Wrong** side along the bottom raw edge and press. Then, fold the edge up again 3" and press. Pin the folded edge in place. Topstitch along the inner folded edge of the sleeve. Repeat this step to hem the bottom raw edges on the right sleeve. (FIGURE 11B)

c. Then, turn the robe **Right** side facing out and press the entire robe.

Step 12. Make the belt.*

a. Find the center of the belt by folding it in half lengthwise with the **Wrong** sides together and press a center crease. Unfold the belt.

b. Next, fold the long side raw edges in to meet the center crease and press. Then, fold each short raw end ½" in and press. Then, refold the belt in half again at the center crease and press.

c. Topstitch completely around the belt close to the folded edges.

See page 170 for an explanation of how to make a drawstring (you'll use the same process to make your belt).

Step 13. Make the belt loops.

Follow the instructions in step 12 to make and finish both of the belt loops.

Step 14. Attach the belt loops to each side of the robe.

a. Try on your robe again. Tie the belt around your waist, and raise and lower your arms to allow enough room on the sides for you to move comfortably. On the left side seam, mark the location just above where your belt is placed. Alternatively, measure 8" down on the left side seam, from the seam that attaches the sleeve to the front and back panels, and make a mark. Repeat this step to mark the placement for your other belt loop on the right side of the robe. Remove the robe.

b. Place one short end of the first belt loop just under the mark on the left side seam, centering it over the side seam, and pin it in place across both short ends. Stitch close to the finished edge on each end of the belt loop, backstitching at each end. (FIGURE 14B)

c. Follow the instructions in step 14b to attach the other belt loop to the right-hand side of the robe.

Step 15. Hem the bottom of the robe.

a. Fold the bottom raw edge on the robe ½" in toward the **Wrong** side and press. Fold the edge in again 1½" toward the **Wrong** side and press. Pin along the inner folded edge.

b. Then, topstitch close to the inner folded edge to finish the robe. (FIGURE 15B)

HANGING TOILETRY BASKET

FINISHED SIZE: 8" WIDE X 15" TALL X 2" DEEP

This sturdy, handy basket offers a lovely way to store your cosmetics, lotions, and other bathroom necessities within easy reach! Made to hang on a doorknob or hook, it's perfect for personalizing small spaces such as dorm rooms. It travels well, too—just pack it in your suitcase along with your favorite toiletries, and stock it when you're settling into your hotel room.

FABRICS AND NOTIONS

- ⅜ yard (44"-wide) light to mid-weight cotton print for the front and bottom panels and pocket
- ½ yard (44"-wide) coordinating cotton solid for the back panels, pocket, and bottom lining panel
- ½ yard (44"- or 58"-wide) 10-ounce cotton canvas or duck cloth
- ½ yard (13"-wide) Timtex* or other extra-heavy interfacing
- ¼ yard boning

*See page 172 for an explanation of Timtex.

OTHER SUPPLIES

- Coordinating thread
- Scissors
- Yardstick or ruler
- Chalk pencil or fabric marker
- Masking tape
- Straight pins
- Seam ripper
- Turning tool (such as a closed pair of scissors)
- Quarter

NOTES

- All seams are ½" unless otherwise stated. (The ½" seam allowance is included in all of the cutting measurements and the pattern piece.)
- Preshrink your fabric by washing, drying, and pressing it before starting your project. To wash Timtex after completing your project, machine wash warm, then reshape your project and air dry. Your project will press back into shape with a steam iron. Once you steam the project, support it with wadded-up tissue paper or a folded towel while air drying in order to keep the shape that you want.

Step 1. Cut out all pieces from the fabric.

a. First, cut out the back panel pattern piece provided in the pocket at the front of this book.

b. Simply measure and mark the dimensions below directly onto the **Wrong** side of your fabric, using a yardstick and a chalk pencil. Then, using your scissors, cut out each panel following the marked lines. (Use FIGURE 1B to see all the parts of the project.)

FROM THE FABRIC FOR THE EXTERIOR FRONT, POCKET, AND BOTTOM PANELS

- Cut 1 exterior front panel: 13″ wide x 10½″ long
- Cut 1 exterior pocket panel: 13″ wide x 6½″ long
- Cut 1 exterior bottom panel: 3″ wide x 9″ long

FROM THE FABRIC FOR THE EXTERIOR BACK, FRONT LINING, POCKET LINING, AND BOTTOM LINING

- Cut 2 exterior back panels: Use the entire pattern piece provided in the pocket at the front of this book.
- Cut 1 front lining panel: 13″ wide x 11½″ long
- Cut 1 pocket lining: 13″ wide x 7½″ long
- Cut 1 bottom lining panel: 3″ wide x 9″ long

FROM THE CANVAS

- Cut 1 front panel: 13″ wide x 10½″ long
- Cut 1 pocket panel: 13″ wide x 6½″ long
- Cut 1 top panel: Use the top of the back panel pattern piece provided in the pocket at the front of this book. (Fold the back panel pattern piece at the fold line and cut around the top part of the pattern to make the top panel.)

~ CONTINUED

- *Cut 2 panels: 8˝ wide x 10˝ long*
- *Cut 2 bottom panels: 2˝ wide x 8˝ long*

c. In order to keep your pieces organized, mark each piece by writing the name on a piece of masking tape and attaching to the **Wrong** side of each panel as it is cut.

Step 2: Attach the canvas and Timtex interfacing to the exterior panels.

a. Center one of the short edges of the first Timtex panel on the bottom raw edge of the canvas top panel, overlapping it ½˝. Stitch a seam across the top cut edge of the Timtex, attaching the 2 pieces together. Then, turn the panel over and repeat this step to attach the other Timtex panel to the other side of the canvas top panel. (FIGURE 2A)

b. Cut a 9" piece of boning* with the casing attached. Slide the boning out of the casing a couple of inches on one end and cut 1¼˝ off the end of the boning. Push the boning back inside the casing. Then, fold under ⅝˝ of the casing on each end of the boning and pin it in place. Machine baste* across both ends of the boning to hold the folded ends in place. (FIGURE 2B)

* See pages 170 and 171 for explanations of boning and machine basting.

c. Center the boning across the top cut edge of the Timtex panel where it is attached to the **Wrong** side of the canvas and pin the boning in place. Stitch across both long sides of the boning and each end of the boning, backstitching at each end.

d. Place the canvas-and-Timtex back panel onto the **Wrong** side of the exterior back panel, matching up the top raw edge of the canvas with the top raw edge of the back panel. Center the attached Timtex on the bottom part of the back panel, leaving ½˝ of the back panel exposed around the side and bottom edges of the Timtex, and pin it in place. Then, machine baste a ½˝ seam around the canvas raw edges, attaching it to the exterior back panel, and continue to stitch around the cut edge on the Timtex. Set the panel aside. (FIGURE 2D)

e. To give the bottom of your Hanging Toiletry Basket added support, machine baste both of the Timtex bottom panels together. Then, center the Timtex panels on the **Wrong** side of the exterior bottom panel, leaving ½˝ of the exterior bottom panel exposed all the way around the Timtex, as in the previous step. Pin the panels in place. Next, machine baste the Timtex around the cut edge to secure it in place. Then, set the panel aside. (FIGURE 2E)

f. Place the canvas front panel onto the **Wrong** side of the exterior front panel, matching up the raw edges, and pin it in place. Then, machine baste a ½˝ seam completely around the edges of the front panel.

g. Place the canvas pocket panel onto the **Wrong** side of the exterior pocket panel, matching up the raw edges, and pin it in place. Then, machine baste a ½˝ seam completely around the edges of the exterior pocket panel.

Step 3. Attach the front lining panel to the exterior front panel.

a. Place the front lining panel and the exterior front panel with **Right** sides together, making sure to match up the top raw edges, and pin them in place. Stitch a ½˝ seam across the top raw edges, backstitching at each end.

NOTE: *The front lining panel is 1" longer than the exterior front panel, in order to create the contrasting edge across the top of the panel.*

b. Then, flip the lining over the seam allowance at the top raw edge of the exterior front panel (with canvas attached). (This will leave ½˝ of the [solid-color] lining showing on the top of the exterior front panel.) Match up the side and bottom raw edges and then machine baste the raw edges together by stitching a ½˝ seam down both sides and across the bottom of the front panel. (FIGURE 3B)

c. Follow the instructions in steps 3a and 3b to attach the pocket lining to the exterior pocket panel.

d. Trim the canvas in the seam allowance of both the front panel and front pocket panel.

Step 4. Attach the pocket panel to the front panel.

Place the lined side of the pocket panel onto the **Right** side of the front panel, matching up the side and bottom raw edges, and pin the panels together. Stitch a ½˝ seam down both sides and across the bottom raw edges, backstitching at each end.

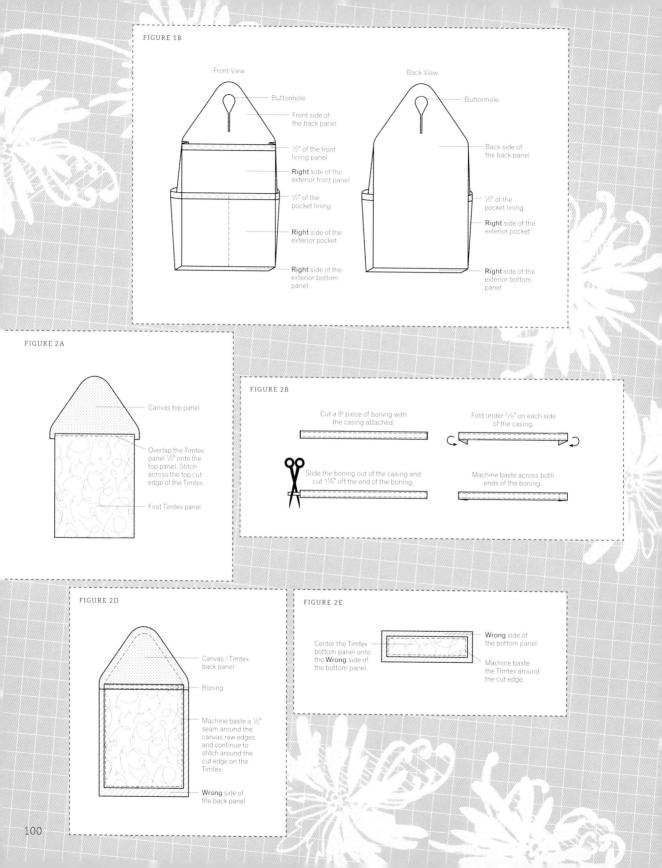

FIGURE 1B

Front View

Buttonhole

Front side of the back panel

½" of the front lining panel

Right side of the exterior front panel

½" of the pocket lining

Right side of the exterior pocket

Right side of the exterior bottom panel

Back View

Buttonhole

Back side of the back panel

½" of the pocket lining

Right side of the exterior pocket

Right side of the exterior bottom panel

FIGURE 2A

Canvas top panel

Overlap the Timtex panel ⅓" onto the top panel. Stitch across the top cut edge of the Timtex.

First Timtex panel

FIGURE 2B

Cut a 9" piece of boning with the casing attached.

Fold under ⅝" on each side of the casing.

Slide the boning out of the casing and cut 1¼" off the end of the boning.

Machine baste across both ends of the boning.

FIGURE 2D

Canvas / Timtex back panel

Boning

Machine baste a ½" seam around the canvas raw edges and continue to stitch around the cut edge on the Timtex.

Wrong side of the back panel

FIGURE 2E

Center the Timtex bottom panel onto the **Wrong** side of the bottom panel.

Wrong side of the bottom panel

Machine baste the Timtex around the cut edge.

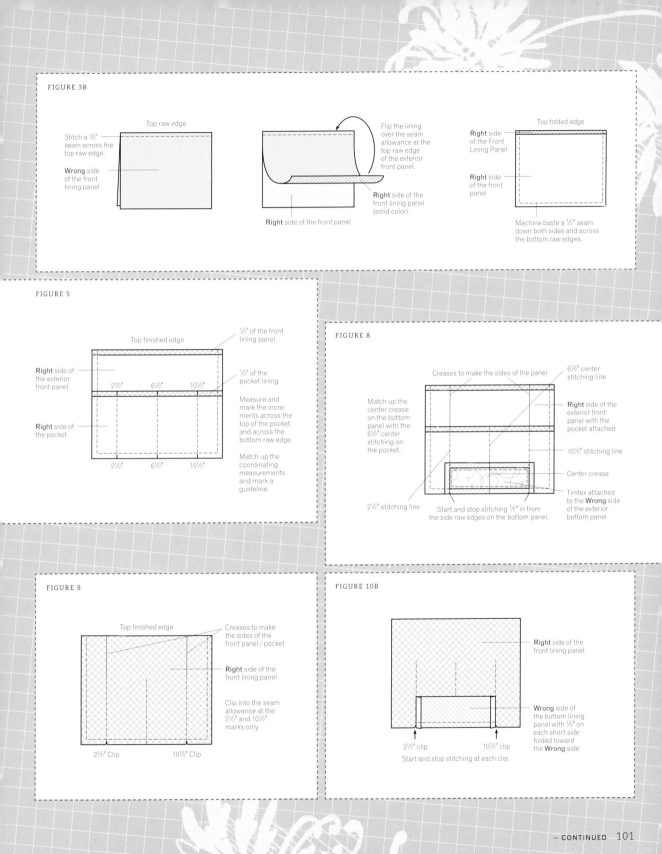

FIGURE 3B

Top raw edge

Stitch a ½" seam across the top raw edge.

Wrong side of the front lining panel

Flip the lining over the seam allowance at the top raw edge of the exterior front panel.

Right side of the front panel

Right side of the front lining panel (solid color)

Top folded edge

Right side of the Front Lining Panel

Right side of the front panel

Machine baste a ½" seam down both sides and across the bottom raw edges.

FIGURE 5

Top finished edge

½" of the front lining panel

½" of the pocket lining

Right side of the exterior front panel

2½"   6½"   10½"

Right side of the pocket

2½"   6½"   10½"

Measure and mark the increments across the top of the pocket and across the bottom raw edge.

Match up the coordinating measurements and mark a guideline.

FIGURE 8

Creases to make the sides of the panel

6½" center stitching line

Match up the center crease on the bottom panel with the 6½" center stitching on the pocket.

Right side of the exterior front panel with the pocket attached

10½" stitching line

Center crease

Timtex attached to the **Wrong** side of the exterior bottom panel

2½" stitching line

Start and stop stitching ⅛" in from the side raw edges on the bottom panel.

FIGURE 9

Top finished edge

Creases to make the sides of the front panel / pocket

Right side of the front lining panel

Clip into the seam allowance at the 2½" and 10½" marks only.

2½" Clip   10½" Clip

FIGURE 10B

Right side of the front lining panel

Wrong side of the bottom lining panel with ½" on each short side folded toward the **Wrong** side

2½" clip   10½" clip

Start and stop stitching at each clip.

~ CONTINUED

Step 5. Make the pocket compartments.

On the **Right** side of the front panel, with the pocket attached, measure and mark across the top of your pocket at the following increments, starting from the left side: 2½", 6½", and 10½". Then, measure and mark the same increments across the bottom raw edge. Using a yardstick, match up the coordinating measurements and mark chalk guidelines down the length of your pocket. Next, stitch the pocket compartments from at the bottom of the first guideline to the top of the pocket, backstitching at each end. Repeat this step to stitch the other 2 guidelines on the pocket to make the compartments. (FIGURE 5)

Step 6. Fold the sides for the front panel/pocket.

Fold the front panel/pocket back toward the lined side at the 2½" and 10½" stitch lines that made the pocket compartments. Press a hard crease along the stitching all the way to the top of the front panel. This will create each side on the front panel/pocket. (You will attach the bottom raw edge of the front panel between the 2½" and 10½" stitch line to the long side raw edge of the exterior bottom panel in step 8, and the bottom raw edge of these sides to the short side raw edge of the exterior bottom panel in step 11.)

Step 7. Find the center of the exterior bottom panel.

Fold the exterior bottom panel in half across the width and gently press a crease. Then, open up the panel.

Step 8. Attach the exterior bottom panel to the bottom of the front panel.

With the **Right** sides together, match up one of the long side raw edges of the bottom panel with the bottom raw edge of the front panel/pocket. Place the center crease on the bottom panel onto the center stitching (the 6½" marks made for the pocket compartments in step 6) on the pocket and pin it in place. Begin stitching a ½" seam, starting ½" in from the side raw edge on the bottom panel, stopping ½" in from the other side raw edge, and backstitching at each end. Then, turn the panel over to the lining side of the front panel. (FIGURE 8)

Step 9. Clip the seam allowance* on the front panel/pocket.

Using your scissors, clip into the bottom seam allowance on the front panel/pocket only at the 2½" and 10½" marks that you made in step 6, making sure not to clip your stitching. Do not clip the bottom panel. These clips will allow the front panel to turn at the bottom corners when the bottom panel is attached. (FIGURE 9)

See page 170 for an explanation of clipping into the seam allowance.

Step 10. Attach the bottom lining panel to the front lining panel.

a. First, with the **Wrong** side of the bottom lining panel facing up, fold each short side raw edge ½" in toward the **Wrong** side and press.

b. Then, place the **Right** side of the bottom lining panel onto the lined side of the front panel, matching up the long side raw edge of the bottom panel with the bottom raw edge of the front panel, centering it between the clips. Starting at one of the folded side edges of the bottom lining panel, stitch a ½" seam across the matched raw edges, stopping at the other folded edge, backstitching at each end. Make sure to stitch across the folded edges on the bottom lining panel. (FIGURE 10B)

Step 11. Attach the sides of the exterior bottom panel to the front panel with the pocket attached.

a. First, turn the bottom raw edges of the front panel at the first clip back (the 2½" clip), matching up the bottom raw edge with the short side raw edge on the exterior bottom panel, and pin them in place. Starting ½" in from the left side bottom raw edge of the front lining panel, stitch a ½" seam across the matched raw edges, stopping at the first clip (the 2½" clip), backstitching at each end. Repeat this step to attach the bottom raw edge on the other short side of the exterior front panel to the other side of the exterior bottom panel. (FIGURE 11A)

b. Trim the bottom corners.* Using your scissors, trim the seam allowance of the 2 bottom corners of the exterior panels, making sure not to clip your stitching.

See page 172 for an explanation of trimming corners.

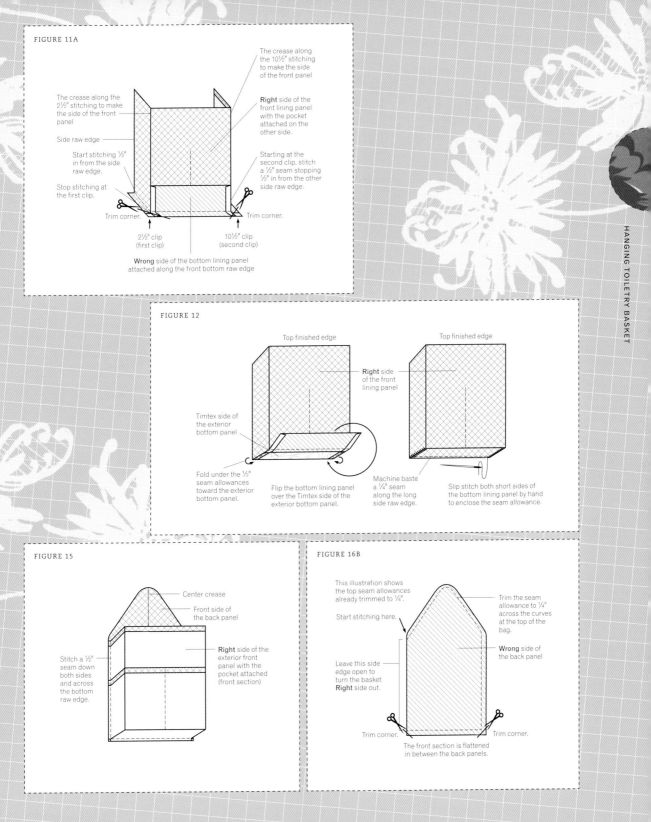

FIGURE 11A

The crease along the 10½" stitching to make the side of the front panel

The crease along the 2½" stitching to make the side of the front panel

Right side of the front lining panel with the pocket attached on the other side

Side raw edge

Start stitching ½" in from the side raw edge.

Starting at the second clip, stitch a ½" seam stopping ½" in from the other side raw edge.

Stop stitching at the first clip.

Trim corner.

Trim corner.

2½" clip (first clip)

10½" clip (second clip)

Wrong side of the bottom lining panel attached along the front bottom raw edge

FIGURE 12

Top finished edge

Top finished edge

Right side of the front lining panel

Timtex side of the exterior bottom panel

Fold under the ½" seam allowances toward the exterior bottom panel.

Flip the bottom lining panel over the Timtex side of the exterior bottom panel.

Machine baste a ¼" seam along the long side raw edge.

Slip stitch both short sides of the bottom lining panel by hand to enclose the seam allowance.

FIGURE 15

Center crease

Front side of the back panel

Right side of the exterior front panel with the pocket attached (front section)

Stitch a ½" seam down both sides and across the bottom raw edge.

FIGURE 16B

This illustration shows the top seam allowances already trimmed to ¼".

Start stitching here.

Trim the seam allowance to ¼" across the curves at the top of the bag.

Wrong side of the back panel

Leave this side edge open to turn the basket **Right** side out.

Trim corner.

Trim corner.

The front section is flattened in between the back panels.

Step 12. Attach the sides of the bottom lining panel to the front lining panel.

First, fold the bottom seam allowances of the front lining panel in toward the Timtex side of the exterior bottom panel and press. Then, flip the bottom lining panel over the Timtex side, matching the folded short side edges of the bottom lining panel with the stitching that attaches the exterior bottom panel and pin it in place. Slip stitch* each short side of the bottom lining panel in place by hand. Then, machine baste a ¼" seam across the matched long side raw edge of the bottom panels. (FIGURE 12)

* See page 171 for an explanation of slip stitching.

Step 13. Turn the attached front section Right side out.

Turn the front panel/pocket with the bottom panel attached **Right** side out, using a turning tool* to push out the corners. Fold the front pocket at the first and last stitching for the pocket compartments and press a hard crease. Press a crease at the bottom panel seams to give this section a boxy look.

* See page 172 for an explanation of a turning tool.

Step 14. Find the center of the first back panel.

Fold the back panel (with the canvas-and-Timtex panel attached) in half lengthwise with **Right** sides together and gently press a center crease. (This center crease will be used in step 18 for centering the buttonhole on the top of the back panel.) Then, open up the panel.

Step 15. Attach the front panel section to the front side of the back panel.

First, place the lined side of the front panel/pocket section (with the bottom panel attached) onto the **Right** side of the first back panel (with the canvas-and-Timtex panel attached). Match up the side and bottom raw edges and pin them in place. Stitch a ½" seam down one side, across the bottom raw edges, and back up the other side, turning the panels at the seam that attaches the bottom panel to the front panel to make the corners of the basket, backstitching at each end. (FIGURE 15)

Step 16. Attach the other back panel to the first back panel.

a. First, fold in the front section to flatten it. Pin the front section to the attached back panel to keep it in place and out of your way. Then, with the **Right** sides together, place the unattached back panel onto the back panel with the front section attached, and pin the panels together. (This will enclose the front pocket section in between the 2 back panels.)

b. Starting at the top left corner of the back panel, where the boning is attached, stitch a ½" seam over the top of the panel, down the right side, and across the bottom raw edges, backstitching at each end. (The panels will be stiff and bulky at this point.) (FIGURE 16B)

c. Using your scissors, trim the 2 bottom corners of the back panels, making sure not to clip your stitching. Then, trim the seam allowances to ¼" across the curve at the top of the bag and along the outside curve on the side of the panels.

Step 17. Turn your Hanging Toiletry Basket Right side out.

Pull the **Right** side of the Hanging Toiletry Basket through the opening on the left side of the attached back panels. Use a turning tool to push out the seams and corners on the panels, and press the seams flat. Then, fold under ½" at the open raw edge on the second back panel and pin the opening closed. Slip stitch the opening closed by hand.

Step 18. Make a large buttonhole* at the top of your Hanging Toiletry Basket.

a. Starting at the top of the back panel, measure down from the top finished edge on the center crease and make marks at 1", 2½", and 4". Then, center a quarter over the center crease below the 1" mark and using your chalk pencil draw a circle completely around the quarter.

* See page 170 for an explanation of making a buttonhole.

b. Next, starting on the left side of the circle, draw a line toward the center crease to the 2½" mark. Then, draw a vertical line from the 2½" mark down to the 4" mark on the left side of the center crease. Repeat this step on the right side of the circle; use the buttonhole drawn on your pattern piece as a visual guide. This will be your guideline to make your buttonhole. Erase any chalk marks inside the buttonhole. **(FIGURE 18B)**

c. Using a small, tight zigzag stitch on your machine and starting at the 4" mark, stitch up the left vertical chalk line, following it around the left side, over the top of the circle, and down the right side. Once you stitch to the bottom of the chalk guideline on the right side of the center crease at the 4" mark, use a wide zigzag stitch to stitch in place 5 or 6 times to secure the 2 ends of the buttonhole.

d. To cut open the buttonhole, start at the 4" mark in the middle of the 2 zigzag stitch lines, insert the pointed end of your seam ripper through all of the layers of the back panel, and cut through the back panel to open up the bottom part of the buttonhole, and then use your scissors to cut out the inside of the circle at the top part of the buttonhole, making sure not to clip your stitches with either tool.

Step 19. Make a pleat on each side of the Hanging Toiletry Basket.

Turn the Hanging Toiletry Basket so the lining side is facing out. Match up the side crease of the basket with the back seam that attaches the basket to the back panel and pin it together. Starting at the top finished edge of the basket, stitch a seam 1½" down along the side crease, backstitching at each end. Then, to finish the project, turn the Hanging Toiletry Basket **Right** side out, using a turning tool to push out the 4 bottom corners, and press. **(FIGURE 19)**

FIGURE 18B

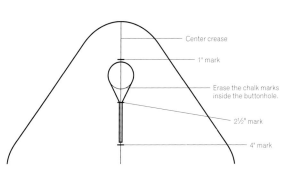

Center crease

1" mark

Erase the chalk marks inside the buttonhole.

2½" mark

4" mark

FIGURE 19

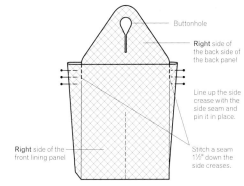

Buttonhole

Right side of the back side of the back panel

Line up the side crease with the side seam and pin it in place.

Right side of the front lining panel

Stitch a seam 1½" down the side creases.

OVERSIZED LAUNDRY BAG

FINISHED SIZE: 20½" WIDE X 30½" TALL | BOTTOM PANEL: 13" DIAMETER

With its heavy-duty construction, this biggie can handle a mountain of laundry. The comfy shoulder strap and simple drawstring closure will make those dreaded trips to the launderette much more bearable. Of course, it's not just for laundry—you can use it to carry all sorts of stuff. Soon you'll be wondering how you ever got by without it!

FABRICS

- 3 yards (44"- or 60"-wide) sturdy cotton fabric for the outer top and bottom panels, the lining, the strap, and the drawstring (referred to as the "main fabric")
- ½ yard (44"- or 60"-wide) coordinating sturdy cotton fabric for the outer center panel
- 1½ yards (44"- or 60"-wide) 10 oz. cotton canvas for the interfacing
- ½ yard (22"-wide) Timtex* or other extra-heavy interfacing

See page 172 for an explanation of Timtex.

OTHER SUPPLIES

- Coordinating thread
- Scissors
- Yardstick or ruler
- Chalk pencil or fabric marker
- Straight pins
- Large safety pin
- Masking tape
- Small buttons for the end of the drawstring (optional)
- Hand sewing needle

NOTES

- All seams are ½" unless otherwise stated. (The ½" seam allowance is included in all pattern pieces and cutting measurements.)
- Preshrink your fabric by washing, drying, and pressing it before starting your project. To wash Timtex after completing your project, machine wash warm, then reshape your project and air dry. Your project will press back into shape with a steam iron. Once you steam the project, support it with wadded-up tissue paper or a folded towel while air drying in order to keep the shape that you want.

Step 1. Cut out all pieces from the fabric.

a. First, cut out the bottom panel pattern piece provided in the pocket at the front of this book.

b. Next, lay the main fabric on a hard, flat surface. Fold the fabric in half, **Right** sides together, matching the selvage edges*, and gently press the fold.

See page 171 for an explanation of a selvage edge.

c. Now, referring to FIGURE 1C, using your yardstick and chalk pencil to measure and mark the measurements in steps 1e, 1f, and 1g directly on the **Wrong** side of the fabric. You will be marking the measurements on the fold of the fabric so when you cut out each panel and open it up you will have one full-size panel.

d. As you mark the measurements for each panel, take a piece of masking tape and place it onto the **Wrong** side of each panel. Mark the name of the panel on the tape to identify each of your pieces.

e. Using your scissors, cut out each panel following the marked lines.

FROM THE MAIN FABRIC:

- *Cut 2 panels (top and bottom): 11" wide x 42" long*
- *Cut 1 lining panel: 31" wide x 42" long*
- *Cut 2 bottom panels: Use the pattern piece provided in the pocket at the front of this book.*

f. Open up the remaining piece of fabric. Working with a single layer of the fabric, measuring on the lengthwise grain* (parallel to the selvage edges), measure and mark the following dimensions directly onto the **Wrong** side of

~ CONTINUED

your fabric, using a yardstick and a chalk pencil. Then, using your scissors, cut out each panel following the marked lines.

- *Cut 1 strap: 10" wide x 32" long*
- *Cut 2 drawstrings: 3" wide x 30" long*
* *See page 171 for an explanation of the lengthwise grain.*

g. Following the instructions in steps 1b through 1e (except for the canvas and interfacing bottom panels), measure, mark, and cut the following:

FROM THE FABRIC FOR THE OUTER CENTER PANEL

- *Cut 1 panel: 11" wide x 42" long*

FROM THE CANVAS

- *Cut 1 panel: 31" wide x 42" long*
- *Cut 1 bottom panel: Use the pattern piece provided in the pocket at the front of this book. (Cut a single layer.)*

FROM THE TIMTEX

- *Cut 1 bottom panel: Use the pattern piece provided in the pocket at the front of this book. (Cut a single layer.)*

Step 2. Stitch the outer panel.

a. First, place one 11" x 42" main fabric panel and the 11" x 42" center panel with **Right** sides together, matching the long raw edges. Pin one long raw edge, and stitch a ½" seam along the raw edge, backstitching at each end. Press the seam open.

b. Now, place the second 11" x 42" main fabric panel along the opposite long raw edge of the center panel, with the **Right** sides together, and matching the raw edges. Pin in place and stitch along the long raw edges with a ½" seam, backstitching at each end of the seam. Press the seam open.

c. Then, place the 31" x 42" canvas panel on the **Wrong** side of the outer (pieced) panel, matching all the raw edges, and pin it in place completely around the panel.

d. Using the longest stitch available on your sewing machine, machine baste* the canvas to the outer panel, stitching ¼" from the raw edge. Then, fold the outer panel in half, with the **Right** sides together, matching the seams.

* *See page 171 for an explanation of machine basting.*

e. Stitch a ½" seam from the top to the bottom. Press the seam open.

f. At the bottom edge of the outer panel, stitch a stay stitching* line, ½" from the cut edge, all the way around the outer panel. Then, clip into the bottom cut edge of the fabric every 1" to 2", making sure not to cut into the stitching line. **(FIGURE 2F, G, H)**

* *See page 172 for an explanation of stay stitching.*

g. Now, mark the bottom of the outer panel into fourths. To do this, turn the outer panel so that the **Wrong** side is facing out and flatten it so that the seam is on the left side. Then, make a mark on the bottom edge, at the fold, opposite the seam. **(FIGURE 2F, G, H)**

h. Flatten the outer panel again, this time matching the seam to the mark you just made opposite it. Then make a mark on each of the folds that result. You will now have 3 marks and one seam, dividing the bottom of the outer panel into fourths. **(FIGURE 2F, G, H)**

i. Turn the outer panel **Right** side out and set it aside.

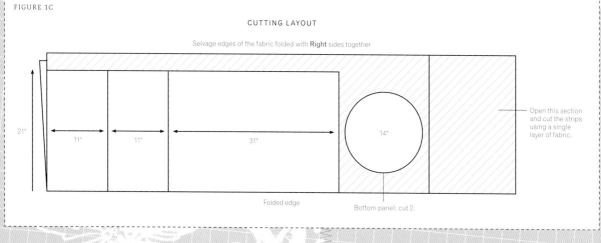

FIGURE 1C

CUTTING LAYOUT

Selvage edges of the fabric folded with **Right** sides together

21"

11" 11" 31" 14"

Open this section
and cut the strips
using a single
layer of fabric.

Folded edge

Bottom panel: cut 2.

Step 3. Make the strap.

a. First, fold the 10" x 32" strap in half lengthwise with the **Wrong** sides together, and press a center crease.

b. Open the folded strap and then fold each long raw edge in to meet the center crease and press.

c. Now, fold the strap in half again along the center crease, enclosing the long raw edges, and pin.

d. Then, edge stitch* close to the folded edge, along both long edges of the strap, creating a 2½" wide x 32" long strap, backstitching at each end.

* See page 170 for an explanation of edge stitching.

Step 4. Attach the strap to the outer panel.

a. Place the strap on the **Right** side of the outer panel, centering it over the side seam and matching the raw edges at the ends of the strap to the raw edges at the top and bottom of the outer panel. Pin the strap in place.

b. Stitch the strap in place with a ½" seam across the top and the bottom raw edges, backstitching at each end. (FIGURE 4B)

c. Turn the outer panel **Wrong** side out.

Step 5. Prepare and attach the bottom panel.

a. First, take one main-fabric bottom panel and mark it into fourths. To do this, fold the bottom panel in half and make a mark at each end of the fold. Then, open the bottom panel and fold it in half again, matching the 2 marks you just made. Make 2 more marks at each end of the new fold.

b. Now, place the Timtex bottom panel onto the **Wrong** side of the marked main-fabric bottom panel. Then, place the canvas bottom panel onto the Timtex bottom panel.

c. Pin the 3 layers together and stitch a ½" seam around the outer edge.

d. Place the layered bottom panel and the bottom edge of the outer panel with **Right** sides together, lining up the marks that divide the panels in fourths. Pin the panels together. (FIGURE 5D)

e. Attach the panels by stitching a ½" seam completely around the bottom panel. Then, stitch a second time to reinforce* the seam, backstitching at each end. (FIGURE 5E)

* See page 171 for an explanation of reinforcement stitching.

f. Then turn the bag **Right** side out.

Step 6. Make the buttonholes for the drawstring casing.

a. First, fold the bag in half with the seam (and strap) to your right.

b. Lightly press a crease at the fold opposite the seam. This crease will be your guide for the buttonhole placement.

c. With the bag still folded and the strap to your right, measure 2" down from the top raw edge, near the creased edge, and make a mark. Then measure 1" down from the first mark and make a second mark at 3".

d. Flip the bag over so that the fold is to your right and the strap is to your left. Measure down as you did in step 6c and make the same marks on this side of the bag near the creased edge.

e. Then, open up the bag and place it with the seam and strap in the back. The crease and marks will be at the front.

f. Make 2 vertical buttonholes,* one on each side of the crease, ½" from the crease, with the top of each buttonhole at the top (2") mark and the bottom of the buttonhole at the bottom (3") mark. (FIGURE 6F)

* See page 170 for an explanation of making a buttonhole.

Step 7. Make the lining for the bag.

a. Fold the 31" x 42" lining panel with **Right** sides together, matching the short raw edges.

b. Then, following the instructions in steps 2e through 2h, stitch the seam, reinforce the bottom raw edge, clip the bottom raw edge, and mark the bag lining into fourths.

c. Follow the instructions in step 5a to mark the lining bottom panel into fourths, and then follow the instructions in steps 5d and 5e to attach the lining bottom panel to the bag lining. Leave the bag lining with the **Wrong** side facing out.

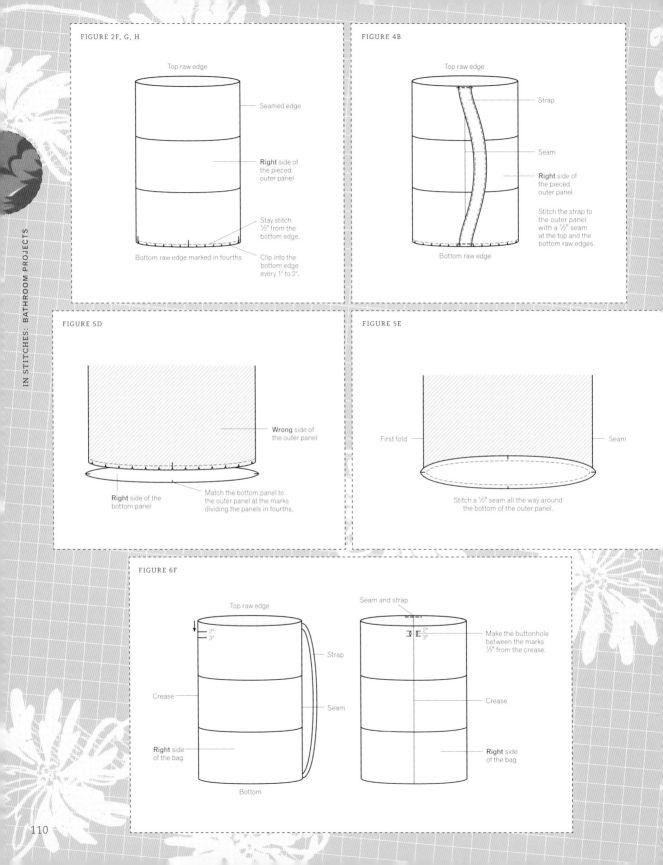

FIGURE 2F, G, H

Top raw edge

Seamed edge

Right side of the pieced outer panel

Stay stitch ½" from the bottom edge.

Clip into the bottom edge every 1" to 2".

Bottom raw edge marked in fourths

FIGURE 4B

Top raw edge

Strap

Seam

Right side of the pieced outer panel

Stitch the strap to the outer panel with a ½" seam at the top and the bottom raw edges.

Bottom raw edge

FIGURE 5D

Wrong side of the outer panel

Right side of the bottom panel

Match the bottom panel to the outer panel at the marks dividing the panels in fourths.

FIGURE 5E

First fold

Seam

Stitch a ½" seam all the way around the bottom of the outer panel.

FIGURE 6F

Top raw edge

2"
3"

Strap

Crease

Seam

Right side of the bag

Bottom

Seam and strap

2"
3"

Make the buttonhole between the marks ½" from the crease.

Crease

Right side of the bag

Step 8. Attach the lining to the bag.

a. With the exterior of the bag **Right** side facing out and the lining **Wrong** side facing out, slip the bag inside the lining. (The **Right** sides of the bag and the lining will be together.) Match the seams and pin them in place.

b. Now, stitch a ½" seam around the top raw edge, leaving a 6" opening for turning the bag **Right** side out, backstitching at each end. (FIGURE 8B)

c. Reach through and pull the bag out through the 6" opening. The lining will turn **Right** side out as the bag is pulled through the opening.

d. Then, tuck the lining down inside the bag.

e. Turn under the raw edges of the opening ½" and press. Slip stitch* the opening closed by hand.

* See page 171 for an explanation of slip stitching.

f. Press the top seam.

Step 9. Stitch the drawstring casing.

a. Measure 1⅜" down from the top finished edge and lightly mark a line all the way around the bag. This will be the topstitching line for the drawstring casing. This line should be at the top of the buttonholes.

b. Now, measure 1¼" down from the first line and lightly mark a second line all the way around the bag. This will be the bottom stitching line and should be at the bottom of the buttonholes.

c. Press completely around the top of the bag. Match the side seams on the bag and lining, and pin them in place. Then continue to pin the bag to the lining around the marked topstitching lines. Center the strap over the side seam and pin it in place.

d. Then, stitch along each line, all the way around the bag. Make sure that the strap is flat against the bag. Stitch through the strap to secure it. Then, stitch across the strap again over the original stitching line to give it extra reinforcement. (FIGURE 9D)

Step 10. Make and insert the drawstring* to complete the bag.

* See page 170 for an explanation of how to make a drawstring.

a. First, place the 2 3"x 30" drawstring strips **Right** sides together, matching up one short raw end on each strip, and pin them in place. Stitch a ½" seam across the matched edges, creating a single 3"x 59" strip. Press the seam open.

b. Now, fold the strip in half lengthwise, with **Wrong** sides together, and press a center crease.

c. Open the strip and fold each long raw edge in to meet the center crease, and press.

d. Then, at each short end, fold under ½" to the **Wrong** side, and press.

e. Now, fold the strip in half again at the center crease (enclosing all the raw edges), and press well. Pin the folded edges together and edge stitch close to the folded edges completely around the drawstring. The drawstring should now measure approximately ¾" wide x 58" long.

f. Attach a large safety pin to one end of the drawstring and insert it into one of the buttonholes. Thread the drawstring through the casing and out the other buttonhole. Remove the safety pin.

g. If you wish, sew a small button or two to each end of the drawstring for detail.

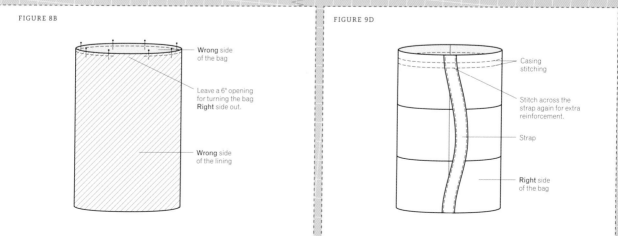

FIGURE 8B

Wrong side of the bag

Leave a 6" opening for turning the bag **Right** side out.

Wrong side of the lining

FIGURE 9D

Casing stitching

Stitch across the strap again for extra reinforcement.

Strap

Right side of the bag

DECORATIVE HANGING TOWELS

FINISHED SIZE: THE FINISHED SIZE WILL BE THE SAME AS THAT OF THE BATH OR HAND TOWEL USED.
BATH TOWEL FINISHED BAND: 5" WIDE | HAND TOWEL FINISHED BAND: 2½" WIDE

Here's a simple way to give your plain towels a splash of color—decorate them with gorgeous fabrics that highlight the hues in your bath. And the added towel loops make for easy hanging.

FABRICS

FOR A BATH TOWEL

- Bath towel of your choice
- 1 yard (44"-wide) cotton fabric for the decorative band and hanging loop

FOR A HAND TOWEL

- Hand towel of your choice
- ⅓ yard (44"-wide) cotton fabric for the decorative band and hanging loop

OTHER SUPPLIES

- Coordinating thread
- Yardstick or ruler
- Chalk pencil or fabric marker
- Scissors
- Straight pins
- Iron
- Turning tool (such as a closed pair of scissors)

NOTES

- All seams are ½" unless otherwise stated. (The ½" seam allowance is included in all cutting measurements.)
- Preshrink your fabric by washing, drying, and pressing it before starting your project.

Step 1. Determine the length of the towel bands and cut the strips.

a. First, measure the width of the end of your towel, across the short end from one corner to the other.

b. Then, add 1" to this measurement for seam allowances. This will be the length measurement for the band to be cut.

c. Simply measure and mark the dimensions below directly onto the **Wrong** side of the fabric, using a yardstick and a chalk pencil. Then, using your scissors, cut out each panel following the marked lines.

FROM THE FABRIC FOR THE BATH TOWEL BANDS

- *Cut 2 bands: 15½" wide x the length measurement from step 1b*

FROM THE FABRIC FOR THE HAND TOWEL BANDS

- *Cut 2 bands: 8" wide x the length measurement from step 1b*

d. Set the bands aside.

Step 2. Cut the fabric for the loop.

Measure and mark the dimensions below directly onto the **Wrong** side of the fabric, using a yardstick and a chalk pencil. Then, using your scissors, cut out each panel following the marked lines.

FROM THE FABRIC FOR THE BATH TOWEL

- *Cut 1 panel: 3½" wide x 6" long*

FROM THE FABRIC FOR THE HAND TOWEL

- *Cut 1 panel: 3" wide x 4" long*

Step 3. Make the loop for the towel.*

* See page 170 for an explanation of how to make a drawstring (you'll use the same process to make your loop).

a. First, fold the loop panel in half lengthwise, with the **Wrong** sides together, matching the long raw edges.

b. Now, press a crease at the center fold.

c. Unfold the fabric, fold each long edge in toward the center crease, and press.

~ CONTINUED

d. Then, fold the fabric piece in half again, enclosing the long raw edges, and press well. Pin the folded edges together.

e. Stitch along each long edge of the loop, stitching as close to the edge as possible and backstitching at each end.

Step 4. Make the fabric towel bands and attach the loop.

a. First, press one long raw edge of a towel band under ½" toward the **Wrong** side. Then, unfold the edge, leaving the pressed crease.

b. Now, fold the towel band in half, matching the short raw ends, and gently press a center crease.

c. Using a yardstick and a chalk pencil, measure over 1½" on each side of the center crease and mark.

d. Place the loop and the marked towel band with the **Right** sides together, lining up the raw ends of the loop with the raw edges of the towel band, placing the ends of the loop as follows:

For the bath towel, place the loop ends just outside the marks on either side of the center crease and pin them in place. (FIGURE 4D-01)

For the hand towel, place the loop ends just inside the marks on either side of the center crease and pin them in place. (FIGURE 4D-02)

e. Stitch the loop in place with a ½" seam, backstitching at each end. The edges of the loop will be turned under at the ½" pressed crease of the long edge in step 6.

Step 5. Attach the towel bands to the end of the towel.

a. First, fold the end of the towel in half lengthwise and make a small mark or place a straight pin to mark the center of each end of the towel.

b. Then, place the uncreased long raw edge of the towel band along one short end of the towel, with the **Right** side of the towel band facing the back side of the towel. Match up the center crease on the towel band with the marked center of the towel and the raw edge of the towel band to the end of the towel. The towel band will extend ½" past each side of the towel. Pin the towel band in place.

> NOTE: *Not all towels have a Front and Back side. If your towel does not have these, you may attach the towel band to either side of the towel.*

c. Using a yardstick and a chalk pencil, make the following measurements:

For the bath towel, measure in from the end of the towel 5" at each side edge and make a mark. Draw a line between the 2 marks on the towel band, creating a stitching line.

For the hand towel, measure in from the end of the towel 2½" at each side edge and make a mark. Draw a line between the 2 marks on the towel band, creating a stitching line.

d. Then, stitch across the line you have drawn, backstitching at each end, to attach the towel band to the towel. (FIGURE 5D)

e. Fold the towel band at the stitching line back over itself, toward the end of the towel, with the **Wrong** sides facing each other, and press across the folded edge.

f. Now, press under the ½" again at the long edge of the towel band toward the **Wrong** side, pressing under the ends of the loop. (FIGURE 5F)

g. Then, fold the towel band back, with **Right** sides together, matching the long folded edge to the seam you stitched in step 5d.

Step 6. Sew the ends of the towel band and finish the Decorative Hanging Towel.

a. First, pin the towel band together at the short ends, matching the raw edges, making sure that the ½" pressed edge you made in step 5f remains folded to the **Wrong** side.

b. Stitch a ½" seam across both short ends, backstitching at each end. (FIGURE 6B)

c. Now, turn the towel band **Right** side out, so that the end of the towel is tucked inside the towel band. Use a turning tool* to push out the corners, and press.
* See page 172 for an explanation of a turning tool.

d. Match the long folded edge of the towel band to the stitching line on the front of the towel and pin in place.

e. Then, topstitch* close to the folded edge, stitching through all the layers of the towel band and the towel, and backstitching at each end. (FIGURE 6E)
* See page 172 for an explanation of topstitching.

Step 7. Attach the second towel band to the other end of the towel.

a. Press ½" under toward the **Wrong** side on one long edge of the second towel band.

b. Then, follow the instructions in steps 5 and 6 to attach the second towel band to the other end of the towel, omitting the loop.

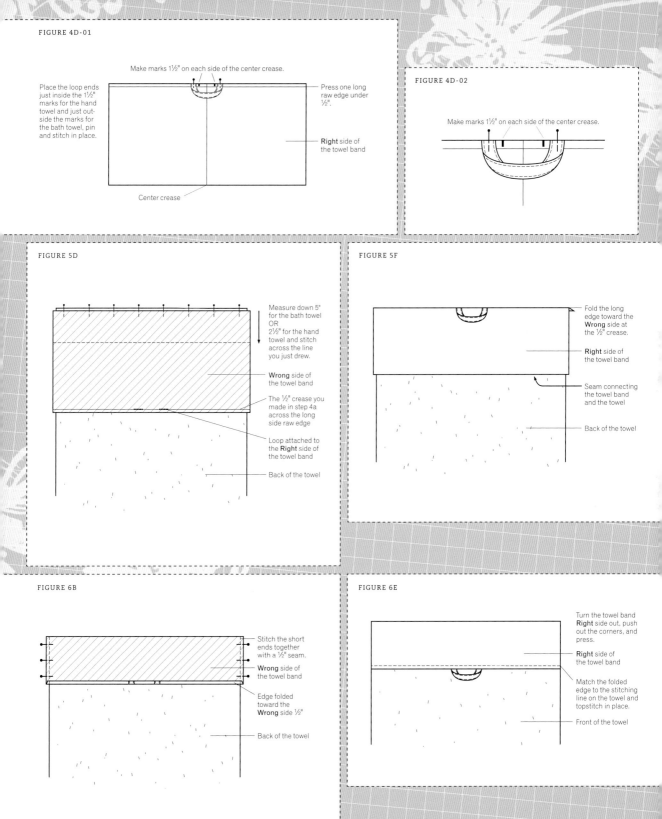

FIGURE 4D-01

Make marks 1½" on each side of the center crease.

Place the loop ends just inside the 1½" marks for the hand towel and just outside the marks for the bath towel, pin and stitch in place.

Press one long raw edge under ½".

Right side of the towel band

Center crease

FIGURE 4D-02

Make marks 1½" on each side of the center crease.

FIGURE 5D

Measure down 5" for the bath towel OR 2½" for the hand towel and stitch across the line you just drew.

Wrong side of the towel band

The ½" crease you made in step 4a across the long side raw edge

Loop attached to the **Right** side of the towel band

Back of the towel

FIGURE 5F

Fold the long edge toward the **Wrong** side at the ½" crease.

Right side of the towel band

Seam connecting the towel band and the towel

Back of the towel

FIGURE 6B

Stitch the short ends together with a ½" seam.

Wrong side of the towel band

Edge folded toward the **Wrong** side ½"

Back of the towel

FIGURE 6E

Turn the towel band **Right** side out, push out the corners, and press.

Right side of the towel band

Match the folded edge to the stitching line on the towel and topstitch in place.

Front of the towel

115

CHAPTER 5

OFFICE
Projects

Who says practical can't be beautiful? Fill your office with sleek, stylish storage accessories, and you'll soon feel confident, productive, and organized. The secret? If you have a place for everything, then it's a snap to get everything in its place. In the pages that follow you'll find fabric baskets that will tame desk clutter, a document duvet that will add a personal touch to your reports, and a photo file that's perfect for sorting and stashing photos. Of course, you'll want to bring your spot-on fashion sense with you when you head out for that client lunch or press conference, which makes the envelope business card holder and the fashion check-book clutch (it looks like a high-end organizer but it actually holds a checkbook, lipstick, and compact!) essential accessories. Work has never looked so good.

CD HOLDER

FINISHED SIZE: 6¼" WIDE X 6¼" LONG X 6¼" DEEP

Keep your clutter under control—and do it with style! Here are two beautiful and useful baskets (see photo, page 117) that you can use as a CD Holder and a **DESKTOP ORGANIZER** (page 122) to hold notepads, pens and pencils, and other office supplies. Of course, they can easily be shifted to the bath, bedroom, or pantry. Feel free to make multiples! You'll want to have these all over your home.

FABRICS

- ¼ yard (54"-wide) home-decor-weight cotton print for the exterior
- ¼ yard (54"-wide) coordinating heavyweight cotton for the lining
- ¾ yard (13"-wide) Timtex* or similar extra-heavy interfacing

See page 172 for an explanation of Timtex.

OTHER SUPPLIES

- Coordinating thread
- Yardstick
- Chalk pencil or fabric marker
- Scissors
- Straight pins
- Turning tool (such as a closed pair of scissors)
- Hand sewing needle

NOTES

- All seams are ½" unless otherwise stated. (The ½" seam allowance is included in all cutting measurements.)

- Preshrink your fabric by washing, drying, and pressing it before starting your project. To wash Timtex after completing your project, machine wash warm, then reshape your project and air dry. Your project will press back into shape with a steam iron. Once you steam the project, support it with wadded-up tissue paper or a folded towel while air drying in order to keep the shape that you want.

Step 1. Cut out all pieces from the fabric.

Simply measure and mark the dimensions below directly onto the **Wrong** side of the fabric, using a yardstick and a chalk pencil. Then, using your scissors, cut out each panel following the marked lines.

FROM THE FABRIC FOR THE EXTERIOR
- *Cut 1 side panel: 26″ wide x 7¼″ long*
- *Cut 1 bottom panel: 7¼″ wide x 7¼″ long*
- *Cut 2 handles: 6″ wide x 4″ long*

FROM THE FABRIC FOR THE LINING
- *Cut 1 side panel: 26″ wide x 7¼″ long*
- *Cut 1 bottom panel: 7¼″ wide x 7¼″ long*

FROM THE TIMTEX
- *Cut 1 side panel: 25¼″ wide x 6½″ long*
- *Cut 1 bottom panel: 6½″ wide x 6½″ long*
- *Cut 2 handles: 5″ wide x 1″ long*

Step 2. Measure and mark the clips for 3 of the corners on the exterior side panel.

a. First, stitch a ½" seam across one of the long raw edges (which will then be the bottom of the side panel) for reinforcement.*

See page 171 for an explanation of a reinforcement stitch.

b. Then, on the **Wrong** side of the side panel, starting at the short right side raw edge, measure and mark the following increments across both the top and bottom raw edges: 6¾", 13", and 19¼".

c. Next, at the marks you made across the bottom raw edge only, clip into the seam allowance,* making sure not to cut your reinforcement stitching. (These clips will allow you to turn the panel at each of the bottom corners when attaching the bottom panel.) (FIGURE 2C)

See page 170 for an explanation of clipping in the seam allowance.

d. To create the 4 different sides of the CD Holder, fold the side panel **Wrong** sides together and press a crease at each of the coordinating marks starting with the first (6¾") mark. (These creases create 3 of the corners for the CD Holder. The fourth corner will be the seam attaching the side panel together.) (FIGURE 2D)

Step 3. Attach the side panel together.

First, with **Right** sides together, fold the side panel in half, matching up the short side raw edges, and pin it in place. Stitch a ½" seam down the matched side raw edges, stopping ½" from the bottom raw edge, backstitching at each end. Then, press the seam allowance open. (Stopping ½" up from the bottom raw edge will serve as the clip on the fourth corner of the CD Holder.)

Step 4. Attach the exterior side panel to the exterior bottom panel.

a. Place the bottom panel inside the attached side panel so the **Right** sides are together. Starting with the unstitched end of the seam on the side panel, place it ½" in along one of the side raw edges of the bottom panel. Then place the 6¾" clip ½" in from the other side of the same side raw edge of the bottom panel. Match up the raw edges and pin them in place.

b. Starting at the side seam on the side panel, stitch a ½" seam across the matched raw edges, stopping at the 6¾" clip on the side panel, backstitching at each end. (FIGURE 4B)

c. Turn the side panel at the 6¾" clip and match up the bottom raw edge of the second folded side panel with the corresponding raw edge of the bottom panel, pinning it in place. Again, stitch a ½" seam from the first clip (6¾") across the matched raw edges, stopping at the 13" clip. (FIGURE 4C)

d. Continue with this process by turning the panel at the 13" clip and stitching across the matched raw edges, stopping at the 19¼" clip. Then turn the panel again, matching up the last side raw edge on the bottom panel with the bottom raw edge of the last side panel, stitching across the matched raw edges, and backstitching at each. (FIGURE 4D)

Step 5. Trim the bottom corners* of the holder.

Using scissors, trim the 4 bottom corners of the holder, making sure not to clip the stitching. Then, turn the holder **Right** side out and press a crease on the side panel at each corner of the holder.

See page 172 for an explanation of trimming corners.

Step 6. Measure and mark for the clips for the corners on the Timtex side panel.

a. First, stitch a ⅛" seam across the bottom long edge of the Timtex side panel for reinforcement. Then, starting at the right side edge, measure and mark the following increments along the bottom raw edge: 6¾", 12⅝", and 18⅞".

b. Next, clip into the seam allowance at each mark, making sure not to clip the stitching. These clips will allow you to turn the panel at each corner when attaching the Timtex bottom panel to the side panel. (You may find it awkward to clip into such a small seam allowance. Just clip through the cut edge; this will allow the Timtex to stretch apart for the corners.)

Step 7. Make the Timtex panel.

Follow the instructions in steps 3 and 4 to make the Timtex panel, but stitch it together with a ⅛" seam and stop ⅛" from the bottom edge on the Timtex. Then, follow the instructions in step 5 to trim the corners of the Timtex panel and turn the Timtex **Right** side out.

Step 8. Attach the Timtex panel to the Wrong side of the exterior CD Holder.

With the exterior of the CD Holder **Right** side out, place the Timtex panel inside the exterior panel onto the **Wrong** side. Push the Timtex down inside, matching up the seams, exposing ⅜" of the exterior fabric around the top edge, and pin it in place. Machine baste* across the cut top edge on the Timtex, stitching one side at a time. (With the Timtex attached the CD Holder will be more difficult to turn.) (FIGURE 8)

See page 171 for an explanation of machine basting.

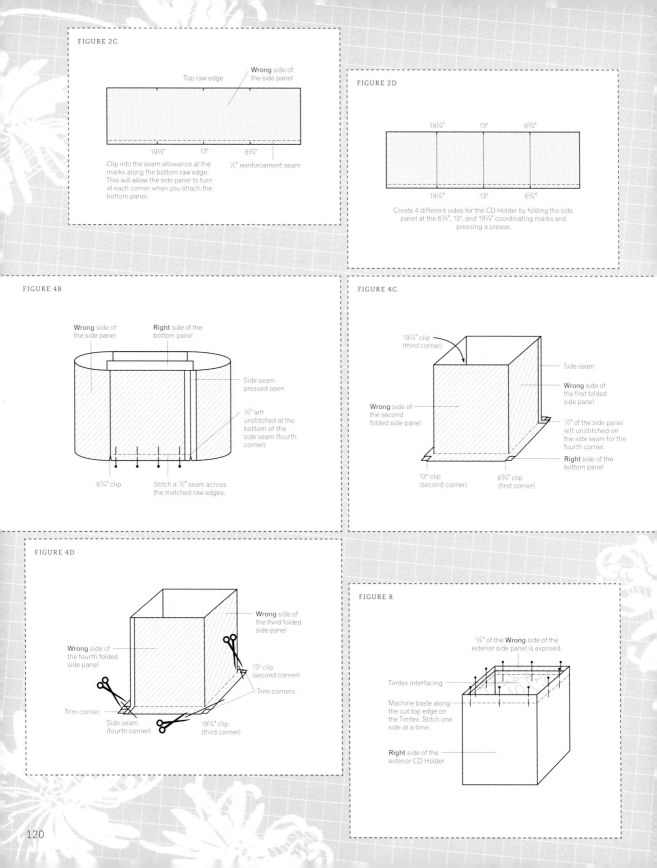

FIGURE 2C

Top raw edge

Wrong side of the side panel

19¼" 13" 6¾"

Clip into the seam allowance at the marks along the bottom raw edge. This will allow the side panel to turn at each corner when you attach the bottom panel.

½" reinforcement seam

FIGURE 2D

19¼" 13" 6¾"

19¼" 13" 6¾"

Create 4 different sides for the CD Holder by folding the side panel at the 6¾", 13", and 19¼" coordinating marks and pressing a crease.

FIGURE 4B

Wrong side of the side panel

Right side of the bottom panel

Side seam pressed open

½" left unstitched at the bottom of the side seam (fourth corner)

6¾" clip

Stitch a ½" seam across the matched raw edges.

FIGURE 4C

19¼" clip (third corner)

Side seam

Wrong side of the first folded side panel

Wrong side of the second folded side panel

½" of the side panel left unstitched on the side seam for the fourth corner.

Right side of the bottom panel

13" clip (second corner)

6¾" clip (first corner)

FIGURE 4D

Wrong side of the third folded side panel

Wrong side of the fourth folded side panel

13" clip (second corner)

Trim corners.

Trim corner.

Side seam (fourth corner)

19¼" clip (third corner)

FIGURE 8

⅜" of the **Wrong** side of the exterior side panel is exposed.

Timtex interfacing

Machine baste along the cut top edge on the Timtex. Stitch one side at a time.

Right side of the exterior CD Holder

Step 9. Make the lining for the CD Holder.

Follow the instructions in steps 2 through 5 to make the lining for the CD Holder.

Step 10. Attach the lining to the exterior CD Holder with the Timtex attached.

With the **Right** side of the exterior facing out and the **Wrong** side of the lining facing out, slip the lining over the exterior, matching up the side seams and pinning in place along the top raw edge. Attach the lining to the exterior by stitching a ½" seam around the top raw edges on 3 sides of the CD Holder, backstitching at each end. (The last side is left unstitched to allow you to turn your CD Holder **Right** side out.)

Step 11. Finish the CD Holder.

a. First, turn the CD Holder **Right** side out by pulling it through the unstitched side at the top edge. Push the lining down inside the holder and press. Fold under the top raw edges of the opening and pin the opening closed.

b. Then, topstitch completely around the top finished edges of the CD Holder to close the opening. "Stitch in the ditch"* by hand at each bottom corner to hold the lining in place. Press the CD Holder to crease the Timtex at each of the edges of the CD Holder.

See page 172 for an explanation of "stitching in the ditch."

Step 12. Make the first handle.

a. First, with **Right** sides together, fold the handle in half, matching up the long side raw edges, and pin them in place. Stitch a ½" seam down both short side raw edges, back-stitching at each end.

b. Then, trim the 2 corners of the handle in the seam allowance, making sure not to clip the stitching.

c. Turn the handle **Right** side out, using a turning tool* to push out the corners of the handle. Then, insert the Timtex into the opened edge of the handle, placing the Timtex on top of the seam allowances. Fold the raw edges of the opening in toward the inside of the handle and pin it closed.

See page 172 for an explanation of a turning tool.

d. Next, topstitch* completely around the handle to close the opening and secure the Timtex in place.

See page 172 for an explanation of topstitching.

Step 13. Attach the handle to the side panel of the CD Holder.

Measure 1½" down from the top finished edge on one side of the CD Holder and make a mark. Then, measure ⅝" in from each side crease and mark. Place the handle onto the side of the CD Holder below the 1½" mark and in between the ⅝" marks on each side. Pin the short sides of the handle in place. (The handle will have a little gap between it and the side of the CD Holder, to make it easier to grasp.) Attach by stitching a ⅛" seam down both of the short ends of the handle, backstitching at each end of your stitching. (The holder will be stiff when you are attaching the handles to the sides. Be persistent!) (FIGURE 13)

Step 14. Follow the instructions in steps 12 and 13 to make and attach the other handle on the opposite side of the CD Holder.

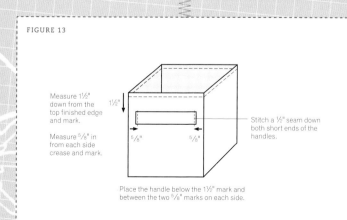

FIGURE 13

Measure 1½" down from the top finished edge and mark.

1½"

Measure ⅝" in from each side crease and mark.

⅝"   ⅝"

Stitch a ½" seam down both short ends of the handles.

Place the handle below the 1½" mark and between the two ⅝" marks on each side.

DESKTOP ORGANIZER

FINISHED SIZE: 14" WIDE X 5" LONG X 5" DEEP

FABRICS

- ⅜ yard (54"-wide) heavyweight cotton print for the exterior

- ⅜ yard (54"-wide) coordinating heavyweight cotton for the lining

- 1⅛ yards (13"-wide) Timtex* or other extra-heavy interfacing

See page 172 for an explanation of Timtex.

OTHER SUPPLIES

- Coordinating thread

- Yardstick

- Chalk pencil or fabric marker

- Scissors

- Straight pins

- Turning tool (such as a closed pair of scissors)

- Hand sewing needle

NOTES

- Preshrink your fabric by washing, drying, and pressing it before starting your project. To wash Timtex after completing your project, machine wash warm, then reshape your project and air dry. Your project will press back into shape with a steam iron. Once you steam the project, support it with wadded-up tissue paper or a folded towel while air drying in order to keep the shape that you want.

Step 1. Cut out all pieces from the fabric.

Simply measure and mark the dimensions below directly onto the **Wrong** side of the fabric, using a yardstick and a chalk pencil. Then, using your scissors, cut out each panel following the marked lines.

FROM THE FABRIC FOR THE EXTERIOR

- Cut 1 side panel: 39˝ wide x 6˝ long
- Cut 1 bottom panel: 15˝ wide x 6˝ long
- Cut 2 handles: 5˝ wide x 4˝ long

FROM THE FABRIC FOR THE LINING

- Cut 1 side panel: 39˝ wide x 6˝ long
- Cut 1 bottom panel: 15˝ wide x 6˝ long

FROM THE TIMTEX

- Cut 1 side panel: 38¼˝ wide x 5¼˝ long
- Cut 1 bottom panel: 14¼˝ wide x 5¼˝ long
- Cut 2 handles: 4˝ wide x 1˝ long

Step 2. Measure and mark for the clips for 3 of the corners on the exterior side panel.

a. First, stitch a ½" seam across one of the long raw edges (which will then be the bottom of the side panel) for reinforcement.

b. Then, on the **Wrong** side of the side panel, starting at the short right side raw edge, measure and mark the following increments across both the top and bottom raw edges: 5½", 19½", and 24½".

c. Next, at the marks you made across the bottom raw edge only, clip into the seam allowance, making sure not to cut your reinforcement stitching. (These clips will allow you to turn the panel at each bottom corner when attaching the bottom panel.) (FIGURE 2C)

d. To create the 4 different sides of the Desktop Organizer, fold the side panel **Wrong** sides together and press a crease at each of the coordinating marks starting with the first (5½") mark. (These creases create 3 of the corners for the Desktop Organizer. The fourth corner will be the seam attaching the side panel together.) (FIGURE 2D)

Step 3. Make the exterior of the Desktop Organizer.

Follow the instructions in steps 3 through 5 for the CD Holder to attach the side panels and bottom panels together to make the exterior of the Desktop Organizer, using the increments marked for the Desktop Organizer in step 2b.

Step 4. Measure and mark for the clips for the corners on the Timtex side panel.

a. First, stitch a ⅛" seam across the bottom edge of the Timtex side panel for reinforcement. Then, starting on the right side edge, measure and mark the following increments along the bottom raw edge: 5⅛", 19⅛", and 24⅛".

b. Next, clip into the seam allowance at each mark, making sure not to clip the stitching. These clips will allow you to turn the panel at each corner when attaching the Timtex bottom panel to the side panel. (You may find it awkward to clip into such a small seam allowance. Just clip through the cut edge; this will allow the Timtex to stretch apart for the corners.)

Step 5. Make the Timtex panel.

Follow the instructions in steps 3 and 4 for the CD Holder to make the Timtex panel, using a ⅛" seam, stopping ⅛" from the bottom edge on the Timtex, and using the increments marked for the Desktop Organizer in step 2b. Then, follow the instructions in step 5 for the CD Holder to trim the corners of the Timtex panel and turn the Timtex panel **Right** side out.

Step 6. Attach the Timtex panel to the Wrong side of the exterior Desktop Organizer.

Follow the instructions in step 8 for the CD Holder to attach the Timtex panel and exterior Desktop Organizer together.

Step 7. Make the lining for the Desktop Organizer.

Follow the instructions in step 2 for the Desktop Organizer to mark for the side panels and clips. Then, follow the instructions in steps 3 through 5 for the CD Holder to make the lining for the Desktop Organizer, using the increments marked for the Desktop Organizer in step 2b.

Step 8. Attach the lining to the exterior Desktop Organizer with the Timtex attached.

Follow the instructions in steps 10 and 11 for the CD Holder to attach the lining and finish the Desktop Organizer.

Step 9. Make the handles.

Follow the instructions in step 12 for the CD Holder to make the handles for the Desktop Organizer.

Step 10. Attach the handles to the short sides of the Desktop Organizer.

Follow the instructions in step 13 for the CD Holder to attach both of the handles to the short sides of the Desktop Organizer.

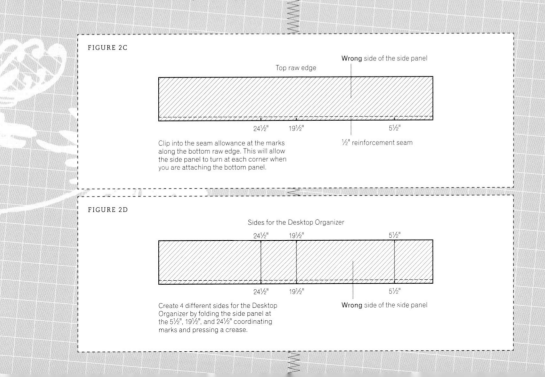

FIGURE 2C

Top raw edge

Wrong side of the side panel

24½"   19½"   5½"

½" reinforcement seam

Clip into the seam allowance at the marks along the bottom raw edge. This will allow the side panel to turn at each corner when you are attaching the bottom panel.

FIGURE 2D

Sides for the Desktop Organizer

24½"   19½"   5½"

24½"   19½"   5½"

Wrong side of the side panel

Create 4 different sides for the Desktop Organizer by folding the side panel at the 5½", 19½", and 24½" coordinating marks and pressing a crease.

DOCUMENT DUVET

FINISHED SIZE: 9½" WIDE X 12½" LONG

Why settle for boring old manila envelopes and file folders? Dress up your documents! This Document Duvet holds 8½" x 11" papers and large photos and is fastened at the top, making it handy to bring along to presentations, meetings, and working lunches. The **PHOTO FILE** (page 128) holds 3" x 5" or 4" x 6" photos, so it's perfect for toting your favorite pictures of your little ones, friends, or pets. Tuck it in your purse or briefcase and sneak a glance at those friendly faces whenever you need a little cheer.

FABRICS

- ½ yard (54"-wide) home-decor-weight cotton fabric for the back panel, flap, and inside pocket
- ½ yard (54"-wide) coordinating home-decor-weight cotton for the front panel
- ¼ yard heavyweight fusible interfacing (such as Pellon's Craft Fuse)
- ⅝ yard (½"-wide) satin ribbon

OTHER SUPPLIES

- Coordinating thread
- 3 (½") grommets
- 9" x 11¾" piece heavy cardboard or chipboard
- Scissors
- Straight pins
- Masking tape
- Ruler or tape measure
- Chalk pencil or fabric marker
- Turning tool (such as a closed pair of scissors)

NOTES

- All seams are ½" unless otherwise stated. (The ½" seam allowance is included in all of the pattern pieces.)
- Preshrink your fabric by washing, drying, and pressing it before starting your project.

Step 1. Cut out all pieces from the fabric.

a. First, cut out the Document Duvet pattern pieces provided in the pocket at the front of this book.

- *Large main panel*
- *Flap*

b. Pin the pattern pieces to the fabric according to the instructions below. Then, using your scissors, cut the fabric according to the outlines on the pattern pieces, in the quantities given below.

FROM THE FABRIC FOR THE BACK PANEL, FLAP, AND INSIDE POCKET

- *Cut 1 back panel on the fold*: Use large main panel pattern piece.*
- *Cut 1 inside pocket on the fold: Use large main panel pattern piece.*
- *Cut 2 flaps on the fold: Use flap pattern piece.*

FROM THE COORDINATING FABRIC FOR THE FRONT PANEL

- *Cut 1 front panel on the fold: Use large main panel pattern piece.*

FROM THE HEAVYWEIGHT FUSIBLE INTERFACING

- *Cut 1 flap on the fold: Use flap pattern piece.*

  ** To cut your pattern piece on the fold of your fabric, first fold the fabric with **Wrong** sides together and the selvage edges aligned. Then lay your pattern piece so that the edge to be cut on the fold is even with the folded edge of your fabric. Once the piece is cut out, open it up to make one full panel.*

c. In order to keep your pieces organized, mark each piece by writing the name on a piece of masking tape and attaching to the **Wrong** side of each panel as it is cut.

~ CONTINUED

Step 2. Finish the top raw edge on the front panel.

With the **Wrong** side of the front panel facing up, fold one of the short side raw edges (to be used as the top raw edge) ¼" in toward the **Wrong** side of the panel and press. Fold the edge ¼" in again and press. Topstitch* along the inner folded edge.

* See page 172 for an explanation of topstitching.

Step 3. Add the grommets to the front panel.

a. First, fold the front panel in half lengthwise and gently press a center crease.

b. Using a ruler and a chalk pencil, starting at the top finished edge on the center crease, measure down and mark the following increments: 1¾" and 3".

c. Center 2 of the grommets over the center crease and the marks you made in step 3b. Follow the manufacturer's instructions to attach the grommets to the **Right** side of the front panel. Place the finished side of the grommets onto the **Right** side of the panel. (FIGURE 3C)

Set the front panel aside.

Step 4. Attach the first flap to the back panel.

a. Place the fusible side of the interfacing onto the **Wrong** side of the first flap. Follow the manufacturer's instructions to fuse the interfacing to the flap.

b. With **Right** sides together, match up the long, top raw edge of the first flap to one of the short raw edges of the back panel (which will become the top raw edge) and pin them in place. Stitch a ½" seam across the top raw edges, backstitching at each end. Press the seam allowances toward the back panel. (FIGURE 4B)

Set the back panel with the first flap attached aside.

Step 5. Attach the other flap to the inside pocket.

With **Right** sides together, match up the long, top raw edge of the other flap to one of the short raw edges of the inside pocket (which will become the top raw edge) and pin them in place. Starting on the left side of the inside pocket, stitch a ½" seam, extending ½" in from each of the side raw edges, backstitching at each end. (This will leave an opening to insert the cardboard inside the pocket.) Open up the flap and press the seam allowances toward the inside pocket. (FIGURE 5)

Step 6. Attach the front panel to the inside pocket with the flap attached.

Place the **Wrong** side of the front panel onto the **Right** side of the inside pocket. Machine baste* with a ¼" seam down both sides and across the bottom raw edges. (FIGURE 6)

* See page 171 for an explanation of machine basting.

Step 7. Attach the inside pocket and flap with the front panel attached to the back panel and flap.

a. Place the front panel (attached to the inside pocket and flap) and the back panel and flap with **Right** sides together, matching up the raw edges of the panels and flaps, and pin them in place. Stitch a ½" seam completely around the outside raw edges of the panels and flaps, backstitching at each end.

> NOTE: *The matched raw edges between the inside pocket and flap will be left unstitched in order to allow you to insert the cardboard in step 8. You will close the opening in step 9.*

b. Using your scissors, trim the corners* in the seam allowance, making sure not to clip your stitching.

* See page 172 for an explanation of trimming corners in the seam allowance.

c. Pull the panels through the opening you left at the top of the inside pocket in step 5, use a turning tool* to push out the corners and press the Document Duvet flat.

* See page 172 for an explanation of a turning tool.

d. Fold the flap in half lengthwise and gently press a center crease. (You will use this center crease in step 9b to mark the placement for the grommets.)

Step 8. Insert the cardboard.

Insert the cardboard into the opening you left at the top of the inside pocket. Push the cardboard completely inside, folding the seam allowances down on top of the cardboard, and pin the opening closed.

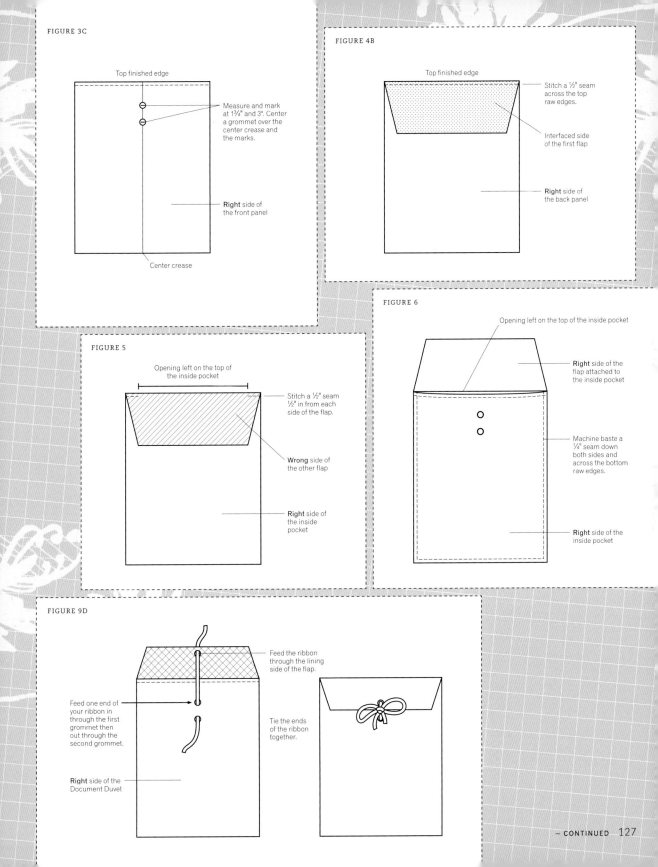

FIGURE 3C

Top finished edge

Measure and mark at 1¾" and 3". Center a grommet over the center crease and the marks.

Right side of the front panel

Center crease

FIGURE 4B

Top finished edge

Stitch a ½" seam across the top raw edges.

Interfaced side of the first flap

Right side of the back panel

FIGURE 5

Opening left on the top of the inside pocket

Stitch a ½" seam ½" in from each side of the flap.

Wrong side of the other flap

Right side of the inside pocket

FIGURE 6

Opening left on the top of the inside pocket

Right side of the flap attached to the inside pocket

Machine baste a ¼" seam down both sides and across the bottom raw edges.

Right side of the inside pocket

FIGURE 9D

Feed the ribbon through the lining side of the flap.

Feed one end of your ribbon in through the first grommet then out through the second grommet.

Tie the ends of the ribbon together.

Right side of the Document Duvet

~ CONTINUED

Step 9. Finish the Document Duvet.

a. Edge stitch* close to the folded edge of the opening at the top of the inside pocket. (This will keep the cardboard inside the duvet and close the opening.)

* See page 170 for an explanation of edge stitching.

b. Using your ruler and chalk pencil, starting at the top finished edge on the center crease, measure and mark ½" down on the **Right** side of the flap.

c. Center your third grommet over the center crease at the ½" mark you made in step 9b. Follow the manufacturer's instructions to attach the grommet to the flap, placing the finished side of the grommet onto the **Right** side of the flap.

d. Feed one end of your ribbon in through the first grommet on the **Right** side of the front panel and then out through the second grommet. Lay the flap onto the front panel and feed the other end of the ribbon through the grommet on the flap. Tie the ends of the ribbon together and make a bow. (FIGURE 9D)

PHOTO FILE

FINISHED SIZE: 5" WIDE X 7" LONG

FABRICS

- ¼ yard (44"-wide) cotton fabric for the front and back panel
- ¼ yard (44"-wide) coordinating cotton for the inside pocket and flaps
- ¼ yard heavyweight fusible interfacing (such as Pellon's Craft Fuse)
- ⅝ yard (½"-wide) satin ribbon

OTHER SUPPLIES

- Coordinating thread
- 2 (½") grommets
- 4½" x 6½" piece heavy cardboard or chipboard
- Scissors
- Straight pins
- Ruler or tape measure
- Masking tape
- Turning tool (such as a closed pair of scissors)

- Chalk pencil or fabric marker

NOTES

- All seams are ½" unless otherwise stated. (The ½" seam allowance is included in all of the pattern pieces.)
- Preshrink your fabric by washing, drying, and pressing it before starting your project.

Step 1. Cut out all pieces from the fabric.

a. First, cut out the Photo File pattern pieces provided in the pocket at the front of this book.

- Main panel
- Flap

b. Pin the pattern pieces to the fabric according to the instructions below. Then, using your scissors, cut the fabric according to the outlines on the pattern pieces, in the quantities given below.

FROM THE FABRIC FOR THE FRONT AND BACK PANELS

- Cut 1 front panel on the fold*: Use main panel pattern piece.
- Cut 1 back panel on the fold: Use main panel pattern piece.

FROM THE FABRIC FOR THE INSIDE POCKET AND FLAPS

- Cut 1 inside pocket on the fold: Use main panel pattern piece.
- Cut 4 flaps on the fold: Use flap pattern piece.

FROM THE HEAVYWEIGHT FUSIBLE INTERFACING

• *Cut 2 flaps on the fold: Use flap pattern piece.*

  ** To cut your pattern piece on the fold of your fabric, first fold the fabric with **Wrong** sides together and the selvage edges aligned. Then lay your pattern piece so that the edge to be cut on the fold is even with the folded edge of your fabric. Once the piece is cut out, open it up to make one full panel.*

c. In order to keep your pieces organized, mark each piece by writing the name on a piece of masking tape and attaching to the **Wrong** side of each panel as it is cut.

Step 2. Attach the interfacing to 2 of the flaps.

Place the fusible side of the interfacing onto the **Wrong** side of the first flap. Follow the manufacturer's instructions to fuse the interfacing to the flap. Repeat this step to attach the other interfacing flap to a second flap.

Step 3. Attach the first interfaced flap to the back panel.

With **Right** sides together, match up the raw edges on one long side of the interfaced flap and the back panel and pin them in place. Stitch a ½" seam across the matched raw edges, backstitching at each end. Press the seam allowances toward the back panel. Repeat this step to attach the second interfaced flap to the other long side. (FIGURE 3)

Step 4. Finish the long side raw edge on the front panel.

With the **Wrong** side of the front panel facing up, fold the raw edge of one long side ¼" in toward the **Wrong** side of the panel and press. Fold the edge ¼" in again and press. Topstitch along the inner folded edge.

Step 5. Attach the first flap to the inside pocket.

With **Right** sides together, match up one of the long side raw edges of the inside pocket with the top raw edge on the first flap and pin them in place. Starting on the left side of the inside pocket, stitch a ½" seam, ½" in from each of the side raw edges, backstitching at each end. (This will leave an opening to insert the cardboard inside the pocket.) Press the seam allowances toward the inside pocket. (FIGURE 5)

Step 6. Attach the front panel to the inside pocket.

Place the **Right** side of the inside pocket (with flap attached) onto the **Wrong** side of the front panel. Match up the seam connecting the flap to the inside pocket with the finished edge of the front panel and pin them in place. Machine baste with a ¼" seam down both short sides and across the bottom raw edges.

Step 7. Attach the other flap lining to the front panel.

With **Right** sides together, match up the raw edge of the long side on the front panel (with the inside pocket attached) with the top raw edge on the flap and pin them in place. Stitch a ½" seam across the matched raw edges, backstitching at each end. Press the seam allowances toward the inside pocket. (FIGURE 7)

Step 8. Attach the front panel to the back panel.

a. Place the front panel (with the inside pocket and non-interfaced flaps attached) onto the back panel (with the interfaced flaps attached), **Right** sides together, matching up the raw edges, and pin them in place. Stitch a ½" seam completely around the outside raw edges, backstitching at each end.

b. Using your scissors, trim the corners* in the seam allowance, making sure not to clip your stitching.

* See page 172 for an explanation of trimming corners in the seam allowance.

c. Pull the Photo File through the opening you left at the top of the inside pocket in step 5, using a turning tool* to push out the corners, and press the Photo File flat.

* See page 172 for an explanation of a turning tool.

d. Fold the Photo File across the width, finding the center of both of the flaps. Gently press a center crease across both flaps. (You will use this crease in step 10b to mark the placement for the grommets.)

Step 9. Insert the cardboard.

a. First, turn your Photo File with the **Right** side of the back panel facing up, match up the seam along the bottom flap with the seam on the front panel, and pin it in place. "Stitch in the ditch"* along the seam on the back panel, backstitching at each end.

* See page 172 for an explanation of "stitching in the ditch."

b. Insert the cardboard into the opening you left on the side of the inside pocket. Push the cardboard completely inside, placing the seam allowances all on one side of the cardboard.

Step 10. Finish the Photo File.

a. Next, fold the seam allowances on the opening inside the inside pocket and pin the opening closed. Topstitch close to the folded edge of the inside pocket. (This will keep the cardboard inside the file and close the opening.)

b. On the **Right** side of the flap, starting at the top finished edge on the center crease, measure and mark ½" down using your ruler and chalk pencil. Repeat this step to measure and mark the placement for the other grommet on the other flap.

c. Center your first grommet over the center crease and the ½" mark you made in step 10b. Follow the manufacturer's instructions to attach the grommet to the **Right** side of the flap. Place the finished side of the grommet on the **Right** side of the flap. Repeat this step to attach another grommet onto the **Right** side of the other flap.

d. Fold the flaps toward the front panel. Then, feed one end of your ribbon in through the first grommet on the lining side of the first flap and out the **Right** side. Then feed the other end of your ribbon through the second grommet on the lining side of the second flap and out through the grommet to the **Right** side of the flap. Take the 2 ends of the ribbon and tie them together to make a bow. (**FIGURE 10D**)

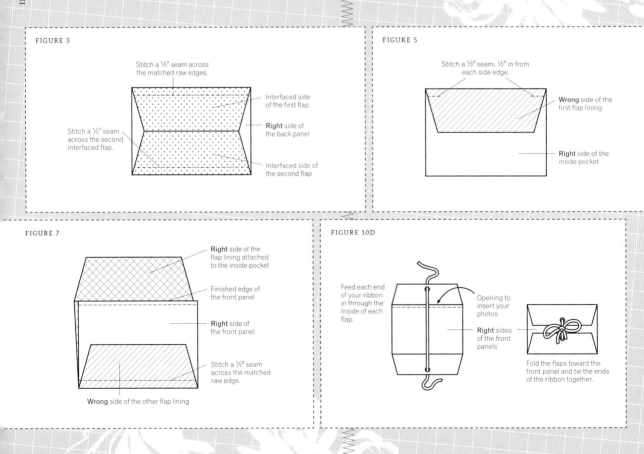

FIGURE 3

Stitch a ½" seam across the matched raw edges.

Interfaced side of the first flap

Right side of the back panel

Stitch a ½" seam across the second interfaced flap.

Interfaced side of the second flap

FIGURE 5

Stitch a ½" seam, ½" in from each side edge.

Wrong side of the first flap lining

Right side of the inside pocket

FIGURE 7

Right side of the flap lining attached to the inside pocket

Finished edge of the front panel

Right side of the front panel

Stitch a ½" seam across the matched raw edge.

Wrong side of the other flap lining

FIGURE 10D

Feed each end of your ribbon in through the Inside of each flap.

Opening to insert your photos

Right sides of the front panels

Fold the flaps toward the front panel and tie the ends of the ribbon together.

FASHION CHECKBOOK CLUTCH

FINISHED SIZE: 12" WIDE X 6¼" TALL X 1" DEEP

Maintain your polished, professional image, and leave that bulky purse at home! When all you need is the basics—checkbook, credit cards, pens, compact, lipstick, and driver's license—this is your perfect fashion accessory! It's feminine, sleek, and functional.

FABRICS

- ⅔ yard (54"-wide) home-decor-weight cotton for the exterior
- 1½ yards (44"-wide) light- to mid-weight coordinating cotton solid for the lining
- ¼ yard (44"-wide) cotton canvas or cotton duck cloth for the flap interfacing
- 1½ yards heavyweight fusible interfacing (such as Pellon's Craft Fuse)
- ½ yard (13"-wide) Timtex* or other extra-heavy interfacing
- 5" (¾"-wide) sew-on Velcro
- ¼ yard (½"-wide) coordinating extra-wide, double-folded bias tape

See page 172 for an explanation of Timtex.

OTHER SUPPLIES

- Coordinating thread
- Button/carpet heavy thread
- 26" coordinating heavyweight plastic or metal jacket zipper
- ½" zipper pull clasp for the handle
- Yardstick or ruler
- Chalk pencil or fabric marker
- Scissors
- Masking tape
- Straight pins
- Turning tool (such as a closed pair of scissors)
- Hand sewing needle

NOTES

- All seams are ½" unless otherwise stated. (The ½" seam allowance is included in all cutting measurements.)
- Preshrink your fabric by washing, drying, and pressing it before starting your project. To wash Timtex after completing your project, machine wash warm, then reshape your project and air dry. Your project will press back into shape with a steam iron. Once you steam the project, support it with wadded-up tissue paper or a folded towel while air drying in order to keep the shape that you want.

Step 1. Cut out all pieces from the fabric.

a. Simply measure and mark the dimensions below directly onto the **Wrong** side of the fabric, using a yardstick and a chalk pencil. Then, using your scissors, cut out each panel following the marked lines.

FROM THE FABRIC FOR THE EXTERIOR

- *Cut 1 front main panel with back flap: 13˝ wide x 11˝ long*
- *Cut 1 back main panel: 13˝ wide x 7½˝ long*
- *Cut 2 back pocket panels: 13˝ wide x 6¾˝ long*
- *Cut 1 flap lining: 13˝ wide x 4½˝ long*
- *Cut 1 ruffle: 2˝ wide x 44˝ long (Cut across the width of your fabric.)*
- *Cut 1 handle: 2˝ wide x 14˝ long (Cut across the width of your fabric.)*

FROM THE FABRIC FOR THE LINING

- *Cut 1 lining panel: 13˝ wide x 47¼˝ long*
- *Cut 1 pen holder tab: 3˝ wide x 3½˝ long*

FROM THE CANVAS

- *Cut 1 flap: 13˝ wide x 4½˝ long*

FROM THE FUSIBLE INTERFACING

- *Cut 1 interfacing panel: 11½˝ wide x 45¾˝ long*

FROM THE TIMTEX

- *Cut 1 Timtex panel: 12˝ wide x 13½˝ long*

— CONTINUED

b. In order to keep your pieces organized, mark each piece by writing the name on a piece of masking tape and attaching it to the **Wrong** side of each panel as it is cut.

Step 2. Make the back pocket and attach it onto the Timtex panel.

a. Place the **Right** sides of the back pocket panels together, matching up each of the 13"-wide raw edges (to be used for the top raw edges), and pin them in place. Topstitch a ½" seam across this top raw edge, backstitching at each end. Then, turn the pocket panels **Right** side out, matching up the side and bottom raw edges, and press. Machine baste* a ¼" seam down the sides and across the bottom raw edges.

* See page 171 for an explanation of machine basting.

b. On the **Right** side of the back pocket, measure 1½" down from the top finished edge on each side of the pocket and make a mark. Using your ruler and chalk pencil, draw a guideline across the width connecting the 2 marks. (FIGURE 2B, C)

c. Then, measure 1" in from the left side raw edge on the 1½" guideline and mark. Place a 2½" piece of the female half of the Velcro below the 1½" guideline and to the inside of the 1" mark and pin it in place. Attach by stitching completely around the edge of the Velcro, backstitching at each end. Repeat this step to attach another 2½" piece of the female half of the Velcro onto the right-hand side of the back pocket. (FIGURE 2B, C)

d. Place the lining side (the side without the Velcro) of the back pocket onto the **Right** side of the back panel, lining up the side and bottom raw edges. Machine baste a ½" seam down both sides and across the bottom of the pocket.

e. Place the Timtex panel onto the **Wrong** side of the back panel, ½" up from the bottom raw edge. Match the 12"-long cut edge on the Timtex panel with the ½" basting stitch, leaving ½" of the back panel exposed around the side and bottom edges of the Timtex panel, and pin it in place. (The back panel covers the bottom half of the Timtex panel.) (FIGURE 2E, F)

f. Then, fold the raw edges of the back panel and pocket over the cut edge of the Timtex and pin it in place. Machine baste a ⅜" seam down both sides and across the bottom raw edges on the back panel. (FIGURE 2E, F)

g. Then, turn the panel over so the **Right** side of the back panel (with the pocket attached) is facing up. Pin across the top raw edge on the back panel. Then stitch close to the top raw edge of the back panel, attaching it to the Timtex panel.

Set the Timtex panel (with the back panel and pocket attached) aside.

Step 3. Make the flap on the front panel.

a. First, place the canvas flap onto the **Wrong** side of the flap lining and pin it in place. Then, machine baste the canvas by stitching a ½" seam completely around the flap lining to act as a reinforcement stitch*.

* See page 171 for an explanation of reinforcement stitching.

b. On the **Right** side of the flap lining, measure ¾" up from the bottom raw edge on each side of the flap lining and mark. Using your ruler and chalk pencil, draw a guideline across the width connecting the 2 marks. (FIGURE 3B, C)

c. Then, measure 1" in from the raw edge on the left side on the ¾" guideline and make a mark. Place a 2½" piece of the male half of the Velcro above the ¾" guideline and to the inside of the 1" mark and pin it in place. Attach by stitching completely around the edge of the Velcro, backstitching at each end. Repeat this step to attach another 2½" piece of the male half of the Velcro onto the right side of the flap lining. (FIGURE 3B, C)

d. With **Right** sides together, match up the bottom raw edge (the edge with the Velcro attached) on the flap lining with the top raw edge of the front panel and pin it in place. With the **Wrong** side of the front panel facing up, measure 3¼" down from the top raw edge on each side and make a mark. Starting at the mark on the right side of the front panel, stitch a ½" seam up the right side, across the top, and down the left side raw edges, to the mark on the left side, backstitching at each end. (FIGURE 3D, E)

e. Using your scissors, trim the 2 top corners* of the flap in the seam allowance, making sure not to clip your stitching. Then, clip into the seam allowance* at the 2 side marks you made in step 3d. (FIGURE 3D, E)

* See pages 172 and 170 for explanations of trimming and clipping into the seam allowance.

f. First, turn the flap **Right** side out, using a turning tool* to push out the corners and press. Then, topstitch* with a ⅛" seam around the finished edge of the flap, backstitching at each end. (FIGURE 3F)

* See page 172 for explanations of a turning tool and topstitching.

g. Next, on the **Right** side of the front panel at the top finished edge of the flap, using your ruler and chalk pencil, match up the 2 clips on each side of the flap and draw a line connecting them. (You will stitch across this guideline in step 5b to attach the top of the flap onto the Timtex panel. This guideline will also be one of the folded edges to make the spine for the clutch.)

Step 4. Make the ruffle and attach it to the front panel and the Timtex panel.

a. First, fold the ruffle in half lengthwise with **Right** sides together. Stitch a ½" seam across each short end of the ruffle, backstitching at each end. Trim the corners on each end of the ruffle and then turn the ruffle **Right** side out. Match up the raw edges of the 2 long sides of the ruffle and pin them together.

b. To gather* the ruffle, place a length of the heavy thread, ½" in from the pinned long side raw edge of the ruffle, leaving 8" to 10" extra on each end of the ruffle strip. Then, with a large zigzag stitch, stitch back and forth across the heavy thread, ½" in along the edge of the ruffle strip, backstitching at each end. (The zigzag stitching makes a casing over the thread.) Be careful not to stitch through the heavy thread; otherwise you won't be able to pull the thread to gather the ruffle. (FIGURE 4B)

See page 171 for an explanation of a gathering stitch.

c. Remove the straight pins. Then, pull the heavy thread on each end of the strip, gathering in the ruffle strip and moving the gathers in toward the center of the strip. Gather it until the ruffle strip measures 24½".

d. To keep the gathering from loosening up, tie off the ends of the gathering thread by placing a straight pin at one end of the ruffle. Take the heavy thread used to gather the ruffle strip and loop it around the ends of the straight pin in a figure-8 pattern (up and around the top of the straight pin and down and across the bottom of the pin). Do this a number of times to hold the gathering in place. Repeat this step with a second straight pin to tie off the other end of the gathering thread on the other end of the ruffle. Keep the straight pins in place until after you stitch the ruffle to the front panel.

e. On the **Right** side of the front panel, measure 1" down from the first set of clips on each side edge of the flap and mark. Using your ruler and chalk pencil, draw a line connecting the 2 marks. (This will be the second fold line to make the spine for the clutch in step 5b.) (FIGURE 4E)

f. Clip into the exterior front panel, ½" in on each side of the guideline you made in step 4e.

g. Starting on the right edge of the front panel at the marks you just made in step 4e, place the first end of the ruffle onto the **Right** side of the front panel. Match up the raw edge of the ruffle with the raw edge of the front panel and pin the ruffle in place. Slightly round the 2 bottom corners on the front panel with the ruffle as you pin it in place. Attach the ruffle by stitching a ½" seam down both sides and across the bottom raw edges, backstitching at each end.

h. Velcro the flap on the front panel to the back pocket (already attached to one end of the Timtex panel). Then, pin the edges of the flap in place on the back pocket, to keep from pulling the front panel too much when attaching it to the Timtex panel. Turn the attached panels over so the **Wrong** side is facing up. Place the other end of the Timtex panel onto the **Wrong** side of the front panel (with the finished flap), matching the cut edge of the Timtex with the stitching line that is attaching the ruffle to the front panel, and pin the Timtex in place. (FIGURE 4H, I)

i. Fold the raw edges of the ruffle on the front panel over the Timtex panel and pin them in place. (The ruffle will be standing out from the front panel.) Then, machine baste a loose ⅜" seam down both sides and across the bottom raw edge on the front panel to secure the Timtex to the front panel. (FIGURE 4H, I)

Step 5. Make the spine for the clutch.

a. Fold under ¼" of the 1"-long section of the raw edge on one side between the 2 clips, toward the Timtex side, and press. Fold it under another ¼", covering the cut edge of the Timtex panel, and press. Topstitch across the inner folded edge between the 2 clips. Repeat this step to finish the raw edge between the clips on the other side of the spine. (FIGURE 5A)

b. Now, turn the panel over so the **Right** side is facing up, and stitch along the guideline you made in step 3g across the top of the flap to attach the front panel to the Timtex panel. Then, stitch along the guideline you made in step 4e, backstitching at each end. (The 2 stitch lines will be the fold lines to make the spine for the clutch.) (FIGURE 5B)

c. Fold the exterior of the clutch toward the Timtex side at both of the stitch lines and press a hard crease. This will make the spine for the clutch.

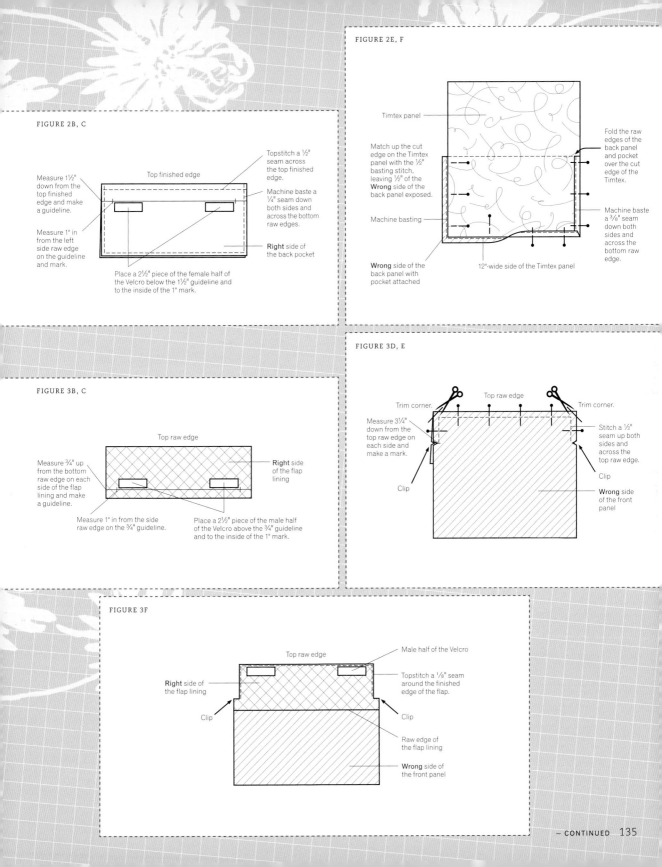

FIGURE 2B, C

Top finished edge

Measure 1½" down from the top finished edge and make a guideline.

Measure 1" in from the left side raw edge on the guideline and mark.

Topstitch a ½" seam across the top finished edge.

Machine baste a ¼" seam down both sides and across the bottom raw edges.

Right side of the back pocket

Place a 2½" piece of the female half of the Velcro below the 1½" guideline and to the inside of the 1" mark.

FIGURE 2E, F

Timtex panel

Match up the cut edge on the Timtex panel with the ½" basting stitch, leaving ½" of the **Wrong** side of the back panel exposed.

Machine basting

Wrong side of the back panel with pocket attached

Fold the raw edges of the back panel and pocket over the cut edge of the Timtex.

Machine baste a ³/₈" seam down both sides and across the bottom raw edge.

12"-wide side of the Timtex panel

FIGURE 3B, C

Top raw edge

Measure ¾" up from the bottom raw edge on each side of the flap lining and make a guideline.

Measure 1" in from the side raw edge on the ¾" guideline.

Right side of the flap lining

Place a 2½" piece of the male half of the Velcro above the ¾" guideline and to the inside of the 1" mark.

FIGURE 3D, E

Trim corner.

Top raw edge

Trim corner.

Measure 3¼" down from the top raw edge on each side and make a mark.

Clip

Stitch a ½" seam up both sides and across the top raw edge.

Clip

Wrong side of the front panel

FIGURE 3F

Top raw edge

Male half of the Velcro

Right side of the flap lining

Topstitch a ⅛" seam around the finished edge of the flap.

Clip

Clip

Raw edge of the flap lining

Wrong side of the front panel

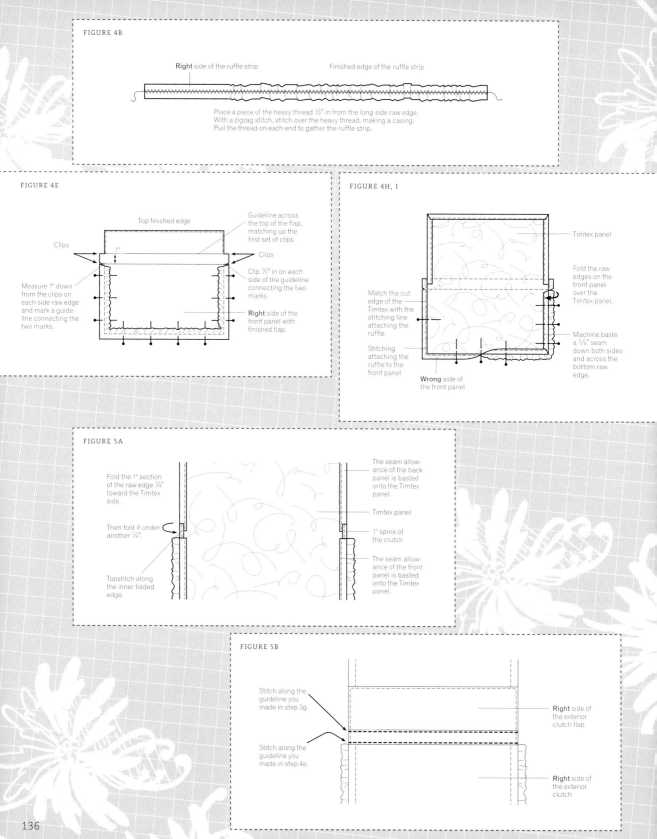

FIGURE 4B

Right side of the ruffle strip   Finished edge of the ruffle strip

Place a piece of the heavy thread ½" in from the long side raw edge.
With a zigzag stitch, stitch over the heavy thread, making a casing.
Pull the thread on each end to gather the ruffle strip.

FIGURE 4E

Top finished edge

Clips

Guideline across
the top of the flap,
matching up the
first set of clips

1"

Clips

Clip ½" in on each
side of the guideline
connecting the two
marks.

Measure 1" down
from the clips on
each side raw edge
and mark a guide-
line connecting the
two marks.

Right side of the
front panel with
finished flap

FIGURE 4H, I

Timtex panel

Fold the raw
edges on the
front panel over
the Timtex panel.

Match the cut
edge of the
Timtex with the
stitching line
attaching the
ruffle.

Stitching
attaching the
ruffle to the
front panel

Wrong side of
the front panel

Machine baste
a ³/₈" seam
down both sides
and across the
bottom raw
edge.

FIGURE 5A

Fold the 1" section
of the raw edge ¼"
toward the Timtex
side.

Then fold it under
another ¼".

Topstitch along
the inner folded
edge.

The seam allow-
ance of the back
panel is basted
onto the Timtex
panel.

Timtex panel

1" spine of
the clutch

The seam allow-
ance of the front
panel is basted
onto the Timtex
panel.

FIGURE 5B

Stitch along the
guideline you
made in step 3g.

Stitch along the
guideline you
made in step 4e.

Right side of
the exterior
clutch flap

Right side of
the exterior
clutch

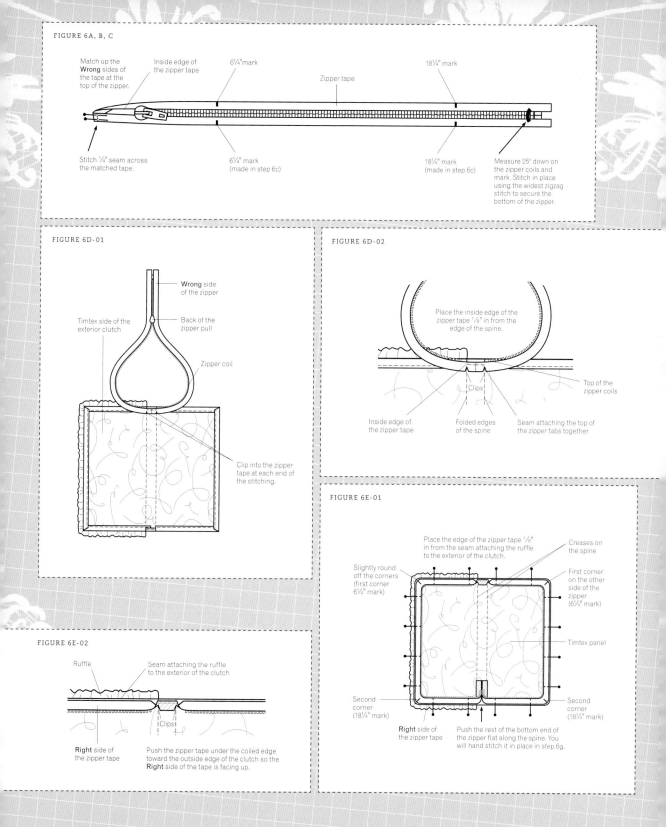

Step 6. Attach the zipper onto the exterior of the clutch. (SEE FIGURE 6A, B, C FOR STEPS a, b, AND c)

a. First, with the zipper in the closed position, match up the **Wrong** sides of the zipper tape at the top of the zipper and pin them in place. Stitch a ¼" seam across the matched ends, backstitching at each end.

b. Measure 25" down on the zipper coils and make a mark. Place your machine to the widest zigzag stitch and stitch in place back and forth across the coils at the mark. Do not hit the zipper coils with your needle.

c. Using your ruler and chalk pencil, starting at the top of the zipper coils, measure down the right side on the zipper tape and make a mark at the following increments: 6¼" and 18¼". Repeat this step to mark the zipper tape on the left side of the coils. (These measurements are where the corners of the clutch will be. It is important that the corners on both the front and back of the clutch turn at the same marks, so the clutch will open correctly.)

d. Unzip the zipper and place the exterior checkbook clutch in the open position with the Timtex side facing up and the ruffled side of the exterior to your left. Center the **Right** side of the sewn-together top of the zipper tape onto the 1" spine, placing the tape ⅛" in from the folded edge, and pin it in place. Attach the top of the zipper by stitching along the inside edge of the tape, across the finished edge on the spine. This will then line up the top of the zipper coils at each of the creases for the spine on the Timtex side of the clutch. Then, using your scissors, clip into the zipper tape at each end of the stitch line to turn the tape **Right** side facing out, making sure not to clip the stitching. (FIGURES 6D-01 AND 6D-02)

e. Flip the zipper down on the Timtex side of the exterior clutch so the **Right** side of the zipper is facing up. Starting on the left side of the clutch (the side with the ruffle attached) on the left side of the clip at the top of the zipper tape, push the zipper tape under the coiled edge toward the outside edge of the clutch so the **Right** side of the tape is facing up. Place the edge of the tape ⅛" in from the seam attaching the ruffle to the exterior of the clutch. Starting at the crease on the spine, pin the tape in place. Turn the zipper tape at the first corner (6¼" mark) slightly rounding the corner, and continue to pin the tape ⅛" in from the seam attaching

the ruffle to the exterior clutch down to the second corner (18¼" mark). Slightly round off the corner and finish pinning the tape across the last side, stopping at the crease for the spine. Then repeat this process for pinning the other side of the zipper ⅛" in from the outside edge on the Timtex side of the back of the clutch. (The corners should turn at the same marks on the front and back of the clutch.) (FIGURES 6E-01 AND 6E-02)

f. Open up the flap on the back of the clutch to keep it out of your way when stitching the zipper in place. With the clutch still in the opened position, starting at the top of the zipper on the Timtex side of the back of the clutch, stitch along the edge on the **Right** side of the zipper tape, starting and stopping at each end of the crease for the spine, backstitching at each end. Now, turn the checkbook clutch and stitch along the edge on the **Right** side of the zipper tape on the ruffled side of the clutch.

g. Push the rest of the bottom end of the zipper flat along the spine, toward the inside of the clutch. Slip stitch* the zipper tape to the Timtex by hand along the spine to secure it in place. (REFER TO FIGURE 6E-01)

See page 171 for an explanation of slip stitching.

h. Now, remove the machine-basting on the front and back of the exterior of the clutch. Set the exterior of the clutch aside. (FIGURE 6H)

Step 7. Measure and mark to make the inside pockets on the lining panel.

a. Center the interfacing panel with the fusible side down onto the **Wrong** side of the lining panel, leaving ¾" of the **Wrong** side of the lining panel showing completely around the interfacing. Follow the manufacturer's instructions to fuse the interfacing onto the lining panel.

b. Starting with the top raw edge of the lining panel on the right side, measure and mark down both side raw edges of the lining panel at the following increments: 6¼", 9¾", 13¾", 17¼", 19¾", 21¾", 24¼", 26¼", 28¾", 30¾", 38½", and 42". (You will be folding the lining panel like an accordion at these measurements.) (FIGURE 7B)

Step 8. Make the credit card pocket compartments.

NOTE: *You will make the credit card pockets first because you will be making smaller compartments from these larger pocket sections.*

a. Starting on the **Right** side of the lining panel, fold the lining **Right** sides together at the 19¾" marks. Press a crease across the folded edge on the **Wrong** side of the lining panel. Topstitch* a ¼" seam across the folded edge on the **Wrong** side of the panel.

* See page 172 for an explanation of topstitching.

b. Then, fold the lining panel **Wrong** sides together at the 21¾" marks. Press a crease across the folded edge on the **Right** side of the lining panel. Topstitch a ¼" seam across the folded edge on the **Right** side of the panel.

c. Follow the instructions in step 8a to fold the lining panel at the 24¼" and 28¾" marks.

d. Follow the instructions in step 8b to fold the lining panel at the 26¼" and 30¾" marks. (FIGURE 8D)

e. Lay the folded panel so the openings of the pockets are facing the top raw edge of the lining panel, and pin the folds in place. Then, machine baste a ½" seam down both sides of the panel to hold the folded pockets in place.

f. To make the credit card pocket compartments, measure across the top finished edge of the first folded pocket and mark the following increments: 4½" and 8½". Then, measure and mark the same increments 3¼" down from the top edge of the first pocket.

g. Using your ruler and chalk pencil, match up the first 2 coordinating marks (4½") and draw a vertical line between them. Repeat this step to match up and draw a vertical line between the second set of marks (8½"). Then, line up the marks for the second set of increments that you made 3¼" down from the top finished edge of the first pocket and draw a horizontal line connecting them across the width of the lining panel. These guidelines are the stitching lines to make the credit card compartments.

h. Starting at the bottom guideline, stitch up both the 4½" and 8½" guidelines to make the credit card compartments, and then stitch across the bottom guideline, backstitching at each end.

Step 9. Fold the lining panel to make the top 2 pockets.

a. Starting on the **Right** side of the lining panel, fold the lining **Right** sides together at the 6¼" marks that you made in step 7b. Press a crease along the folded edge on the **Wrong** side of the lining panel. Topstitch a ¼" seam along the folded edge on the **Wrong** side of the panel.

b. Then, fold the lining panel **Wrong** sides together at the 9¾" marks. Press a crease along the folded edge on the **Right** side of the lining panel. Topstitch a ¼" seam along the folded edge on the **Right** side of the panel.

c. Follow the instructions in step 9a to fold the lining panel at the 13¾" marks.

d. Follow the instructions in step 9b to fold the lining panel at the 17¼" marks.

e. Lay the folded panel so the openings of the pockets are facing the top raw edge of the lining panel and pin the folds in place. Machine baste a ½" seam down both sides of the panel to hold the folded pockets in place.

Step 10. Fold the pockets for the bottom section of the inside of the clutch.

(SEE FIGURE 10 FOR STEPS c, d, AND e)

a. Starting on the **Right** side of the lining panel, fold the lining **Right** sides together at the 38½" marks. Press a crease across the folded edge on the **Wrong** side of the lining panel. Topstitch a ¼" seam across the folded edge on the **Wrong** side of the panel.

b. Then, for the last fold, fold the lining panel **Wrong** sides together at the 42" marks. Press a crease across the folded edge on the **Right** side of the lining panel. Topstitch a ¼" seam across the folded edge on the **Right** side of the panel.

c. Lay the folded lining panel so the openings of the pockets are facing the top of the panel, and pin the folds in place. Machine baste a ½" seam down both sides of the panel to hold the folded pockets in place.

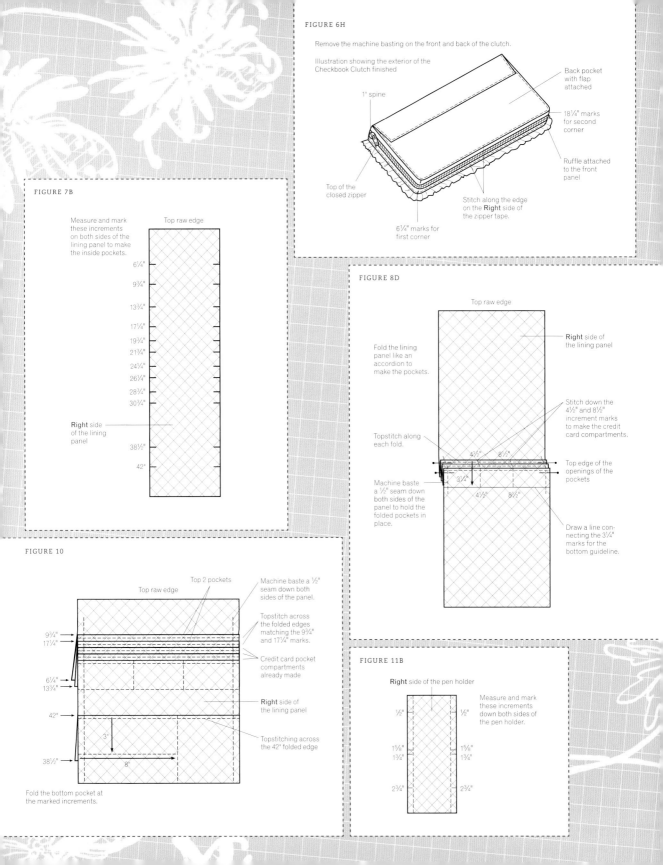

FIGURE 6H

Remove the machine basting on the front and back of the clutch.

Illustration showing the exterior of the Checkbook Clutch finished

1" spine

Back pocket with flap attached

18¼" marks for second corner

Ruffle attached to the front panel

Top of the closed zipper

Stitch along the edge on the **Right** side of the zipper tape.

6¼" marks for first corner

FIGURE 7B

Measure and mark these increments on both sides of the lining panel to make the inside pockets.

Top raw edge

6¼"
9¾"
13¾"
17¼"
19¾"
21¾"
24¼"
26¼"
28¾"
30¾"

Right side of the lining panel

38½"
42"

FIGURE 8D

Top raw edge

Right side of the lining panel

Fold the lining panel like an accordion to make the pockets.

Stitch down the 4½" and 8½" increment marks to make the credit card compartments.

Topstitch along each fold.

Top edge of the openings of the pockets

4½"   8½"

3¼"

Machine baste a ½" seam down both sides of the panel to hold the folded pockets in place.

4½"   8½"

Draw a line connecting the 3¼" marks for the bottom guideline.

FIGURE 10

Top raw edge

Top 2 pockets

Machine baste a ½" seam down both sides of the panel.

Topstitch across the folded edges matching the 9¾" and 17¼" marks.

9¾"
17¼"

Credit card pocket compartments already made

6¼"
13¾"

Right side of the lining panel

42"

3"

38½"

8"

Topstitching across the 42" folded edge

Fold the bottom pocket at the marked increments.

FIGURE 11B

Right side of the pen holder

Measure and mark these increments down both sides of the pen holder.

½"   ½"

1⅝"   1⅝"
1¾"   1¾"

2¾"   2¾"

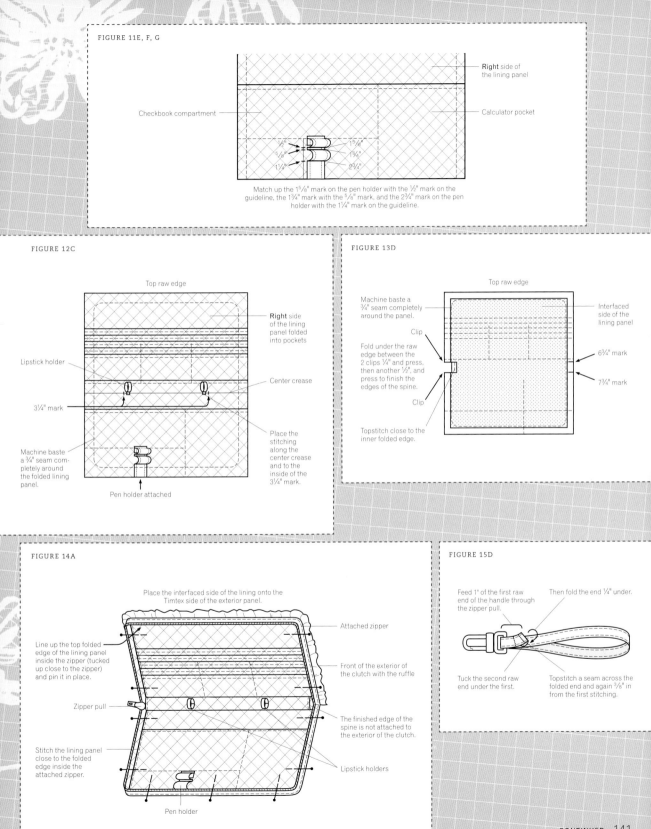

FIGURE 11E, F, G

Right side of the lining panel

Checkbook compartment

Calculator pocket

¹⁄₂" 1⁵⁄₈"
⁵⁄₈" 1³⁄₄"
1¹⁄₄" 2³⁄₄"

Match up the 1⁵⁄₈" mark on the pen holder with the ¹⁄₂" mark on the guideline, the 1³⁄₄" mark with the ⁵⁄₈" mark, and the 2³⁄₄" mark on the pen holder with the 1¹⁄₄" mark on the guideline.

FIGURE 12C

Top raw edge

Right side of the lining panel folded into pockets

Lipstick holder

Center crease

3¹⁄₄" mark

Place the stitching along the center crease and to the inside of the 3¹⁄₄" mark.

Machine baste a ³⁄₄" seam completely around the folded lining panel.

Pen holder attached

FIGURE 13D

Top raw edge

Machine baste a ³⁄₄" seam completely around the panel.

Clip

Fold under the raw edge between the 2 clips ¹⁄₄" and press, then another ¹⁄₂", and press to finish the edges of the spine.

Clip

Topstitch close to the inner folded edge.

Interfaced side of the lining panel

6³⁄₄" mark

7³⁄₄" mark

FIGURE 14A

Place the interfaced side of the lining onto the Timtex side of the exterior panel.

Attached zipper

Line up the top folded edge of the lining panel inside the zipper (tucked up close to the zipper) and pin it in place.

Front of the exterior of the clutch with the ruffle

Zipper pull

The finished edge of the spine is not attached to the exterior of the clutch.

Stitch the lining panel close to the folded edge inside the attached zipper.

Lipstick holders

Pen holder

FIGURE 15D

Feed 1" of the first raw end of the handle through the zipper pull.

Then fold the end ¹⁄₄" under.

Tuck the second raw end under the first.

Topstitch a seam across the folded end and again ³⁄₈" in from the first stitching.

~ CONTINUED

d. To make the compartments for your checkbook and calculator, using your ruler and chalk pencil, measure 8" over from the raw edge on the left side across the top of the last folded edge and make a mark. Move your ruler down along the bottom raw edge and measure 8" over again and make a mark. Line up the 2 marks and draw a guideline from the folded edge to the bottom raw edge of the lining panel. Topstitch down the length of the guideline, backstitching at each end. (FIGURE 10)

e. Then, measure 3" down on the topstitching you just made and make a mark. Then, on the raw edge on the left side, starting at the top finished edge of the last pocket, measure 3" down and make another mark. Draw a guideline connecting the 2 marks from the raw edge on the left side to the topstitching, and topstitch along the guideline, backstitching at each end.

Step 11. Make and attach the holder for the pens.

a. First, fold the pen holder panel in half lengthwise with **Right** sides together. Stitch a ½" seam down the length of the pen holder. Turn the pen holder **Right** side out and press it flat. Topstitch a ½" seam down both long sides of the pen holder, backstitching at each end.

b. Then, on the **Right** side of the pen holder, mark the following increments down both sides of the holder: ½", 1⅝", 1¾", and 2¾". (FIGURE 11B)

c. On the **Right** side of the lining panel, measure and mark 3¾" in from the raw edge on the left side, across the stitch line for the bottom of your checkbook that you made in step 10e, and make a mark. Then measure 3¾" in again across the bottom raw edge and make another mark. Using a ruler and a chalk pencil, line up the 2 marks and draw a line connecting them. This guideline will be used to place the pen holder.

d. Fold the top short end of the pen holder at the ½" mark, back toward the **Wrong** side, and press it in place. Then, place the top folded edge of the pen holder onto the **Right** side of the lining panel, even with the stitching line you made in step 10e and to the inside of the guideline you made in step 11c. Stitch along the folded end at the stitching line, backstitching at each end.

e. Measure down on the guideline you made in step 11c and mark at the following increments: ½", ⅝", and 1¼". Match up the 1⅝" mark on the pen holder with the ½" mark on the lining panel and pin it in place. Stitch across the pen holder at the 1⅝" mark, backstitching at each end. (FIGURE 11E, F, G)

f. Match up the 1¾" mark on the pen holder with the ⅝" mark on the lining panel and pin it in place. Stitch across at the 1¾" mark, backstitching at each end. (FIGURE 11E, F, G)

g. Then, match up the last mark (2¾") on the pen holder with the last mark (1¼") on the lining panel and pin it in place. Stitch across at the matched marks, backstitching at each end. (FIGURE 11E, F, G)

Step 12. Make and attach the lipstick holders to the center of the lining panel.

a. Fold the lining panel in half across the width, matching up the top and bottom raw edges, and gently press a crease. Open up the lining panel. Measure 3¼" in along the center crease from each side raw edge and make a mark.

b. Then, cut a 2¾"-long piece of extra-wide, double-folded bias tape and edge stitch* down both long folded edges of the tape, backstitching at each end. Fold the piece of bias tape in half, matching up the raw ends. Stitch a ¼" seam along the matched raw ends, backstitching at each end.

See page 170 for an explanation of edge stitching.

c. Starting at the mark on the left side you made in step 12a along the center crease on the lining panel, place the first piece of bias tape with the cut ends attached so the stitching is along the center crease and to the inside of the 3¼" mark. Then, pin the bias tape in place. Attach by stitching across the bias tape on the center crease, backstitching at each end. (FIGURE 12C)

d. Follow the instructions in steps 12b and 12c to attach another 2¾"-long piece of bias tape onto the right side of the lining.

Step 13. Finish the outside raw edges on the lining panel.

a. Machine baste a ¾" seam completely around the lining panel, slightly rounding out the 4 outside corners. This will keep the folded pockets in place and act as a guideline to turn under the raw edges. (FIGURE 12C)

b. Using your scissors, trim away any bulk in the seam allowances where the pockets are folded.

c. On the interfacing side of the lining panel, starting at the top left corner, measure down 6¾" and 7¾" along the side raw edge and mark these increments on both the left and right side raw edges. Clip into the seam allowance ¾" at each of these marks on both the right and left sides, making sure not to clip the basting stitch you made in step 13a.

d. On both sides of the lining panel, fold the raw edges ¼" under between the clips and press. Then, fold the edge under another ½" and press. Topstitch across the inner folded edge. (This area will not be stitched to the exterior clutch. This finished edge will fall on the 1" spine of the clutch. It will allow the zipper room between the panels.) (FIGURE 13D)

e. With the interfacing side of the lining panel facing up, fold in the side raw edges at the basting stitch line and press. Pin the raw edges under around the areas where the seam allowance is thicker and will not stay in place, such as at the pocket folds and the 4 corners.

Step 14. Attach the lining onto the inside of the clutch.

a. Open up the exterior part of the clutch and place it with the Timtex side facing up and the front of the exterior clutch (the ruffled edge) at the top. Then, place the top folded edge of the lining panel close to the inside of the zipper on the inside of the exterior part of the clutch and pin it in place. Place the side and bottom folded edges of the lining tucked up close to the inside of the zipper. Pin the rest of the lining in place. The finished edges on the sides of the lining panel will line up with the 1" finished edges on the sides of the exterior part of the clutch. This is the spine on the clutch. (FIGURE 14A)

b. Starting on the left side of the clutch at the top crease for the spine on the clutch, topstitch close to the folded edge, up both sides, and along the top folded edge of the lining panel, stopping at the top crease on the other side for the spine on the clutch and backstitching at each end.

> NOTE: *An alternative to both steps 14b and 14c would be to slip stitch the lining panel in place by hand, which would eliminate a topstitching line that would otherwise show through on the exterior of the clutch.*

c. Open up the flap to keep it out of your way while attaching the lining onto the exterior of the clutch. Starting on the right-hand side of the clutch at the bottom crease for the spine on the clutch, topstitch close to the folded edge, down both sides and along the bottom folded edge of the lining, stopping at the bottom crease on the other side of the spine on the clutch, and backstitching at each end.

Step 15. Make the handle.*

* See page 170 for an explanation of how to make a drawstring (you'll use the same process to make your handle).

a. Fold the handle panel in half lengthwise with **Wrong** sides together, and press a center crease. Then, unfold up the handle.

b. Fold the raw edges in to meet the center crease with the **Wrong** sides together. Then, fold the handle in half again at the center crease, enclosing the raw edges, and press.

c. Topstitch down both sides of the handle, close to the folded edges, backstitching at each end.

d. Fold the finished handle in half across the width, matching up the raw ends. Then, feed 1" of the first raw end of the handle through the zipper pull, folding the handle back, and pin it close to the end of the handle. (FIGURE 15D)

e. Now, tuck the second raw edge under the first end of the handle at the folded edge and pin it in place. Finish the first raw end by folding ¼" under toward the inside of the handle and pin it in place. This will enclose both raw ends of the handle.

f. Stitch a seam across the folded edge on the first end of the handle and again ⅜" in from the first stitching toward the zipper pull, backstitching at each end of these 2 seams. Attach the handle to the zipper pull by clipping the clasp through the hole on the end of your zipper pull, and you have a handle for your Fashion Checkbook Clutch.

CHAPTER 6

PERSONAL STYLE

Projects

It's the accessories that make the outfit. And you *always* need new accessories to express your ever-changing preferences and moods. Here's a bunch of fabulous ways to spice up your wardrobe. We all love handbags, and there's something for everyone in this chapter—a clutch bag with fabric flower for dressing up, a leather-handled shoulder bag for busy days on the go, and a funky patchwork handbag for anytime—all create different style impressions depending on your distinctive fabric choices. You can also accent your look with the beaded sash. You'll turn heads wherever you go.

CLUTCH HANDBAG WITH FABRIC FLOWER

FINISHED SIZE: 17½" WIDE X 7" TALL

With its lovely fabric flower, this elegant evening clutch (see photo, page 145) can double as a daytime run-around bag. It's wonderfully versatile—you can make it in black for evening, gray for business, or a flouncy floral print for a springtime garden party.

FABRICS

- ½ yard (54"-wide) home-decor-weight cotton for the exterior and fabric flower
- ½ yard (44"-wide) light- to mid-weight coordinating cotton for the lining and divider
- ¾ yard (60"-wide) cotton batting
- ¼ yard (22"-wide) Timtex* or other extra-heavy interfacing
- 2¾" (¾"-wide) sew-on Velcro

* See page 172 for an explanation of Timtex.

OTHER SUPPLIES

- Coordinating thread
- Scissors
- Yardstick or ruler
- Chalk pencil or fabric marker
- Straight pins
- Turning tool (such as a closed pair of scissors)
- Hand sewing needle
- Hot glue gun and glue

NOTES

- All seams are ½" unless otherwise stated. (The ½" seam allowance is included in all cutting measurements and the pattern pieces.)
- Preshrink your fabric by washing, drying, and pressing it before starting your project. To wash Timtex after completing your project, machine wash warm, then reshape your project and air dry. Your project will press back into shape with a steam iron. Once you steam the project, support it with wadded-up tissue paper or a folded towel while air drying in order to keep the shape that you want.

Step 1. Cut out all pieces from the fabric.

a. First, cut out the Clutch Handbag pattern pieces provided in the pocket at the front of this book.

- *Main panel*
- *Tab closure*
- *Lining/divider panel*

b. Pin the pattern pieces to the fabric according to the instructions below. Then, using your scissors, cut the fabric according to the outlines on the pattern pieces, in the quantities given below.

FROM THE FABRIC FOR THE EXTERIOR

- *Cut 2 main panels on the fold:* Use the main panel pattern piece provided in the pocket at the front of this book.*
- *Cut 2 tab closures: Use the tab closure pattern piece provided in the pocket at the front of this book.*
- *Cut 1 fabric flower strip: 4" wide x 38" long (Measure across the width of your fabric and mark these dimensions directly onto the Wrong side of the fabric, using a yardstick and a chalk pencil. Then, using your scissors, cut out the panel following the marked lines.)*

FROM THE FABRIC FOR THE LINING

- *Cut 2 lining panels on the fold:* Use the entire lining/divider panel pattern piece provided in the pocket at the front of this book.*
- *Cut 2 divider panels on the fold:* Use the lining/divider pattern piece, first folding it down at the guideline.*

FROM THE BATTING

- *Cut 4 main panels on the fold:* Use the main panel pattern piece.*
- *Cut 2 tab closures: Use the tab closure pattern piece.*

FROM THE TIMTEX

- *Cut 1 divider panel on the fold:* Use the lining/divider pattern piece, first folding it down at the guideline.*

  ** To cut your pattern piece on the fold of your fabric, first fold the fabric with **Wrong** sides together and the selvage edges aligned. Then lay your pattern piece so that the edge to be cut on the fold is even with the folded edge of your fabric. Once the piece is cut out, open it up to make one full panel.*

Step 2: Attach the batting and Timtex to the main panels, tabs, and divider panel.

a. Place 2 batting main panels onto the **Wrong** side of the first exterior main panel, matching up the raw edges, and pin the batting in place. Then, machine baste* a ⅜" seam completely around the batting on the main panel.

* See page 171 for an explanation of machine basting.

b. Using your scissors, trim the batting in the seam allowance close to the basting stitch to help reduce bulk in the seams.

c. Follow the instructions in steps 2a and 2b to attach the other 2 batting main panels onto the other exterior main panel.

d. Follow the instructions in steps 2a and 2b to attach one piece of batting onto the **Wrong** side of each of the tab closures.

e. Place the Timtex divider panel onto the **Wrong** side of the first divider panel and pin it in place. Then, machine baste a ½" seam completely around the Timtex panel.

f. Using your scissors, trim the Timtex only in the seam allowance close to the basting stitch to help reduce bulk in the seams.

Step 3. Attach the Velcro to the front main panel and one of the tab closures.

a. First, fold the front main panel in half lengthwise, **Right** sides together, matching up the side raw edges, and gently press a center crease for use in centering the Velcro. Then, open up the front main panel and, using your ruler and chalk pencil, measure 2¼" down from the top raw edge along the center crease and make a mark. Center a 2¾" piece of the male half of the Velcro over the center crease and below the 2¼" mark and pin it in place. Attach it by stitching completely around the edge of the Velcro, backstitching at each end. (FIGURE 3A)

Set the main panel aside.

b. Fold one of the tab closures in half lengthwise, with **Right** sides together, matching up the side raw edges. Gently press a crease to use for centering the Velcro. Then, open up the tab closure and, using a yardstick and a chalk pencil, measure ¾" up from the bottom raw edge on the center crease and make a mark. Center a 2¾" piece of the female half of the Velcro over the center crease and above the ¾" mark and pin it in place. Attach it by stitching completely around the edge of the Velcro, backstitching at each end. This is now the tab closure lining. (FIGURE 3B)

Step 4. Make and attach the tab closure.

a. Place the tab closure and the tab closure lining **Right** sides together, matching up the raw edges, and pin them in place. Attach them by stitching a ½" seam down both sides and around the bottom raw edges, leaving the long top edge open.

b. Using your scissors, trim the seam allowance* to ¼" around the outside curved edges of the tab closure. Clip into the seam allowance* around the inside curved edges, making sure not to clip your stitching. This will allow the curves to turn neatly.

* See pages 172 and 170 for explanations of trimming and clipping the seam allowance.

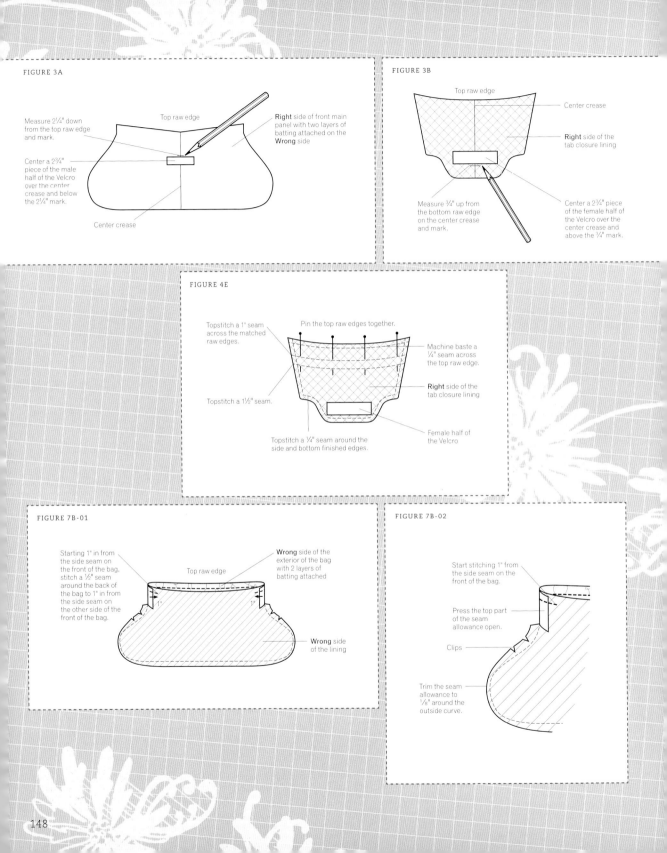

FIGURE 3A

Top raw edge

Measure 2¼" down from the top raw edge and mark.

Right side of front main panel with two layers of batting attached on the **Wrong** side

Center a 2¾" piece of the male half of the Velcro over the center crease and below the 2¼" mark.

Center crease

FIGURE 3B

Top raw edge

Center crease

Right side of the tab closure lining

Measure ¾" up from the bottom raw edge on the center crease and mark.

Center a 2¾" piece of the female half of the Velcro over the center crease and above the ¾" mark.

FIGURE 4E

Topstitch a 1" seam across the matched raw edges.

Pin the top raw edges together.

Machine baste a ¼" seam across the top raw edge.

Right side of the tab closure lining

Topstitch a 1½" seam.

Topstitch a ¼" seam around the side and bottom finished edges.

Female half of the Velcro

FIGURE 7B-01

Starting 1" in from the side seam on the front of the bag, stitch a ½" seam around the back of the bag to 1" in from the side seam on the other side of the front of the bag.

Top raw edge

Wrong side of the exterior of the bag with 2 layers of batting attached

1"   1"

Wrong side of the lining

FIGURE 7B-02

Start stitching 1" from the side seam on the front of the bag.

Press the top part of the seam allowance open.

Clips

Trim the seam allowance to ⅛" around the outside curve.

c. Turn the tab closure **Right** side out using a turning tool*
to push out the curves on the tab. Press the tab flat.

* See page 172 for an explanation of a turning tool.

d. Pin the top raw edges on the tab closure and the tab
closure lining together, then machine baste a ¼" seam
across the matched raw edges. Topstitch* across the tab
closure 1" in from the matched raw edges and then again
1½" down, backstitching at each end.

* See page 172 for an explanation of topstitching.

e. Then, topstitch a ¼" seam around the outside finished
edges of the tab closure, backstitching at each end.
(FIGURE 4E)

f. Next, find the center of the back main panel by folding
the panel in half lengthwise, with **Right** sides together,
matching up the side raw edges. Gently press a center
crease to use in centering the tab closure onto the top of
the back main panel.

g. Place the **Right** sides of the exterior tab closure (the
side without the Velcro attached) and the back main panel
together, matching up the center crease and the top raw
edges on the each panel, and pin them in place. Then,
machine baste a ¼" seam across the top raw edges.

Step 5. Attach the exterior front and back main panels together.

a. Place the **Right** sides of the front and back main panels
together, matching up the side and bottom raw edges, and
pin them in place. Starting on the right side of the panels,
½" down from the top raw edge, stitch a ½" seam down both
sides and along the bottom raw edges, stopping ½" down
from the left-hand top raw edge, backstitching at each end.

b. Using your scissors, trim the seam allowances to ⅛"
around the outside curved edges of the exterior main panels
and press the top part of the side seam allowances open.
(You may find it difficult to maneuver the panels to press
the seam allowances, so use the tip of your iron and press
a little bit at a time.)

Set the exterior of the bag aside.

Step 6. Make and attach the divider to the lining panels.

a. Place the **Right** sides of the divider panels together (one
panel has the Timtex already attached), matching up the
top raw edges, and pin them in place. Attach the divider
panels by stitching a ½" seam across the top raw edges,
backstitching at each end.

b. Turn the divider panel **Right** side out and press along the
top finished edge. Topstitch across the top finished edge
of the divider with a ¼" seam, backstitching at each end.

c. Match up the side and bottom raw edges of the divider
and pin them in place. Then, machine baste a ¼" seam
down both sides and across the bottom raw edges to hold
the panels together.

d. Now, sandwich the divider in between the **Right** sides
of the lining panels, matching up the side and bottom raw
edges, and pin them in place.

e. Starting on the right side of the panels, ½" down from
the top raw edge, stitch a ½" seam down both sides and
across the bottom raw edges, stopping ½" down from the
top raw edge on the left side, backstitching at each end.

f. Using your scissors, trim the seam allowances to ⅛"
around the outside curved edges and clip into the seam
allowance along the inside curves. Then press the top part
of the side seam allowances open. (You may find it difficult
to maneuver the panels to press the seam allowances, so
use the tip of your iron and press a little bit at a time.)

Step 7. Attach the lining to the exterior of the clutch.

a. With the **Right** side of the exterior facing out, you'll need to fold the sides in and the bottom of the bag up to allow room to fit the exterior of the bag inside the lining. Then, with the **Wrong** side of the lining facing out, slip the lining over the exterior of the clutch, matching up the side seams, and pin the exterior to the lining around the top raw edges. (The tab closure is tucked down in between the panels.)

b. Starting 1" in from the side seam on the front of the bag, stitch the top raw edge across the back of the clutch with a ½" seam, stopping on the front of the bag, 1" in from the side seam on the other side of the front of the clutch, back-stitching at each end. This will leave a front section on the front of the bag open, which will allow you to turn the bag **Right** side out. (FIGURE 7B-01 AND 7B-02)

c. Turn the bag **Right** side out by pulling the exterior and lining through the front opening. Place the lining down inside the exterior, using a turning tool to push the bottom corners of the lining into the corners of the exterior clutch, and press. (Your bag will be stiff with the Timtex inside the divider.) (FIGURE 7C, D)

d. Fold the top raw edges in ½" along the front of the clutch, and then pin the opening closed. Topstitch with a ⅛" seam completely around the top finished edge of the clutch to close the opening. (FIGURE 7C, D)

Step 8. Make the fabric flower.

a. First, fold the fabric flower strip in half lengthwise with **Wrong** sides together and press a crease along the folded edge.

b. Then, fold the one raw end of the strip to form a triangle, matching the raw end with the matched raw edges, and pin it in place. Repeat this step to make a triangle on the other end of the fabric flower strip. (FIGURE 8B)

c. Machine baste a long, loose ½" seam across the matched raw edges of the fabric flower strip, leaving about 6" of thread on each end of the strip to be used to gather in the strip.

d. Gather* the strip by pulling the bobbin thread a little at a time, moving the gathers in toward the center of the strip. Draw the strip in to measure 18" in length, making the gathers evenly spaced. The tighter you draw in the strip, the more open your flower will look.

See page 171 for an explanation of gathering.

e. Start rolling one end of the gathered fabric strip, keeping the raw edges together. Begin slip stitching* along the base of the coiled flower by hand to secure the flower. Roll the strip all the way to the other end, slip stitching along the base as you go to keep the base secure. Tie off the end of your thread by stitching a couple times in the same place, and then cut the thread to free your needle. (FIGURES 8E-01 AND 8E-02)

See page 171 for an explanation of slip stitching.

f. Place the flower upside down and use your iron to steam across the bottom raw edges of the flower. This will squash the flower to help spread out the petals and give the flower some shape. Turn the flower over and, using your fingers, spread the flower petals open.

g. Using a hot glue gun, attach the flower to the outside of your clutch, following the placement mark on your main panel pattern piece. Hold the flower in place for just a moment while the hot glue cools and sets.

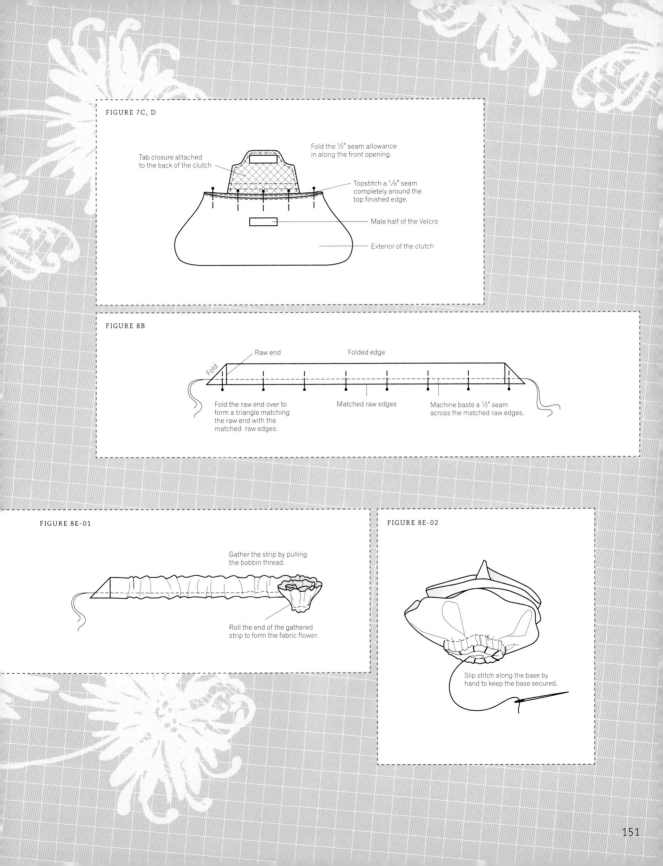

FIGURE 7C, D

Tab closure attached to the back of the clutch

Fold the ½" seam allowance in along the front opening.

Topstitch a ⅛" seam completely around the top finished edge.

Male half of the Velcro

Exterior of the clutch

FIGURE 8B

Fold

Raw end

Folded edge

Fold the raw end over to form a triangle matching the raw end with the matched raw edges.

Matched raw edges

Machine baste a ½" seam across the matched raw edges.

FIGURE 8E-01

Gather the strip by pulling the bobbin thread.

Roll the end of the gathered strip to form the fabric flower.

FIGURE 8E-02

Slip stitch along the base by hand to keep the base secured.

SASH WITH BEADED FRINGE

FINISHED SIZE: 5½" WIDE X 59" LONG

You can use this adorable sash in so many ways! Used as a belt, it makes boring old blue jeans suddenly chic. Worn as a neck scarf, it adds elegance to a plain sweater. Bad hair day? It works as a beautiful head scarf as well. And it makes a simple and quick sewing project that's perfect for gift giving. It's a fashion emergency staple!

FABRICS

- 1⅜ yards (44"-wide) light- to mid-weight cotton for the sash
- ½ yard (1"-wide) decorative beaded trim

OTHER SUPPLIES

- Coordinating thread
- Scissors
- Straight pins
- Yardstick
- Chalk pencil or fabric marker
- Zipper foot
- Turning tool (such as a closed pair of scissors)
- Hand sewing needle

NOTES

- All seams are ½" unless other-wise stated. (The ½" seam allow-ance is included in all cutting measurements and the pattern pieces.)
- Preshrink your fabric by washing, drying, and pressing it before starting your project.

Step 1. Cut out the pattern pieces.

First, cut out the Sash pattern pieces provided in the pocket at the front of this book.

- *Sash right end*
- *Sash left end*

Step 2. Measure and mark the sash onto your fabric.

a. First, open up your piece of fabric. Fold it with the **Right** sides together on the bias of the fabric.* Do this by match-ing one of the selvage edges* with one of the cut edges to make a triangle shape. Press the folded edge and then pin along the fold to keep the fabric from slipping. (FIGURE 2A)

* *See pages 170 and 171 for explanations of bias fold and selvage edge.*

NOTE: *The sash right and left end pattern pieces are provided. You will be measuring the length of the sash directly onto your fabric and then using the pattern pieces to make the point for each end of the Sash with Beaded Fringe.*

b. Place the sash's left end pattern piece with the top edge on the fold of the fabric and pin the pattern piece in place.

c. Then, starting on the folded edge at the dotted line on the pattern piece, using a yardstick and a chalk pencil, measure over 47" and make a mark. Take the sash's right end pattern piece and place the top edge on the fold of the fabric, matching up the dotted line on the pattern piece so it's even with the mark you just made, and pin this pattern piece in place.

~ CONTINUED

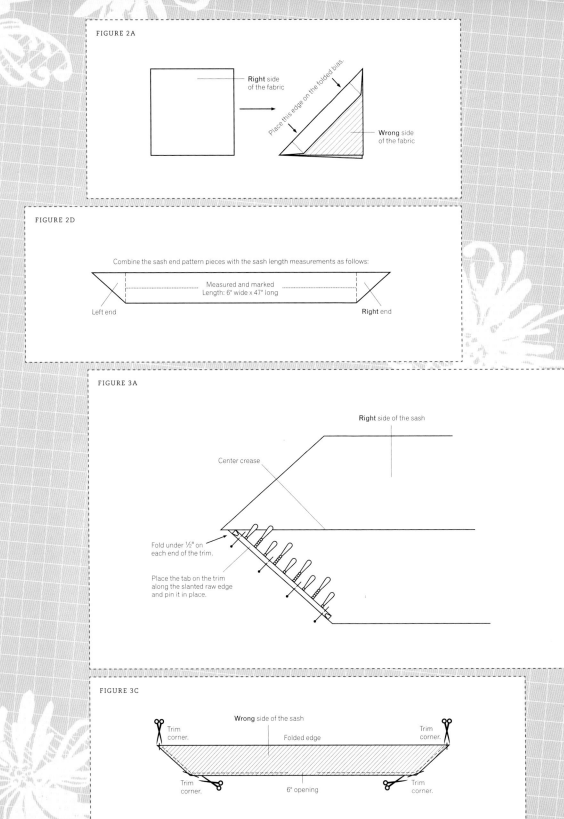

FIGURE 2A

Right side of the fabric

Place this edge on the folded bias.

Wrong side of the fabric

FIGURE 2D

Combine the sash end pattern pieces with the sash length measurements as follows:

Measured and marked
Length: 6" wide x 47" long

Left end

Right end

FIGURE 3A

Right side of the sash

Center crease

Fold under ½" on each end of the trim.

Place the tab on the trim along the slanted raw edge and pin it in place.

FIGURE 3C

Wrong side of the sash

Trim corner.

Folded edge

Trim corner.

Trim corner.

6" opening

Trim corner.

d. Now, using your yardstick, match up the bottom end of the dotted line on the left end pattern piece with the bottom end of the dotted line on the right end pattern pieces. Using your chalk pencil, mark down the side of your yardstick, lining up both ends. (You will have to move your yardstick to finish drawing the line.) Pin the fabric together inside the guideline you made between the pattern pieces at each end of the sash. The marked sash is 6" wide x 47" long. (FIGURE 2D)

e. Cut the sash out along the end of the pattern piece and along the chalk guideline you made in step 2d. Do not cut along the dotted line or on the folded edge of the fabric.

f. Carefully remove the pattern pieces and pins.

Step 3. Make the sash.

a. First, open up the sash panel and place it with the **Right** side facing up. Then, cut a 9" piece of beaded trim. Fold the tab section of the trim ½" in on each end and pin the folded ends in place. Starting on the left end of the sash, place the trim below the center crease (folded bias edge) and along the raw edge on the slanted side, with the beaded trim facing inside the panel. The other folded end of the trim will stop ½" in from the long side raw edge. Pin the trim in place. Using the zipper foot on your machine, stitch across the tab close to the inside edge, backstitching at each end. Repeat this step to cut and attach another 9" piece of beaded trim to the end on the right side of your sash. (FIGURE 3A)

b. Fold the sash panel in half lengthwise with **Wrong** sides together, matching up the raw edges on the long sides and each of the slanted sides. Tuck the beaded trim inside the sash and pin the raw edges in place. Starting at the folded edge on the sash, stitch a ½" seam across both slanted ends and down the long side, leaving a 6" opening in the center of the long side raw edge, backstitching at each end.

c. Using your scissors, trim in the seam allowance* at the 2 pointed ends and at the angled corners at each end of the sash, making sure not to clip the stitching. (FIGURE 3C)

See page 172 for an explanation of trimming in the seam allowance.

d. Pull the **Right** side of the sash through the 6" opening, using a turning tool* to push out the corners of the sash, and press.

See page 172 for an explanation of a turning tool.

e. Then, turn under the raw edges of the opening, press, and pin the opening closed. Slip stitch the opening closed by hand and press your sash flat.

See page 171 for an explanation of slip stitching.

SIMPLE LEATHER-HANDLED SHOULDER BAG

FINISHED SIZE: 12¾" WIDE X 15¼" LONG (EXCLUDING HANDLES)

Here's another simple project with very high style points. Its organic shape makes for a kinetic bag that really shows off your favorite fabric. This will be the one you carry everywhere.

FABRICS

- 1 yard (44"- or 60"-wide) sturdy cotton fabric
- 2 (½" x 32") leather strips

OTHER SUPPLIES

- Coordinating thread
- Button/carpet thread, any color
- Yardstick or ruler
- Chalk pencil or fabric marker
- Scissors
- Straight pins
- Turning tool (such as a closed pair of scissors)
- Leather hand sewing needle (size 3)
- Thimble
- Masking tape (optional)

NOTES

- All seams are ½" unless otherwise stated. (The ½" seam allowance is included in all cutting measurements provided.)
- Preshrink your fabric by washing, drying, and pressing it before starting your project.

Step 1. Cut out all pieces from the fabric.

First, fold your fabric, **Right** sides together, matching the selvage edges,* and place it on a hard, flat surface with the folded edge toward you. Measure and mark the dimensions below directly onto the **Wrong** side of the fabric, using a yardstick and a chalk pencil. Then, using your scissors to cut through both layers, cut out the panels following the marked lines.

- Cut 2 bag panels: 14˝ wide x 32˝ long

* See page 171 for an explanation of a selvage edge.

Step 2. Prepare the panels for stitching.

a. Place the bag panels with the **Right** sides together on a hard, flat surface.

b. Using your yardstick or ruler, measure in from the top left, short, raw edge 11" and make a mark with your chalk pencil on the long raw edge. Now, repeat this step to measure in 11" from the bottom left, top right, and bottom right short, raw edges. You will have made 4 marks in all.

c. Now, beginning at the top right corner, pin the bag panels together along one of the long raw edges, stopping at the first 11" mark. Begin pinning again at the second 11" mark and pin the remainder of the long raw edge. Do not pin between the 11" marks. (FIGURE 2C, D, E)

d. Pin the bag panels together at the short raw edge on the left side. (FIGURE 2C, D, E)

e. Then, pin the second long raw edge together in the same manner as the first, but leave the short raw edge on the right side open. Your bag panels will have a 10" opening at the center of each long raw edge. (FIGURE 2C, D, E)

Step 3. Stitch the panels together and make the bag.

a. First, stitch the panels together with a ½" seam along the pinned raw edges, backstitching at each end. Leave the 10" opening at the center of each long raw edge unstitched and leave the short raw edge on the right side open.

b. Press the seams open. One way to do this is to lay the attached bag panels flat on your ironing board, and, while leaving the bottom panel flat against the board, pull back the seam allowance on the top panel, flatten it against the **Wrong** side of the top bag panel, and press.

– CONTINUED

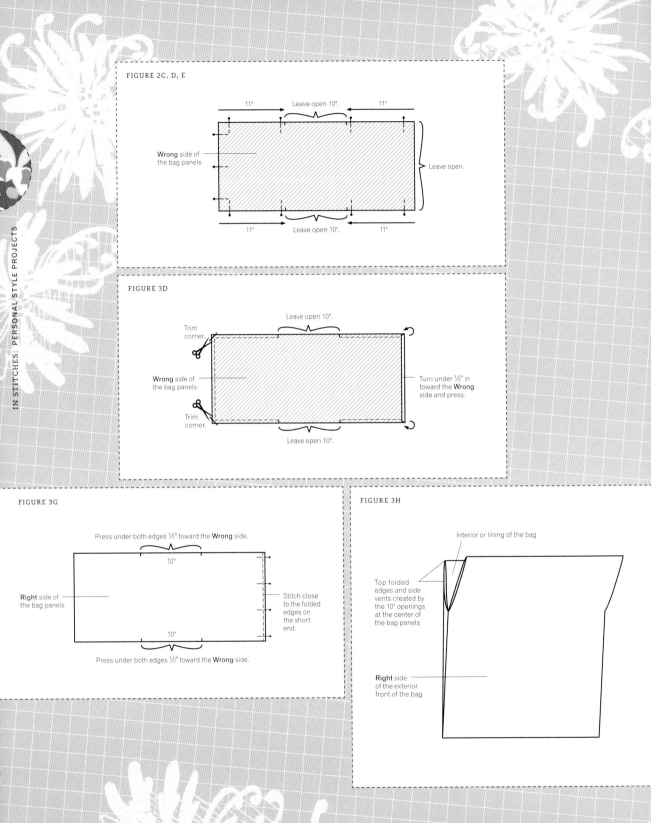

FIGURE 2C, D, E

11"   Leave open 10".   11"

Wrong side of
the bag panels

Leave open.

11"   Leave open 10".   11"

FIGURE 3D

Leave open 10".

Trim
corner.

Wrong side of
the bag panels

Turn under ½" in
toward the Wrong
side and press.

Trim
corner.

Leave open 10".

FIGURE 3G

Press under both edges ½" toward the Wrong side.

10"

Right side of
the bag panels

Stitch close
to the folded
edges on
the short
end.

10"

Press under both edges ½" toward the Wrong side.

FIGURE 3H

Interior or lining of the bag

Top folded
edges and side
vents created by
the 10" openings
at the center of
the bag panels

Right side
of the exterior
front of the bag

c. Trim the corners on the stitched short edge, making sure not to cut into the stitching line.

d. Then, turn the 2 raw edges of the short, unstitched edge ½" in toward the **Wrong** side of the fabric and press. (FIGURE 3D)

e. Turn the bag panels **Right** side out by pulling them through the open short end, and use a turning tool* to push out the corners.

See page 172 for an explanation of a turning tool.

f. Now, turn each edge of both 10" unstitched sections ½" toward the **Wrong** side and press.

g. Pin the folded edges on the short unstitched edge together and stitch close to the folded edges to close the end of the bag panels. (FIGURE 3G)

h. Then, take the short end that you just stitched and push it down inside the opposite short end of the bag panel until the 2 short ends meet, creating an outer bag and a lining. The short ends of the bag panels will become the bottom seams and the 10" unstitched openings will create 2 separate top folded edges connected at the side seams. These will become the casing and the side vents of the finished bag. (FIGURE 3H)

Step 4. Finish the top edges of the bag and make the casing for the leather handles.

a. First, match the bottom and side seams of the bag and the lining. Press the top folded edges of the bag flat, making a nice, crisp edge.

b. Then, using your ruler and chalk pencil, measure down from one top folded edge 1¼" and make a mark. Move the ruler across the top edge and measure down 1¼" again and make another mark. Use your ruler to connect the marks and draw a line from one side edge to the other side edge.

c. Follow the instructions in step 4b to measure and mark the other top edge of the bag.

d. Now, pin the bag and lining together along the marked lines, making sure to keep the front bag and lining pinned separately from the back bag and lining. (FIGURE 4D)

e. Then, stitch along the drawn line on each of the top edges, backstitching at each end. This stitching line creates the casing for the leather handles.

f. Now, pin the folded edges along the side vents from the stitching line at the casing down to the point where the side seam begins. (FIGURE 4F)

g. Stitch close to the folded edges, beginning at the stitching line for the casing. Stitch to a point just below where the side seam begins. Leaving your needle in the down position, lift the presser foot and turn the bag. Stitch straight across the side seam. Again, with the needle in the down position, lift the presser foot and turn the bag. Continue to stitch up the other side of the first vent, close to the folded edge, stitching until you reach the stitching line for the casing. Backstitch at each end of your stitching.

h. Follow the instructions in steps 4f and 4g to stitch the second side vent. (FIGURE 4H)

Step 5. Insert and finish the leather handles.

a. First, insert one of the ½" x 32" lengths of leather into the casing on one side of the bag. Slide the leather through the casing and out the opposite end.

b. Then, being careful not to twist the leather, overlap the ends of the leather ½". Stitch the ends of the handle together with button/carpet thread and a leather hand sewing needle, protecting your fingers with a thimble.

NOTE: *You may find it helpful to secure the ends of the leather with a small piece of masking tape to avoid slipping while you are stitching. Remove the masking tape when you are finished.*

c. Follow the instructions in steps 5a and 5b to insert and finish the second leather handle.

d. Slide the leather handles so that the joined ends are hidden inside the casing of the bag, and gently gather the top edges of the bag along the leather handles.

~ CONTINUED

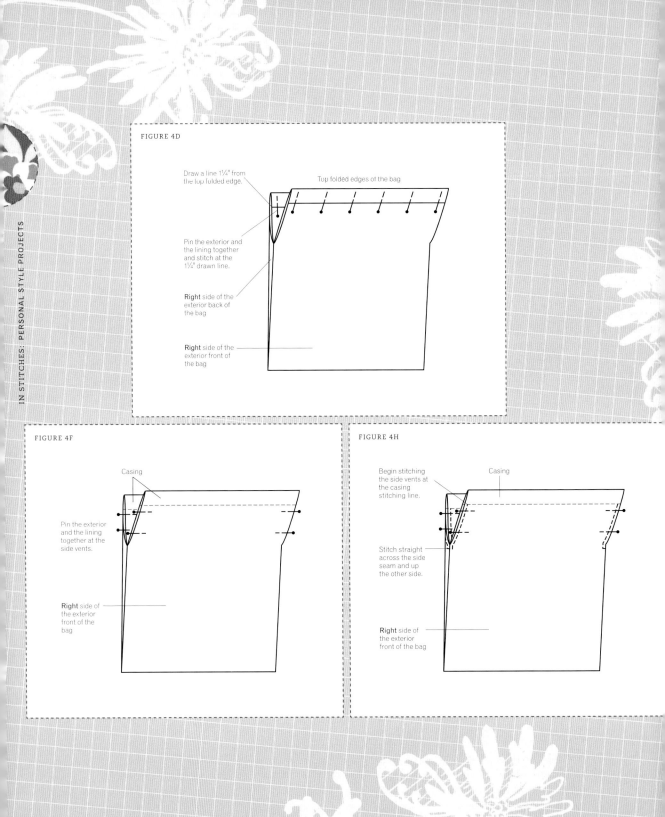

FIGURE 4D

Draw a line 1¼" from the top folded edge.

Top folded edges of the bag

Pin the exterior and the lining together and stitch at the 1¼" drawn line.

Right side of the exterior back of the bag

Right side of the exterior front of the bag

FIGURE 4F

Casing

Pin the exterior and the lining together at the side vents.

Right side of the exterior front of the bag

FIGURE 4H

Begin stitching the side vents at the casing stitching line.

Casing

Stitch straight across the side seam and up the other side.

Right side of the exterior front of the bag

PATCHWORK HANDBAG WITH ZIPPER CHARM

FINISHED SIZE: 5" TALL X 5" WIDE X 15" LONG (EXCLUDING HANDLES)

Funky and practical, this modern, boxy bag will hold it all and is great for everyday use. Its appeal comes from the unique patchwork design, which features heavyweight fabric for great shape support and sturdiness. And the zipper pull gives this stylish bag an added dose of charm!

FABRICS

- 1 yard (44"- or 60"-wide) heavyweight cotton fabric for the top, ends, bottom, and handles
- Small pieces of coordinating heavyweight cotton fabric for the patchwork side panels (enough to complete a patchwork panel measuring 18" wide x 15" long)
- ¾ yard (44"-wide) light- to mid-weight cotton fabric for the lining
- ¼ yard heavyweight fusible interfacing for the handles
- ¾ yard (44"-wide) light- to mid-weight cotton or muslin for the backing of the patchwork panel

- 1 package (34" x 45") cotton batting
- 6" (1mm- or 1½mm-wide) leather string, for the zipper charm

OTHER SUPPLIES

- Coordinating thread
- 20" to 22" coordinating nylon zipper
- Polyfill for the zipper charm
- Yardstick or ruler
- Chalk pencil or fabric marker
- Scissors
- Straight pins
- 1"-wide masking tape

- Zipper foot
- Hand sewing needle
- Turning tool (such as a closed pair of scissors)
- 4¾" x 14¾" piece heavy cardboard

NOTES

- All seams are ½" unless otherwise stated. (The ½" seam allowance is included in all pattern pieces and cutting measurements.)
- Preshrink your fabric by washing, drying, and pressing it before starting your project.

Step 1. Cut out all pieces from the fabric.

a. Measure and mark the dimensions below directly onto the **Wrong** side of the fabric, using a yardstick and a chalk pencil. Then, using your scissors, cut out each panel following the marked lines.

FROM THE FABRIC FOR THE TOP, ENDS, BOTTOM, AND HANDLES

- *Cut 2 top panels: 3 ½" wide x 20" long*
- *Cut 2 end panels: 4" wide x 6" long*
- *Cut 1 bottom panel: 6" wide x 16" long*
- *Cut 2 handles: 2" wide x 21" long*

FROM THE FABRIC FOR THE LINING

- *Cut 3 panels (sides and bottom): 6" wide x 16" long*
- *Cut 2 end panels: 4" wide x 6" long*
- *Cut 2 top panels: 3 ½" wide x 20" long*
- *Cut 2 bottom sleeve panels: 5¾" wide x 15¾" long*

FROM THE FUSIBLE INTERFACING

- *Cut 2 handles: 2" wide x 21" long*

FROM THE FABRIC FOR THE BACKING

- *Cut 1 bottom panel: 6" wide x 16" long*
- *Cut 2 end panels: 4" wide x 6" long*
- *Cut 1 patchwork side panel: 15" wide x 18" long*

FROM THE BATTING

- *Cut 1 bottom panel: 6" wide x 16" long*
- *Cut 2 top panels: 3½" wide x 20" long*
- *Cut 2 end panels: 4" wide x 6" long*
- *Cut 1 patchwork side panel: 15" wide x 18" long*

~ CONTINUED

b. In order to keep your pieces organized, mark each piece by writing the name on a piece of masking tape and attaching to the **Wrong** side of each panel as it is cut.

Step 2. Make the patchwork panels for the sides of the bag. (FIGURE 2)

NOTE: *You will find it helpful to lay your fabric pieces in place before beginning to stitch, so that you can see what the finished panel will look like and arrange the pieces to achieve the most pleasing pattern.*

NOTE: *FIGURE 2 shows the dimensions of each patchwork piece used to make our sample. This is meant only as a guide. You may wish to follow our layout or create your own. Each side of our sample bag has a different patchwork pattern. The measurements and location for each piece are given, and the patchwork design is shown after the 2 side panels have been cut from the 18" wide x 15" long patchwork piece made in step 2a. The measurements are given with the width listed first and the height listed second. The ¼" seam allowance is included in the measurements listed.*

a. Using the coordinating pieces of fabric, piece together various squares and rectangles in a pleasing pattern. Stitch these pieces together using a ¼" seam and press each seam down toward the bottom of the panel before moving on to the next seam. You will need to create a patchwork panel measuring 15" wide x 18" long.

b. Next, place the backing fabric piece for the patchwork side panel on a hard, flat surface with the **Right** side facing down. Then, layer the batting piece for the patchwork side panel on top of the backing, and place the 15" x 18" patchwork piece on top of the batting with the **Right** side facing up. This creates a "sandwich" of fabric, which will be quilted to make the 2 side panels.

c. Pin the layers together.

d. Now, using the side of your presser foot as a guide, stitch along one long (18") edge of the fabric sandwich.

e. Then, place a 20" strip of masking tape so that the edge of the masking tape is next to the first stitching line. Stitch close to the edge of the tape, creating a 1" channel between the quilting lines.

f. Continue to move the tape and stitch lengthwise channels 1" apart until the entire 15" x 18" panel is quilted in parallel lines. (FIGURE 2F)

NOTE: *The illustration shows a general overview of the patchwork pieces and how to place the masking tape to quilt the channels. The patchwork pieces in this illustration are random.*

g. Now, using a yardstick and a chalk pencil, measure and mark 2 panels, each measuring 6" wide x 16" long, onto the 15" x 18" quilted panel. Be sure to cut the panels lengthwise so that the quilting lines are parallel to the 16"- long edge.

h. Use your scissors to cut both 6" x 16" quilted side panels, and set them aside. (FIGURE 2H)

Step 3. Layer and quilt the top, ends, and bottom panels.

a. Following the instructions in step 2b, layer the backing, batting, and exterior fabrics for the top panels, the end panels, and the bottom panel, making sure that the **Right** side of the backing and the exterior fabrics are facing away from the batting.

NOTE: *You will use the lining fabric as the backing on the top panels, because it will be visible after the bag is completed. All other panels may be backed with muslin or another backing fabric.*

b. Following the instructions in steps 2c, 2d, and 2e, use the masking tape to quilt lengthwise lines 1" apart on all the fabric panels. Make sure to quilt lengthwise. (Refer to the cutting measurements to be certain of the lengthwise direction.)

FIGURE 2

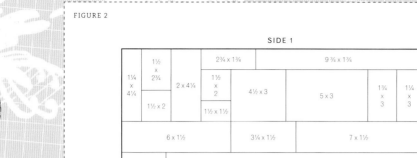

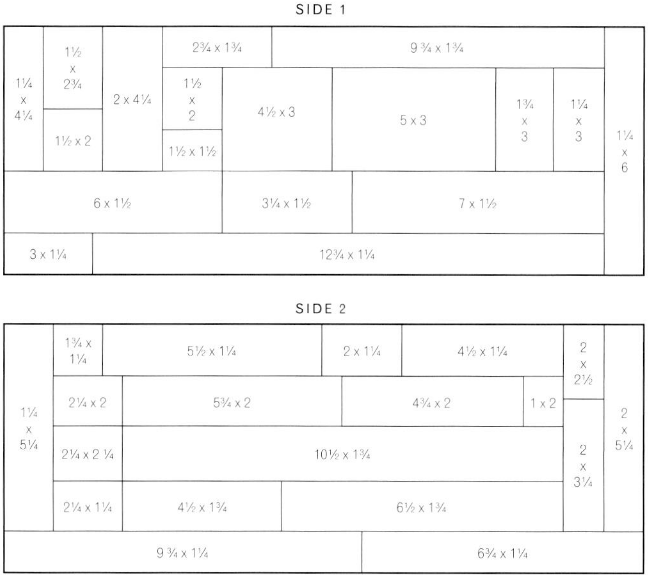
SIDE 1
1¼ x 4¼
1½ x 2¾
1½ x 2
2 x 4¼
2¾ x 1¾
9 ¾ x 1¾
1½ x 2
1½ x 1½
4½ x 3
5 x 3
1¾ x 3
1¼ x 3
1¼ x 6
6 x 1½
3¼ x 1½
7 x 1½
3 x 1¼
12¾ x 1¼
SIDE 2
1¼ x 5¼
1¾ x 1¼
5½ x 1¼
2 x 1¼
4½ x 1¼
2 x 2½
2 x 5¼
2¼ x 2
5¾ x 2
4¾ x 2
1 x 2
2¼ x 2 ¼
10½ x 1¾
2 x 3¼
2¼ x 1¼
4½ x 1¾
6½ x 1¾
9 ¾ x 1¼
6¾ x 1¼

FIGURE 2F

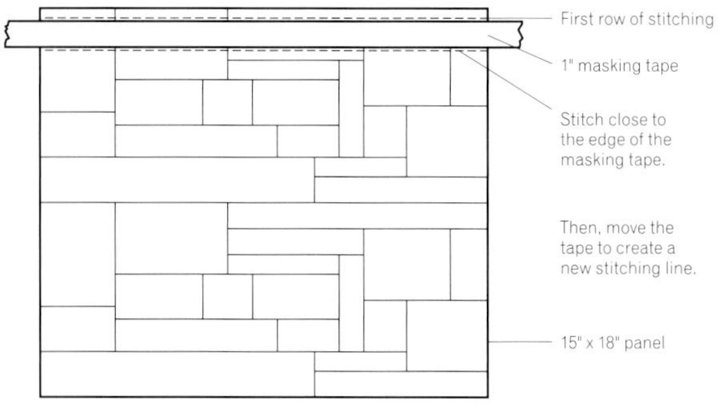
First row of stitching
1" masking tape
Stitch close to the edge of the masking tape.
Then, move the tape to create a new stitching line.
15" x 18" panel

FIGURE 2H

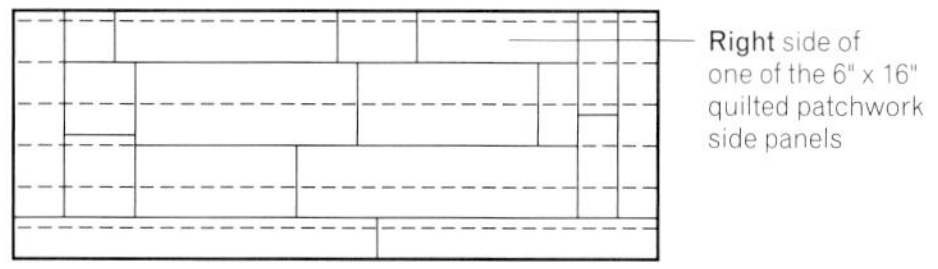
Right side of one of the 6" x 16" quilted patchwork side panels

FIGURE 4C

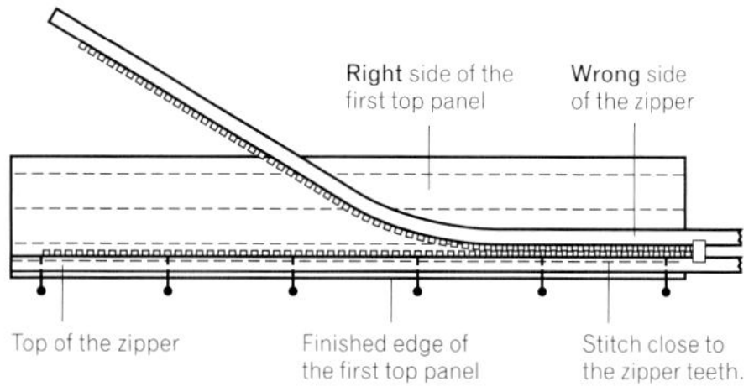
Right side of the first top panel
Wrong side of the zipper
Top of the zipper
Finished edge of the first top panel
Stitch close to the zipper teeth.

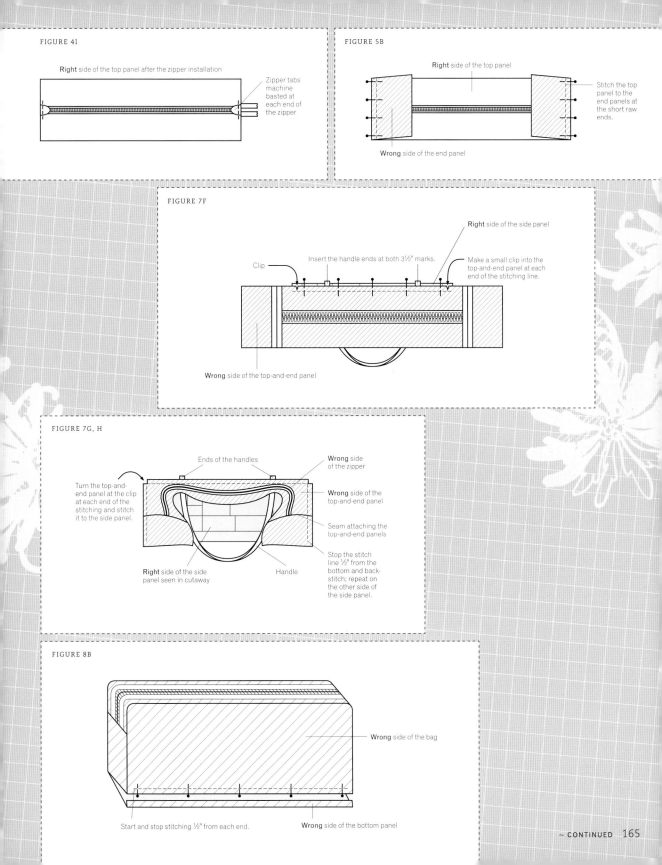

FIGURE 4I

Right side of the top panel after the zipper installation

Zipper tabs machine basted at each end of the zipper

FIGURE 5B

Right side of the top panel

Stitch the top panel to the end panels at the short raw ends.

Wrong side of the end panel

FIGURE 7F

Clip

Insert the handle ends at both 3½" marks.

Right side of the side panel

Make a small clip into the top-and-end panel at each end of the stitching line.

Wrong side of the top-and-end panel

FIGURE 7G, H

Ends of the handles

Wrong side of the zipper

Wrong side of the top-and-end panel

Turn the top-and-end panel at the clip at each end of the stitching and stitch it to the side panel.

Seam attaching the top-and-end panels

Stop the stitch line ½" from the bottom and backstitch; repeat on the other side of the side panel.

Right side of the side panel seen in cutaway

Handle

FIGURE 8B

Wrong side of the bag

Start and stop stitching ½" from each end.

Wrong side of the bottom panel

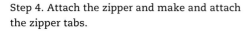

Step 4. Attach the zipper and make and attach the zipper tabs.

a. First, finish one long edge of each top panel by zigzag stitching the raw edge.

b. Then, open the zipper and place it face down on the **Right** side of the long finished edge of the first top panel, with the top of the zipper even with the short end of the panel, and the edge of the zipper tape even with the long, finished edge of the top panel. Pin the zipper in place. (Don't worry if the zipper extends slightly past the end of the panel. The excess zipper can be trimmed after the end panels have been attached to the top panels.)

c. Now, using the zipper foot on your sewing machine, attach the first side of the zipper by stitching close to the zipper teeth for the length of the zipper, closing the zipper as needed to allow the needle to pass. Backstitch at each end. (FIGURE 4C)

d. Follow the instructions in steps 4b and 4c to attach the other side of the zipper to the second top panel, making sure that the zipper is placed so that the short ends of both top panels are even. Your completed top panel with the zipper attached now measures 6" wide x 20" long when the zipper is closed.

e. Using scraps of the exterior fabric, measure, mark, and cut 4 small tab pieces, each measuring 1½" wide x 1¼" tall. Using your scissors, round off 2 of the corners of the rectangles, creating half-moon-shaped pieces measuring 1½" wide x 1¼" tall.

f. Place 2 of the half-moon-shaped tabs with **Right** sides together and stitch a ¼" seam along the curved edge. Then, trim the seam to ⅛".

g. Turn the tab **Right** side out and press well.

h. Now, place the tab at one end of the zipper with the flat raw edge of the tab matched to the raw end of the top panel and the rounded edge lying on top of the end of the zipper. Pin in place. Then, using the longest stitch on your machine, machine baste the tab in place with a ¼" seam.

i. Follow the instructions in steps 4f, 4g, and 4h to make the second tab and attach it to the other end of the zipper. (FIGURE 4I)

Step 5. Attach the end panels to the top panel.

a. Place one end panel on each short end of one of the top panels with the **Right** sides together, matching the 6" raw ends, and pin it in place.

b. Attach the panels by stitching a ½" seam across the 6" ends, backstitching at each end. Press the seams away from the top panel. Trim away any excess zipper extending past the seam. (FIGURE 5B)

Step 6. Make the handles.*

See page 170 for an explanation of how to make a drawstring (you'll use the same process to make your handles).

a. First, place the fusible interfacing pieces, fusible side down, on the **Wrong** side of the handle pieces. Follow the manufacturer's instructions to attach the interfacing to the handles.

b. Now, fold one handle piece in half lengthwise, **Wrong** sides together, and press firmly.

c. Unfold the handle piece, fold both long, unfinished edges in to meet the center crease, and press.

d. Then, fold the handle in half one more time at the center crease, enclosing the long raw edges, and press.

e. Now, stitch close to both long edges, stitching the entire length of the handle.

f. Follow the instructions in steps 6b through 6e to make the second handle. Your handles will measure approximately ½" wide x 21" long and the raw ends will be hidden.

Step 7. Attach the side and top panels and insert the handles.

a. First, find the center of the joined top-and-end panel (with zipper) and then the side panel by folding each of them separately in half, **Right** sides together, matching the short ends, and gently pressing a crease.

b. Then, place the joined top-and-end panel and the side panels **Right** sides together, matching the pressed center creases. Pin the panels together. The top-and-end panel will be longer than the side panels. Make sure that they are matched at the center crease.

c. Use your ruler to measure in 3½" from each end of the side panel and make a mark with your chalk pencil. Mark both side panels. You will have a total of 4 marks.

d. Insert one short raw end of the handle in the pinned seam of the joined side, top, and end panel at the first 3½" mark, placing the smooth, folded edge of the handle facing the center of the side panel and allowing the handle to curve down and away from the top-and-end panel. Insert the other end of the handle at the second 3½" mark at the opposite end of the side panel, making sure not to twist the handle as you insert the ends into the seam.

e. Now, stitch a ½" seam along the pinned edge of the side panel, beginning and ending ½" from each end, backstitching at each end. Stitch a second time over the seam where the handles are attached to reinforce the handle. Press the seam toward the side panel.

f. Then, make a small clip into the edge of the top-and-end panel at each end of the stitching line attaching the first side panel. Clip only into the top-and-end panel; do not clip into the side panel. Clip at each end of the stitching line, making sure not to clip into the stitching line. These clips will be ½" from each end of the side panel and will allow the end panels to turn and attach the side panel at each end. (FIGURE 7F)

g. Now, turn the top-and-end panel at the first clip mark and match this edge to the short raw end of the side panel with the **Right** sides together. Pin in place. (FIGURE 7G, H)

h. Attach this side of the top-and-end panel to the end of the side panel with a ½" seam beginning and ending ½" from each end of the side panel, backstitching at each end. (FIGURE 7G, H)

i. Follow the instructions in steps 7g and 7h to attach the other end of the top-and-end panel to the other side of the first side panel.

j. Follow the instructions in steps 7a through 7h to attach the other top-and-end panel to the other side panel and insert the second handle. Your bag will now look like a box with no bottom.

Step 8. Attach the bag's top section to the bottom panel at the side panels.

a. First, with the **Right** sides together, match one raw edge of the long side of the bottom panel to the bottom edge of the side panel, and pin in place.

b. Then, stitch a ½" seam along the pinned edge, beginning and ending ½" from each end of the bottom panel. Backstitch at each end. (FIGURE 8B)

c. Follow the instructions in steps 8a and 8b to attach the other side panel to the bottom panel.

Step 9. Attach the bag's top section to the bottom panel at the end panels.

NOTE: *Before attaching the bottom panel to the end panels, open the zipper partway to allow you to turn the bag Right side out easily.*

a. First, match the short raw end of the bottom panel to the raw bottom edge of the top-and-end panel. (The ½" unstitched end of the seam on the side and top-and-end panels will allow the top of the bag to turn and meet the bottom panel.) Pin in place.

b. Attach the top-and-end panel to the bottom panel with a ½" seam beginning and ending ½" from each end of the bottom panel. Backstitch at each end.

c. Follow the instructions in steps 9a and 9b to attach the other end of the bottom panel to the top-and-end panel.

d. Now, using your scissors, trim the corners in the seam allowance,* making sure not to clip into your stitching. This will allow the corners to turn easily. Set the bag aside. (FIGURE 9D)

* *See page 172 for an explanation of trimming corners in the seam allowance.*

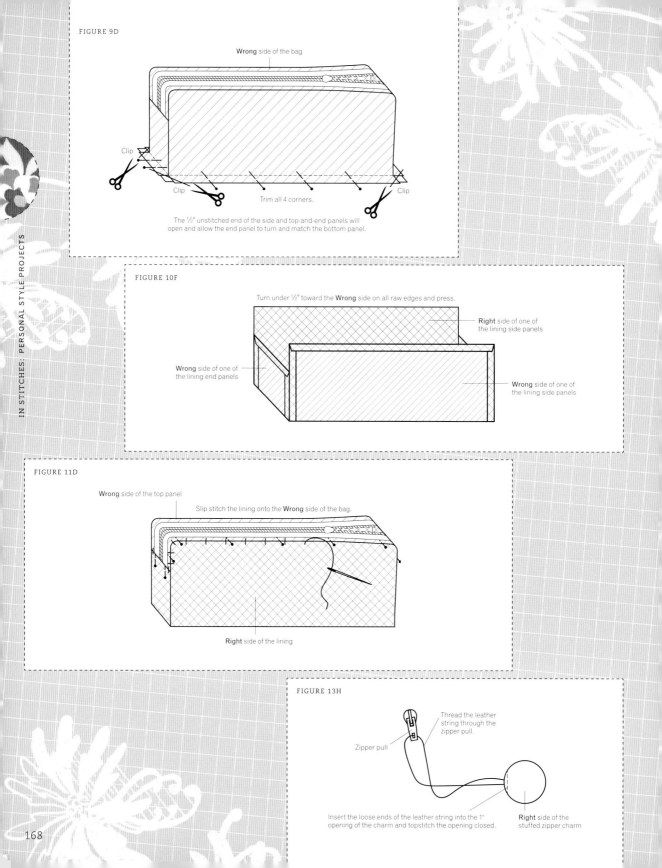

FIGURE 9D

Wrong side of the bag

Clip

Clip

Trim all 4 corners.

Clip

The ½" unstitched end of the side and top-and-end panels will
open and allow the end panel to turn and match the bottom panel.

FIGURE 10F

Turn under ½" toward the **Wrong** side on all raw edges and press.

Right side of one of
the lining side panels

Wrong side of one of
the lining end panels

Wrong side of one of
the lining side panels

FIGURE 11D

Wrong side of the top panel

Slip stitch the lining onto the **Wrong** side of the bag.

Right side of the lining

FIGURE 13H

Thread the leather
string through the
zipper pull.

Zipper pull

Insert the loose ends of the leather string into the 1"
opening of the charm and topstitch the opening closed.

Right side of the
stuffed zipper charm

Step 10: Make the lining for the bag.

a. Place one lining side panel and one lining end panel with **Right** sides together, matching the 4" side of the end panel to the lower edge of the side panel. (The side panel will be taller than the end panel.) Pin in place.

b. Stitch the end panel and side panel together with a ½" seam, beginning ½" from the top edge of the end panel and ending ½" from the bottom edge of the end panel. Backstitch at each end.

c. Follow the instructions in steps 10a and 10b to attach the other end of the lining side panel to the second lining end panel.

d. Follow the instructions in steps 10a through 10c to attach the second lining side panel to the lining end panels.

e. Now, follow the instructions in steps 8 and 9 to attach the lining bottom panel to the lining side and end panels.

f. Turn all unfinished raw edges of the lining ½" toward the **Wrong** side and press. (FIGURE 10F)

Step 11. Attach the lining to the bag.

a. First, turn the bag **Wrong** side out.

b. With the **Wrong** side of the bag facing out and the **Right** side of the lining facing out, slip the bag into the lining so that the **Wrong** sides are facing each other.

c. Match the folded top edges of the lining to the seam lines on the **Wrong** side of the bag and pin it in place.

d. Using a hand needle and coordinating thread, slip stitch* the lining to the **Wrong** side of the bag by hand. (FIGURE 11D)

See page 171 for an explanation of slip stitching.

e. Turn the completed bag **Right** side out, using a turning tool to push out the corners, and press.

Step 12. Make and insert the cardboard into the bottom sleeve.

a. Place the bottom sleeve panels with **Right** sides together, matching the raw edges. Pin along both long edges and along one short end.

b. Now, stitch a ½" seam along the pinned edges, leaving one short end open for turning.

c. Clip the 2 corners on the stitched short end, making sure not to clip the stitching.

d. Then, turn the bottom sleeve **Right** side out, using a turning tool to push out the corners, and press flat.

e. Insert the 4¾" x 14¾" piece of heavy cardboard into the bottom sleeve.

f. Turn under the raw edges of the short open end ½" toward the **Wrong** side, tucking the raw ends inside the sleeve to hide the cardboard, and press. Slip stitch the opening closed by hand.

g. Place the bottom sleeve into the bottom of the bag for support.

Step 13. Make and attach the zipper charm.

a. First, using the pattern piece provided in the pocket at the front of this book, cut 2 circles with a diameter of 2½" from the exterior fabric.

b. Then, place the circles with **Right** sides together and stitch around the outer edge with a ¼" seam, leaving a 1" opening for turning the charm **Right** side out.

c. Trim the seam to ⅛".

d. Turn the charm **Right** side out.

e. Fill the charm with polyfill, stuffing the charm firmly.

f. Now, thread the leather string through the zipper pull on the bag. Tie an overhand knot in the loose ends of the charm and insert the knotted end of the leather into the 1" opening in the charm and pin it in place.

g. Turn the raw ends under ¼" toward the **Wrong** side at the 1" opening and slip stitch a few stitches through the leather and the charm by hand, just enough to hold the leather in place.

h. Then, machine stitch across the opening to close the seam and secure the leather. (FIGURE 13H)

SIMPLE TECHNIQUES AND BASIC EQUIPMENT

To help you understand the terms and techniques used in the projects in this book, here is a quick reference list of the technical terms and phrases.

BACKSTITCH: Backstitching is used to reinforce your sewing in order to help keep it from unraveling. To do this, put your machine in the reverse position and stitch 3 or 4 stitches.

BIAS FOLD: See *fabric grain*.

BONING: A plastic stiffening material used to support your project and keep it from curling up, boning is sold by the yard or precut in packages.

BUTTONHOLE: To make a buttonhole you first need to measure the button you will be using. For example, if your button is ½" wide, you will make the sides of the buttonhole (not including the top and bottom finished ends) measure ½". Once you have figured out where you need to place your buttonhole, measure and mark the width of the button on your project with a chalk pencil. If you do not have a buttonhole setting or foot on your sewing machine, just use the following alternative method for making a buttonhole:

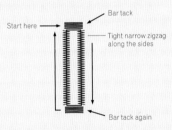

Using the zigzag setting on your sewing machine, make a bar tack (this means using the widest zigzag stitch and stitching a few times in place) at the top of the buttonhole measurement on your project with a tight and wide zigzag stitch. Sew back and forth a few times, and then set your zigzag on a tight, narrower stitch to sew the first side of the buttonhole. At the bottom of the first side, reset the stitch for a tight, wide bar tack, and sew a bar tack again at the bottom. Then reset the stitch for a tight, narrow zigzag, and sew up the second side of the buttonhole. Set your stitch width to zero and sew a couple of stitches in place to "lock" the zigzag stitches and finish the buttonhole. Carefully cut the buttonhole open with a seam ripper.

CLIPPING: Clipping allows some give in your seam allowance, especially if it's curved, in order to make the seam lie flat and make it easier to turn your project **Right** side out. When clipping, use your scissors to cut into the seam allowance only, making cuts up to the stitch line, taking care not to cut your stitching.

CROSSWISE GRAIN: See *fabric grain*.

DOT ON THE PATTERN PIECES: To use the dot marked on a pattern piece, first transfer the dot onto the **Wrong** side of the fabric piece by marking its position with your chalk pencil. Dots are used in a few ways. First, when you are stitching trim pieces together you can use it to indicate your stopping point for your stitching. Second, it can serve as the point where you will pivot and turn your project before you continue stitching. Finally, it can identify where you should end a clip (see *clipping*, above) in order to allow you to turn your project **Right** side out.

DRAWSTRING: To make a drawstring, follow the instructions below:

A. Fold the drawstring strip in half lengthwise, with **Wrong** sides together, and press a crease at the fold.

B. Open the drawstring strip and fold each long, raw edge in to meet the center crease, and press.

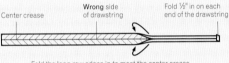

Fold the long raw edges in to meet the center crease.

C. Then, at each short end of the drawstring, fold under ¼" to ½" toward the **Wrong** side and press.

D. Now, fold the strip in half at the center crease, enclosing all of the raw edges, and press well. Pin the folded edges together and edge stitch close to the folded edges completely around your drawstring.

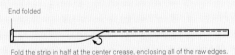

Fold the strip in half at the center crease, enclosing all of the raw edges.

E. You may like to sew a small button or two to each end of the drawstring for detail.

EDGE STITCH: An edge stitch is a very narrow stitch, done by machine close to the edge, in order to finish a project, close an opening, or stitch something in place. For example, you would use edge stitching when sewing a piece of Velcro in place.

FABRIC GRAIN: Most fabric is made using a set of fixed lengthwise threads woven at right angles with a set of crosswise threads. *Grain* indicates the direction of these threads. *Lengthwise grain* (also called *straight of grain*) refers to the lengthwise threads, or the fabric's length, and runs parallel to the selvage edge. *Crosswise grain* refers to the crosswise threads, or the fabric's width, and runs across the fabric. *Bias* refers to any diagonal line crossing either the lengthwise or crosswise grain. In this book, *bias fold* refers to the diagonal fold of a rectangle of fabric to align one selvage edge (or an edge cut on the lengthwise grain) with one edge cut on the crosswise grain, producing a 45-degree-angle fold.

FINGER PRESS: You can "press" open the seam allowance of a seam using your finger or thumbnail to form a crease on fabric that cannot be pressed or is in a tight area where the iron will not fit.

GATHERING STITCH: Using the longest stitch on your machine and loose bobbin tension enables you to pull the bobbin thread and gather in your fabric.

GRAIN: See *fabric grain*.

HAND STITCH: See *slip stitch*.

INTERFACING: A stiffening, fabriclike material used to give your project strength and durability. Interfacing also gives lighter-weight fabrics form and body. There are different types of interfacings, including fusible (press-on) and sew-in interfacings, both of which come in various weights. If you buy fusible interfacing, make sure to ask for directions to correctly apply the interfacing.

LENGTHWISE GRAIN: See *fabric grain*.

MACHINE APPLIQUÉ: Use a tight zigzag stitch to nicely finish the edge of a shape that you are attaching or appliquéing to your project.

MACHINE BASTE: A machine basting stitch is used to hold sections of your project in place until you are ready to complete your final stitches. Use the longest stitch on your machine, so you can easily remove these basting stitches later. You do not have to backstitch at the end of your stitching.

PIVOT: Pivoting is used when you reach a corner or any place where you want to turn and continue stitching in a different direction. To pivot, stop stitching (but keep your fabric in place in the sewing machine) with your needle in the down position, pick up the presser foot, and rotate or move your fabric to continue stitching in a different direction.

PRESHRINK: Wash and dry your fabric to allow for any shrinkage before cutting out your project. We always recommend that you preshrink your fabric, since you will be laundering your project after use. It is important to preshrink because most cotton and other natural fibers will shrink when laundered, which could change the shape of your project.

PRESS: For best results, press your fabrics before you cut out and sew your project, and as you are constructing your project. Pressing before you cut out your fabric pieces removes wrinkles, which could distort your pattern, and pressing your seams as you make your project can give your project a smooth, professional look.

REINFORCEMENT STITCH: This form of stitching is done to add strength and support to specific areas in your project, such as at the end of a clip, or in a spot that will take a lot of wear.

SEAM, STITCHING A ¼" (OR ANY OTHER LENGTH): Stitching a ¼" seam simply means stitching a seam that is ¼" in from the edge of 2 aligned fabrics or parts of a project, in order to join them. The seam allowances, or fabric extending from the stitching line to the edge, can be pressed open or to one side, as indicated in the project directions.

SEAM ALLOWANCE: See *seam, stitching a ¼"*.

SEAM RIPPER: A tool with a sharp, hooked tooth used for removing previously sewn stitches or opening buttonholes. For example, a seam ripper may be used to remove a stitched hem line or to take out stitches that are in the wrong place.

SELVAGE EDGE: The narrow, tightly woven finished edge along each side of the lengthwise grain of your fabric.

SLIP STITCH: A slip stitch is a hand stitch used to join 2 adjacent pieces or edges of fabric. To slip stitch, you will need a long piece of thread and a sharp hand-sewing needle. Follow the instructions below:

A. Feed one end of the thread through the eye of the needle, doubling it back on itself and matching up the cut ends.

B. Then, tie a double overhand knot near the matched ends of the thread.

C. Starting at one end of the area you will be stitching, insert your needle into your fabric and pull the thread through until the knot stops the thread from going completely through the fabric.

D. Then, insert the needle into one of the 2 edges you are stitching together, right above the point where the thread went through the first time, catching only a few threads on the fabric. Pull the thread through until it is taut.

E. Now insert the needle into the other edge going through about ½" of the fabric, hiding the thread inside a fold. Push the needle through the fabric and again pull the thread taut.

F. Insert the needle back into the first edge, slightly above the point where the thread came through, and stitch through again. Again, catch only a few threads and stitch through to the other edge.

G. Repeat this step until you have stitched your fabric together as indicated in your pattern, keeping even spaces between stitches.

H. To finish, tie off your stitching by making a double knot close to the fabric, and cut your excess threads to free your needle.

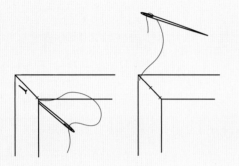

STAY STITCH: Stay stitching is sewn in the seam allowance before construction to stabilize curved or slanted edges so the fabric on these edges does not stretch.

STITCH IN THE DITCH: This stitching, done either by machine or hand as indicated in the pattern instructions, is sewn in the groove formed by the seam. Make sure to line up any seams underneath so both seams will be sewn through neatly.

STRAIGHT OF GRAIN: See *fabric grain*.

TEMPLATE: A pattern piece used for tracing or for marking guidelines.

TIMTEX: A thick, stiff stabilizer used to add support and help projects keep their shape. Timtex is machine washable. After laundering, press your project back into shape with a steam iron, and then allow it to dry, supporting it with wadded-up tissue paper or a folded towel to keep the shape that you want.

TOPSTITCH: Topstitching is used for several purposes. It finishes your project and gives it a neat appearance; it is used to close openings left for turning your project **Right** side out; and it can be used as a reinforcement stitch, by adding another row of stitching to areas that will be used heavily and receive more wear. To topstitch, stitch parallel to an edge or another seam for the distance suggested in the project directions.

TRIM THE CORNERS: This is a great finishing technique used to add shape and definition to corners on your project. Use your scissors to cut off the tip of the corner in the seam allowance in order to take out the bulk. Be careful not to cut into your project or your stitching. Once you turn your project **Right** side out, your corner will have a neat, squared-off look.

TRIM THE SEAM ALLOWANCE: This technique reduces bulk around curved seams, so that they will lie flat when you turn the project **Right** side out. Use your scissors to cut off most of the excess fabric in the seam allowance. Be sure to press out these areas once you've turned them **Right** side out.

TURNING TOOL: A turning tool is a pointed object such as a closed pair of scissors that can be used to push out the corners on your project after you've turned it **Right** side out. Specially made turning tools, usually constructed of plastic or wood, are available at sewing and fabric stores. When using a turning tool, push out the corners *gently*, especially if you're working with delicate, lightweight fabric.

RESOURCE GUIDE

SOURCES OF FABRICS, NOTIONS, TRIMS, AND BEADS

For a selection of the finest niche fabric retailers please visit my Web site, **www.amybutlerdesign.com**, and search under **"Where to Buy"** to find a retailer near you.

Through these purveyors you'll find not only my fabric designs from Kokka Ltd., some of which I used for the projects in this book, but also thousands of beautiful sewing and home-decor fabrics.

RETAIL STORES

ABC CARPET AND HOME
881–888 Broadway
New York, NY 10003
212-473-3000
www.abchome.com
Collections of exotic home-decor fabrics

ANTHROPOLOGIE
1700 Sansom Street
Philadelphia, PA 19103-5214
800-309-2500
www.anthropologie.com
Stores nationwide and mail-order catalog
Wonderful selection of fashion and home goods. A great source of textiles with lovely prints, perfect for repurposing.

BRITEX FABRICS
146 Geary Street
San Francisco, CA 94108
415-392-2910
Large selection of ribbons, trims, and notions

CALICO CORNERS
203 Gale Lane
Kennett Square, PA 19348
800-213-6366
www.calicocorners.com
Stores nationwide
A wide selection of designer and home decor fabrics

FRENCH GENERAL
1621 Vista Del Mar
Hollywood, CA 90028
323-462-0818
www.frenchgeneral.com
Fabulous beads, notion kits, and a gorgeous selection of French textiles

GREEN VELVET
130 E. Broadway
Granville, OH 43023
740-587-0515
www.mygreenvelvet.com
Great ribbons, trims, new and vintage milliner flora, bead kits, and fabrics

HANCOCK FABRICS
2605A West Main Street
Tupelo, MS 38801
662-844-7368
www.hancockfabrics.com
America's largest fabric store

HYMAN HENDLER AND SONS
67 West 38th Street
New York, NY 10018
212-840-8393
www.hymanhendler.com
Basic novelty and vintage trims

ON BOARD FABRICS
Route 27, P.O. Box 14
Edgecomb, ME 04556
207-882-7536
www.onboardfabrics.com
An interesting variety of Balinese cottons, Italian tapestry, and woven plaids

SALSA FABRICS
3100 Holly Avenue
Silver Springs, NV 89429
800-758-3819
www.salsafabrics.com
Original fabrics in cotton, silk, and wool from Guatemala and Indonesia

TINSEL TRADING COMPANY
47 West 38th Street
New York, NY 10018
212-730-1030
Vintage and contemporary trims

URBAN OUTFITTERS
30 Industrial Park Blvd.
Trenton, SC 29847-2164
800-282-2200
www.urbanoutfitters.com
Stores nationwide and mail-order catalog
Great source for urban fashion for you and your home. Fun printed bedspreads and curtains for repurposing.

BEADS BY SANDY

www.beadsbysandy.com

Enormous selection of vintage "dead stock" beads, buttons, and trims

CAROL LANE-SABER DESIGNS

www.saberdesigns.cc

My favorite source for antique Japanese and kimono fabric

DAVA BEAD AND TRADE

www.davabeadandtrade.com

Fantastic resource for beads

EBAY

www.ebay.com

Internet auctions selling vintage fabrics, trims, beads, and buttons

ONLINE CRAFT STORES

www.hobbylobby.com
www.joann.com
www.michaels.com
www.acmoore.com
www.dickblick.com

REPRODEPOT FABRICS

www.reprodepotfabrics.com

The best reproduction fabric source, with a large selection of interesting prints

THE RIBBONERIE INC.

www.theribbonerie.com

Extensive ribbon collections

THE TIMTEX STORE

800-752-3353

www.timtexstore.com

The best online supplier of Timtex interfacing. You can also find Timtex at most larger sewing stores and quilt shops.

WWW.CURIOSCAPE.COM

More than 40,000 listings of stores selling antiques, including vintage textiles and clothing

WWW.TIAS.COM

Large selection of antiques, collectibles, and textiles

WWW.VINTAGEFIBERWORKS. COM

Vintage clothing, accessories, and fabrics

BRIMFIELD ANTIQUE SHOW

www.brimfieldshow.com

A well-known, high-quality outdoor show held in Brimfield, Massachusetts, for about a week each in May, July, and September

INTERNATIONAL QUILT FESTIVAL

www.quilts.com

Held in Houston, Texas, every October, the Quilt Festival is the largest annual new and vintage quilt and textile show in the world.

ROUND TOP MARBURGER ANTIQUE SHOW

www.roundtop-marburger.com

More than 350 dealers from thirty-nine states and Canada selling and trading antiques, collectibles, and textiles

SPRINGFIELD ANTIQUES SHOW AND FLEA MARKET

www.jenkinsshows.com

937-325-0053

A fantastic monthly antique show with a wide selection of vintage fabrics held each year in Ohio

THE VINTAGE FASHION AND TEXTILE SHOW

www.vintagefashionand textiles.com

Held in Sturbridge, Massachusetts, the day before Brimfield opens, with an extensive range of high-quality vendors selling incredible trims, textiles, beads, and buttons

WWW.FLEAMARKETGUIDE. COM

Listing of flea markets held throughout the country

INDEX